Aristotle And His Medieval
Interpreters

Aristotle And His Medieval Interpreters

Edited by
Richard Bosley
and
Martin Tweedale

©1991 Canadian Journal of Philosophy

The University of Calgary Press
Calgary, Alberta, Canada

ISSN 0229-7051   ISBN 0-919491-17-0

©1992 The Canadian Journal of Philosophy
ISBN 0-919491-17-0
ISSN 0229-7051

University of Calgary Press
2500 University Drive N.W.
Calgary, Alberta, Canada T2N 1N4

Canadian Cataloguing in Publication Data

Main entry under title:
Aristotle and his medieval interpreters

(Canadian journal of philosophy. Supplementary volume, ISSN
0229-7051 ; 17)
Includes bibliographical references and index.
ISBN 0-919491-17-0

1. Aristotle. 2. Philosophy, Medieval. 3. Thomas, Aquinas, Saint,
1225?-1274. I. Bosley, Richard. II. Tweedale, Martin, 1937- III. Series.
B485.A75 1992   185   C92-091073-4

Cover design by Art Design Printing Inc., Edmonton, AB

Printed in Canada
This book is printed on acid-free paper.

Table of Contents

Preface

All the papers in this volume were prepared for and delivered for the first time at a conference held at the University of Alberta from September 27 to September 30, 1990. The conference, entitled 'Aristotle and His Medieval Interpreters,' was devoted to the treatment of Aristotle by late ancient and medieval thinkers. The range of the papers at the conference was even broader than the selection published here, including treatments of the topics of immortality and modal logic, among others.

The editors would like to acknowledge the financial assistance given to the conference by the Social Sciences and Research Council of Canada, The University of Alberta Conference Fund, the office of the Vice-President for research at the University of Alberta, and the Department of Philosophy of that same institution.

RICHARD BOSLEY
MARTIN M. TWEEDALE

CANADIAN JOUNRAL OF PHHILOSOPHY
Supplementary Volume 17

Contributors

Marilyn McCord Adams is professor of philosophy at the University of California, Los Angeles. She is the author of *William Ockham* and many articles on medieval philosophy and theology.

E.J. Ashworth is professor of philosophy at the University of Waterloo in Ontario. She is the author of many books and articles on late medieval logic. She recently edited Paul of Venice's *Tractatus de Obligationibus*.

Deborah L. Black is a professor at the Pontifical Institute of Medieval Studies in Toronto. She has written mainly on medieval Arabic philosophy, her most recent book being *Logic and Aristotle's 'Rhetoric' and 'Poetics' in Medieval Arabic Philosophy*.

Norman Kretzmann is professor of philosophy at Cornell University and has written and edited many books and articles on medieval philosophy, including *Meaning and Inference in Medieval Philosophy*.

Gareth B. Matthews is professor of philosophy at the University of Massachusetts in Amherst. He has written extensively in ancient philosophy and is currently producing an English translation of Ammonius's commentary on Aristotle's *Categories*.

Joseph Owens is professor emeritus of the Pontifical Institute of Medieval Studies in Toronto. He has published many books and articles over the years on both ancient and medieval philosophy and particularly on Aristotle and Thomas Aquinas, including *The Doctrine of Being in the Aristotelian Metaphysics*.

Eleonore Stump is professor of philosophy at Virginia Polytechnic Institute and State University. She has published widely in medieval philosophy and theology. Recently some of her essays were collected in a volume entitled *Dialectic and Its Place in the Development of Medieval Logic*.

Note Concerning Footnotes

In the footnotes to the following essays where the name of an author is followed by a number in square brackets (e.g. William Ockham [3]) the reader is referred to the corresponding entry in the bibliography of sources which immediately follows the last essay.

CANADIAN JOURNAL OF PHILOSOPHY
Supplementary Volume 17

The Reception of Aristotle in the Middle Ages

RICHARD BOSLEY
MARTIN TWEEDALE

This collection of papers derives from a conference on the reception of Aristotle in the Middle Ages held at the University of Alberta in September, 1990, and organized by the editors. They conceived of the conference in the light of a general view of Aristotle and medieval thought, a statement of which may serve as an introduction to the papers which follow.

Within the Greek philosophical tradition Aristotle's works became the focus of commentary and discussion; they became, furthermore, the texts of instruction, particularly in logic. Some scholars, of a Neo-Platonist orientation, sought to harmonize the teachings of Plato and Aristotle and to deliver those teachings as a single science or body of knowledge. Just as Aristotle made it a point of good methodology to open his works by sorting out the opinions of his predecessors, so the great commentators, such as Alexander of Aphrodisias (c. 200 AD) and Simplicius (sixth century), did not make their subject-matter, whether that of logic or of metaphysics, independent of the thought of the Greek masters. At the same time the commentators did not emphasize disagreement between Plato and Aristotle, as a philosophy of the ancient skeptical traditions could be expected to do. The skill of a Neo-Platonic commentator shows itself in maximizing consistency and harmony for the purpose of saving as much as possible; the skill of the skeptic emphasizes disharmony in the hope of saving

1

as little as possible. Gareth Matthews's paper, 'Container Metaphysics According to Aristotle's Greek Commentators,' shows us how some of the Greek commentators of the former sort went about explaining a passage in the *Categories* of Aristotle. Matthews's paper emphasizes and argues for the tradition, represented in both ancient and modern commentary, according to which individual substances are the primary realities: everything is either a box, a specific or generic classification of a box, or something contained in a box.

Aristotle's work, along with some of the Greek commentaries, was translated into Arabic and woven into the fabric of Arabic thought, especially medicine, theology, and political philosophy. The promise of a demonstrative science was bound to attract the attention of thinkers of a theoretical bent whether they were by training doctors or lawyers. One of the greatest of the medieval philosophers to work within the confluence of Greek philosophy and a revealed religion, Avicenna (980-1037), was first trained as a doctor; another, Averroes (1126-1198), as a lawyer. Unlike their thirteenth- and fourteenth-century Latin counterparts, these philosophers were not university professors.

Avicenna worked out a metaphysical system based on Aristotle but heavily influenced by Neo-Platonism and its tradition of commentary. When it became available to Latin readers, it filled a metaphysical void and had a profound effect upon the metaphysical thinking of the Christian traditions. Avicenna applied the principles of a demonstrative science to cosmology and undertook to prove the necessary existence of a First Cause. The effort to situate revealed theology in a basically Aristotelian-Neo-Platonic cosmological frame was repeated again and again among both the Islamic and Christian thinkers of the Middle Ages.

Causation appropriate to God is called emanation (a Neo-Platonist notion) and reminds one more of light streaming out from its source than of a builder building a house. The philosophical theologian al-Ghazali (1058-1111) can hardly have thought that Avicenna's metaphysical system lay just below the surface of the theological teachings of the Koran. He himself set out to show, in the *Incoherence of the Philosophers*, that Avicenna's arguments by no means reach the level of demonstrative proof and need not be taken to displace the received teachings of Islamic faith. In the *Incoherence of the Incoherence* Averroes responded to al-Ghazali and undertook to restore the authority of Aristotle by means of commentaries which laid out the correct understanding of his works.

Aristotle directly influenced the Latin traditions in two different periods. First during the late eleventh and early twelfth centuries he was known mainly through Boethius's sixth-century translations of the *Categories* and *De Interpretatione*. Second, from the mid-twelfth to the late thirteenth century the whole Aristotelian corpus, as we now have it, was translated first from Arabic and later directly from the Greek. The earlier translations of the first period helped support reflection on language, especially the relations between grammar and logic. This volume contains Deborah Black's study on similarities and differences which emerge in the Arabic and Latin traditions as they attempt to develop a coherent inquiry into language that combines both the grammatical and the logical approaches. E.J. Ashworth's paper explores thirteenth-century developments on a particular topic in the study of language which was especially important to Aristotle and all later Peripatetics: equivocation and analogy. She shows how the Latin scholastics in their treatments re-worked a rich inheritance of ideas from both Greek and Arabic sources.

The later translations of the second period came at an unusually propitious time: European universities were developing and the utility of reading Aristotle for the pursuit of a degree in a higher faculty (law, medicine, or theology) was recognized. Aristotle's logic had long found a place in the training of the mind and helped to define the medieval trivium of grammar, logic, and rhetoric. Now his work in physics, psychology, metaphysics, and ethics combined with the logic to transform the intellectual agenda of western Europe, but not without problems for the older Augustinian mind-set and orthodox theology. For example, in chapter 9 of *De Interpretatione* Aristotle poses the question of whether the truth of propositions about future contingent events leads to fatalism. The Augustinian Christian can neither accept that the future is already determined (because he sees no way of reconciling that with moral responsibility for our choices) nor allow that no propositions about future contingents are true (since that conflicts with the theological claim that God now knows the future in just the same, all-inclusive way as He knows the past and the present). Aristotle, consequently, is interpreted, with considerable strain, as holding that fatalism does not follow from admitting that what we say about future contingents has a definite truth-value now. This and many other areas of tension between the new Aristotle and the old theology elicited theological brilliance and logical acumen in those thinkers who wished to save both.

In the sciences of man Aristotle's *On the Soul* became required reading, at least in the University of Paris, by the middle of the thirteenth century. Lively discussion of the work raised the question whether the intellect belonging to humanity is one or many. If one emphasizes the teaching concerning knowledge, one is apt to think that Aristotle means that when there is actual knowing, knower and known are one and the same. But if so, then since there is one order of intelligibles, there is only one intellect. This view drew much from the interpretation of Averroes and was advanced by thinkers who have been known as Latin Averroists. The collision between this view and that of theologians, even some like Thomas Aquinas (1225-1274), who accepted Aristotle as the authority in matters knowable by natural reason, was inevitable, since orthodox dogma demanded that each human have their own intellect; otherwise, the doctrine of personal immortality was threatened. Here again, as Aristotle's own texts appeared obscure and inconclusive, medieval thinkers demanded a teaching both clear and also consistent with the body of Christian doctrine.

The topic of knowledge is addressed by several of the papers which follow. Joseph Owens takes up Aristotle's view of the identity of knower and known and sets it before his readers for serious consideration. Because of this perspective skepticism of either the Pyrrhonian or Academic variety never got a serious hearing in the Aristotelian milieu. Foundationalism is the usual rationalist response to skepticism, but where skepticism is not an issue, it would not be surprising if philosophers felt no necessity to develop their epistemology along foundationalist lines. The papers by Eleonore Stump and Norman Kretzmann argue that Aquinas was an example of just such a thinker. His concentration was on the reliability of admittedly fallible cognitive faculties, not on building an edifice of knowledge on some indubitable and absolutely secure base. Their remarks clarify not only the contrast between Aquinas's epistemology and modern thought but also a number of issues in the interpretation of Aristotle himself.

The Averroist movement ultimately engendered a conservative reaction in the 1270s, leading to ecclesiastical condemnation of some doctrines close to the heart of any true Aristotelian as well as many doctrines that are only doubtfully supported by the Aristotelian corpus. The result was a new willingness to experiment with ideas definitely not congenial to the Philosopher. One theological area that engendered such ideas was the doctrine of the Eucharist. Marilyn Adams's paper concludes this volume by showing how Eucharistic theology forced the later scholastics to entertain some very surprising and non-Aristotelian notions. Among these are (1) the idea of change of one substance into another instantaneously and with no persistent substratum, (2) the idea that accidents can exist without being in any subject, (3) the possibility of a body's existing but not in any place, (4) the possibility of a body's existing in two places at once, (5) the possibility of two bodies existing in the same place at once, (6) the idea that bodies can exist with no shape or quantity, etc. If all these are genuine possibilities, then the question naturally arises what sort of scientific status does Aristotelian philosophy retain. The stage was set for a revival of skepticism and the eventual abandoning of a set of ideas which, ever since the death of their author in 322 BC, had been a major, sometimes dominating, force in the development of Islamic and Western thought.

CANADIAN JOURNAL OF PHILOSOPHY
Supplementary Volume 17

Container Metaphysics According to Aristotle's Greek Commentators

GARETH B. MATTHEWS

I

Aristotle's little treatise the *Categories*, which stands, of course, at the very beginning of his corpus, presents a range of interpretive problems that are both interesting in themselves and also philosophically instructive. They can be divided into internal problems and external problems. The external problems are difficulties in harmonizing Aristotle's ideas in the *Categories* with his later views. The internal ones are those presented by the treatise itself, taken, in so far as that is feasible, in isolation.

In my view the main external problems posed by the Categories are those that arise from these three ideas of the later Aristotle:

(1) The idea of matter. The Aristotelian concept of matter first appears in the *Physics*. No doubt Aristotle's initial motivation for introducing the notion of matter has to do with philosophical problems about change. The world of the *Categories* is an almost static realm and, in that respect, the idea of matter might seem quite irrelevant to it. Yet surely matter is among the "things that there are," at least according to later Aristotle. And a classificatory work like the *Categories* should make a place for anything that exists — or so it seems. Whether we could simply add matter to the inventories we are already given in the *Categories* without disrupting the classifica-

Gareth B. Matthews

tory schemes to be found there is an interesting and difficult external problem in interpreting Aristotle's *Categories*.

(2) The primacy of secondary substance. It has seemed to many commentators that later Aristotle comes to view *eidos*, and particularly the *eidos* of the *infima species*, as primary substance, rather than, as in the *Categories*, the concrete individual — this human being, or this horse. The implications of such a shift are staggering. They constitute a major external problem for interpreting the *Categories*.

(3) The idea of a *pollachōs legomenon*. The universal wrench in the philosophical toolbox of the mature Aristotle is the idea that philosophically troublesome *legomena* are said in many ways. It is a task of no small difficulty to get clear on what Aristotle means by '*pollachōs legomenon*.' But certainly he thinks of this diagnosis as an indispensable tool of philosophical analysis.

The *Categories* does introduce the idea of homonyms. In fact, the very first word of the *Categories* is '*homonyma*.' But what seems to be at stake in the discussion of homonyms in this work is only what Aristotle later calls 'chance homonymy.'

In the second part of the treatise, the '*Postpraedicamenta*,' the idea of a *pollachōs legomenon* is clearly put to serious use. But the situation in the first half, the '*Praedicamenta*,' is much harder to assess. At 8b25 Aristotle does say that quality ('*poiotēs*') is among the things said in several ways. But he seems to cash in that claim by dividing quality into four kinds, rather than by assigning to the word 'quality' anything like four different senses. If the four kinds really are to be understood as species of quality, '*poiotēs*' should apply to each in the same sense, or else we have no reason to suppose there is a single genus of which the four kinds are species.[1]

What Aristotle says about quantities ('*posa*' not '*posotēs*,' which does not occur in the *Categories*) at 5a38 sounds much more like a genuine claim of polysemy. But the most interesting thing that looks like a serious claim of polysemy in the first part of the *Categories* seems to

---

1 To complicate things further, Aristotle uses the word '*eidos*' for the first kind (8b26) and the word '*genos*' for the other three (9a14, 9a28, 10a11).

be the assertion that 'substance' (*'ousia'*) is said more strictly of concrete individuals — the 'primary substances' — than of 'secondary substances' (2a11); and that, among secondary substances, species are more strictly called 'substance' than genera.[2] If, as one might have supposed, primary and secondary substance were to be thought of as something like species of substance, then *'ousia'* should be said no less strictly of one species than the other.

Strikingly absent from the *Categories*, however, is any suggestion that 'to be' or 'being' is said in many ways. In Aristotle's later writings, by contrast, he standardly couples the idea of there being different categories with the remark that 'to be' is said in as many ways as there are categories.

Perhaps it would involve only cosmetic changes in the treatise the *Categories* to make room for the idea that 'to be' is a *pollachōs legomenon* and that there is a distinct way of saying 'there exists' to go with each category of thing said to exist. Perhaps — but I think not. I should say that this issue presents an external problem of no small importance for interpreting the treatise.

Before we go on to consider internal problems in interpreting Aristotle's *Categories*, let me say a little about whether the Greek commentaries might help us deal with these three external problems. (By 'Greek commentaries' in this paper I shall mean the commentaries on Aristotle's *Categories* to be found in *Commentaria in Aristotelem Graeca* by Dexippus, Ammonius, Simplicius, Philoponus, and Elias.)

(1) The idea of matter. A standard objection discussed in the Greek commentaries to Aristotle's definition of 'in a subject' at 1a24-5 uses the example of form in matter. Ammonius puts the objection this way:

---

2 I am supposing that, in the light of, e.g., 2b37ff, we can understand 'x is more substance than y' to mean something like 'x is more strictly called "substance" than y.'

> Again it is said, "Form is in matter and is not part of matter and cannot exist apart from matter. Therefore according to the aforesaid definition form, too, is an accident." (27, 30-2)[3]

Ammonius is, of course, buying into a big assumption here, namely, that the definition of 'in a subject' is meant to be a definition of 'accident.' That assumption bears examination, but I shall not examine it here. It is enough for the objection to be telling to point out that species and genera should count as what is 'said of a subject, but not in a subject.' Yet it seems by the above reasoning that species and genera, if they are enmattered, are therefore in a subject.

The commentators do various things with this alleged counterexample. One interesting move is the second line of defense that Philoponus offers the Aristotelian. He says (34, 16ff.) that Aristotle isn't here treating of beings qua beings, but rather of beings as many people refer to them and talk about them — ordinary people, presumably nonphilosophers. As support for this claim he notes that Aristotle, in deference to general opinion, calls individuals, rather than species and genera, primary substance; whereas, as we know — or, anyway as Philoponus thinks we know — this reverses the true priority (34, 19ff.). I shall return to this point about priority below.

Philoponus goes on to suggest that lay people, many of them, wouldn't even have the conception of form and matter, but only that of the composite, the *syntheton* (34, 26ff.). So the readers this treatise was aimed at, Philoponus supposes, wouldn't think of form as a counterexample because they wouldn't think of form anyway.

It seems to be an implication of Philoponus's defense of Aristotle on this point that the treatise the *Categories* is aimed at the uninitiated. It seems also to be an implication of this line of defense that the definition of 'in a subject' at 1a24-5 is only a first approximation. Ammonius suggests, in discussing another putative counterexample to the definition, that Aristotle needs to be using 'in a subject' in the

---

3 Textual citations of the commentators are from these volumes of the *Commentaria in Aristotelem Graeca* (Berlin 1882-1909): Ammonius [1] IV, 4; Dexippus [1] IV, 2; Elias [1] XVIII, 1; Philoponus [1] XIII, 1; Simplicius [1] VIII.

sense of 'inheres [*enuparchein*] in a subject.' According to Ammonius it is only of accidents that we say they 'inhere' in a subject (27, 29-30).

(2) The primacy of secondary substance. We have already broached this point in discussing the form-in-matter counterexample. No doubt the view of many of us today is that Aristotle changed his mind about what substance is primary sometime between first lecturing on the *Categories* and writing *Metaphysics Z*. Ammonius, like Philoponus, supposes that the *Categories* is aimed at beginners in philosophy and that it makes important concessions to their ignorance. Ammonius distinguishes, in a way that he has learned from Aristotle, between what is prior by nature and what is prior to us. Form and matter, he says, are prior in nature, but not to us (36, 7ff.). "Since then," he goes on,

> the explanation is aimed at beginners and to beginners immediate things are more manifest, it is fitting that in the present circumstance he calls particulars primary. For it is from particulars that we are led to universals. (36, 10-3)

The idea that the *Categories* was written for beginners had been around since well before Dexippus (40, 19-25). But I don't see how this can possibly be a correct account of why Aristotle, in the *Categories*, makes the individual human being and the individual horse primary substance. Aristotle's 'container metaphysics,' as I am going to try to bring out in a moment, deliberately shifts the focus from Plato's heaven of the Forms to the individual boxes of this world. Surely that is what is going on here — not just some concession to the ignorance or prejudice of philosophical novices. But more on that in a moment.

(3) The idea of a *pollachōs legomenon*. Aristotle's Greek commentators obviously think they are entitled to full and unbridled use of this notion in their commentaries. A conspicuous use they make of it has to do, again, with their discussion of 1a24-5, the definition of 'in a subject.' (In case it isn't already obvious to you, this definition is the primary focus for my discussion.)

In Aristotle's *Physics*, Book 4, Chapter 3, the preposition 'in' ('*en*') is treated as a *pollachōs legomenon*. Aristotle identifies eight different ways in which it can be used. By the time we get to Ammonius, the list has grown to eleven. Here is Ammonius's list:

Gareth B. Matthews

(1) in a time

(2) in a place

(3) in a vessel

(4) as a part in the whole

(5) as a whole in its parts

(6) as a species in a genus

(7) as a genus in a species

(8) as the "affairs" of the ruled in the "power or control of the ruler"

(9) as form in matter

(10) as in an end

(11) as in a subject

(The same list appears in other commentators: for example, in Philoponus at 32, 7-26.)

The idea that Ammonius and other commentators have seems to be that this is an exhaustive list of the ways 'in' is used and Aristotle's definition of 'in a subject' at 1a24-5 is meant to pick out #11 from all the rest. I'll have more to say in a moment about how successful they think he is.

II

So much for the external problems and a little about what the Greek Commentators have to say about them. I shall now mention three internal problems in interpreting Aristotle's *Categories*.

(1) There is the problem about how the container story in this work fits with the categories story. When Aristotle says at 1a20ff.: "Among the things there are [the *onta*] some are said of a subject but are not in a subject" (and so forth), he lays out his story about 'the little boxes'

— what I am calling his 'Container Metaphysics.' The idea seems to be that everything is either

(i) an individual box;

(ii) a kind of box;

(iii) an individual item within some box; or

(iv) a kind of item within some box.

I shall focus most of the rest of my discussion on this container story in general and, in particular, on whether some of the Greek commentators can help us understand it. But first let me mention a problem about how this container story fits, or fails to fit, with the categories idea.

It is, of course, substances that are supposed to be the containers — the subjects in which other things are to be found. And primary substances are the individual containers — this man or this horse — whereas secondary substance is always a kind of container — man or horse.

So much for substance. That leaves nine categories. Are items in all the remaining categories simply nonsubstantial jewels held by the substantial jewel boxes? That's my way of reading Aristotle. The resulting picture, it must be conceded, requires a bit of getting used to. It is relatively easy to think of qualities as jewels in some little jewel box or other. But to think of quantities, places, times, etc. as also 'contained in' the relevant boxes is another affair. Aristotle is in the Lyceum. How can it be that in the Lyceum is in Aristotle?

The difficulty has two aspects. By talking of 'containers' here, and even of 'jewel boxes,' I am deliberately emphasizing the metaphorical basis for Aristotle's technical use of the preposition 'in.' There is certainly a danger in doing that. Aristotle calls the last of his eight ways in which 'in' can be used the 'strictest' (*kuriōtaton*). This is 'in' as in a vessel [*en aggeiō*] and generally in a place [*en topō*] (210a24). In the longer list of uses of 'in' that the commentators provide, the use of 'in' as in 'in a place' is made distinct from 'in' as in 'in a vessel' and both of these, of course, are made distinct from the use of 'in' as when an accident is said to be 'in a subject.' I certainly don't mean to be ignoring these distinctions. But I do want to suggest that this last use — 'in' as in 'in a subject' — rests on a metaphorical extension of the idea of being in a vessel or container.

The metaphor seems quite apt so long as we stick to qualities. Admittedly the shininess of the apple is not literally and non-technically in the apple. Shininess is a paradigm example of what is on the surface, rather than inside. But the willing student soon becomes accustomed to saying that, in a suitably technical sense of 'in,' the apple's shininess is in the apple.

The unnaturalness is, however, much magnified when we try to say that not only the apple's shininess, but also its measurements, place, time, relation to its mother tree, etc., are also in the apple. The difficulty is partly one of grasping the technical use when its metaphorical basis ceases to be helpful. Partly, and more significantly, it is a problem about how to fit together the categories story with the container story.

It must be admitted that Aristotle doesn't actually say that each being — each thing that there is — is an individual box, a kind of box, an individual content, or a kind of content. He just says that 'among beings' some are said of a subject, but not in any subject, and so on. If we read him as intending this fourfold classification as a total inventory, as I have been suggesting we should, we have an entirely 'this-worldly' account of what there is. It is somewhat reminiscent of Plato's story, say in the *Phaedo* (where there is Simmias and the tall, but also the tall in Simmias — i.e., Simmias's own tallness [102c]). But the story in the *Categories* is also different enough from Plato's story to make it plausible to suppose these are competing stories in metaphysics. On the total-inventory interpretation, Aristotle would be trying to do what Plato was doing, but also trying to do it better.

Alternatively, we can read Aristotle as saying that, among the things there are, are substances (primary and secondary) and qualities (individuals and types). Period. The things neither said of nor in a subject are primary substances. The things said of, but not in, are secondary substances. The things in but not said of are individual qualities. And the things that are both said of and in a subject are kinds of qualities. Other nonsubstantial categories besides quality would then be irrelevant to this fourfold classification.

What is wrong with this last reading?

The said-of-a-subject/not-said-of-any-subject dichotomy seems to be aimed at problems of the one and the many. What is not said of any subject is an individual, whereas what is said of a subject is a species or genus. It seems implausible to think Aristotle wanted to restrict this way of thinking about the one and the many to only two categories, namely, substance and quality.

The in-a-subject/not-in-a-subject dichotomy is a distinction between attribute and substance. Again, it seems implausible to think Aristotle wants to count only qualities as attributes of a substance.

When Aristotle asserts, then, at 2a34, "All the other things, then [*ta d'alla panta*], are either said of the primary substances as subjects or in them as subjects," he seems to be talking about all the things there are — including quantities, places, times, and the rest. The only way I can think of to avoid that implication is to assign a tacit restriction to the occurrence of 'all' here to yield this reading: all the other things we have just been talking about. The result would be this:

> All the other things we have just been talking about (i.e., things said of a subject but not in a subject, in a subject but not said of a subject, and both said of and in a subject) — all these are either said of the primary substances as their subjects or in them as subjects.

Whereas I don't think we can rule out such a reading automatically, it is, I suggest, so minimally informative as to be implausible.

So the first internal problem is this. Do we have in the *Categories* two total inventories, or just one total inventory, plus one partial inventory? Taking the first line we have to suppose that items from all the nine nonsubstance categories are 'in a subject.' Taking the second line we will suppose that it is only qualities that are 'in a subject.' The items in the remaining eight categories, on this alternative, simply fail to fall under the 'in a subject'/'said of a subject' classification scheme.

The Greek commentaries seem uniformly to follow the first interpretation. Though they, like we, prefer qualities as examples of things in a subject, they seem to suppose that there are two total inventories, and that the first fourfold classification classifies the very same items as the second tenfold classification. Here is Ammonius: "The natural sequence would be to produce [right away] an account of the categories themselves, but since [Aristotle] wants to produce a more general fourfold division before his teaching concerning the categories, he puts that in front" (24, 23-4). Ammonius's explanation for this seemingly unnatural way of proceeding is that Aristotle needs to begin with four units so that he can take the components of 4, namely 4, 3, 2, and 1, and add them up to get 10 — the number of the categories! But we can agree with him in supposing that the fourfold classification and the tenfold classification are meant to classify the very same items without accepting his numerological explanation for Aristotle's way of proceeding.

2. The second internal problem concerns how to read the definition of 'in a subject.' Since I'm going to give that rather extensive discussion, I'll pass over it for now and turn immediately to a third internal problem.

3. There is a problem in understanding just what the doctrine of categories is a doctrine of. Ammonius summarizes the ancient debate on this question as follows: "Notice that commentators have differed on this, some saying that the Philosopher is discussing words [*phōnai*], some [saying] things [*pragmata*], and some, concepts [*noēmata*]" (8, 21-9, 1). Ammonius himself pronounces this Solomonic compromise (which had actually been around since Iamblichus): "The Philosopher's aim here, therefore, is to treat words that mean things through mediating concepts" (9, 10-11).

Such a talent for compromise may be useful in labor negotiations or in politics, but it is not really valuable in philosophy. Suppose we want to know what category *nous* belongs to? How do we find out? Suppose we assign it to substance, when it actually belongs to quality, or vice versa. We have made a category mistake. But what kind of mistake is that? An empirical mistake, i.e., a mistake about the *pragmata*? A conceptual mistake, i.e., a mistake about the *noēmata*? Or a linguistic mistake, i.e., a mistake about the *phōnai*?

The commentators certainly have things to say that are relevant to this third problem. But I shall not try to assess their contribution here. I mean only to mention this problem to make clear that it is a problem and that it is something the commentators address.

III

I return now to the second internal problem, the problem about how to interpret this definition:

> By "in a subject" I mean what is in something, not as a part, and cannot exist separately from what it is in. (1a24-5)

Reading this definition correctly is, I think, central to understanding Aristotle's Container Metaphysics and assessing it responsibly. I want to consider now whether Aristotle's Greek commentators can help us in either of these projects.

Before considering what the ancient Greek commentators have to say on this point, though, let's review very briefly the most important points of controversy concerning it in the literature of our own time.

In 1965 G.E.L. Owen published an influential paper called 'Inherence' (*Phronesis* **10** [1965], 97-105), in which he attacked John Ackrill's reading of 1a24-5. Ackrill had understood the last clause to mean

(A) ... cannot exist apart from whatever it is in.

Thus from

(1) Color is in a subject

and

(2) Color is in this balloon

we could conclude:

(3) Color cannot exist apart from this balloon.

Since (3) is false, we have here a reductio argument for the conclusion that (2) is false, that is, that color is not in this balloon. Indeed, as

Ackrill conceded, on his reading of Aristotle, the only thing color would be in is body. Aristotle's claim to the contrary at 2b1-2, "Again, colour is in body and therefore also in an individual body," Ackrill had to write off as "compressed and careless" (*Aristotle's Categories and De Interpretatione* [Oxford: Clarendon Press 1963], 83).

Owen proposed, instead, that the last clause of the definition be read this way:

(O) ... cannot exist apart from being in something or other.

Thus, according to Owen, red and color could both be in a subject and indeed be in this red balloon so long as they can't exist without being in something or other — perhaps now in this balloon, later in a fire hydrant, etc.

More recently Michael Frede has suggested ('Individuals in Aristotle,' *Essays in Ancient Philosophy* [Minneapolis: University of Minnesota Press 1987], 49-71) that we read the last clause of the definition this way:

(F) ... there is something it cannot exist apart from.

Frede's idea is that everything in a subject has at least one so-called 'primary host.' If y is x's primary host, then x cannot exist apart from being in y. But that doesn't mean x isn't in other things besides its primary host. Thus body may be the primary host of color, so that color couldn't exist apart from being in body. However, color, on Frede's reading of Aristotle, could still be in all sorts of other things besides body. It could be in this red balloon, that brown book, yonder green grass, etc.

In what follows I shall refer to Frede's interpretation as the 'Primary-Host Interpretation.' I shall call Ackrill's interpretation the 'Monogamous-Parasite Interpretation' (the idea being that x is faithful to whatever it is in — that is, it can't exist apart from being in that. Owen's interpretation I shall call the 'Promiscuous-Parasite Interpretation.' (The idea is that something that is in a subject needs some host or other to be in to continue to exist; but there is nothing such that, to exist, it needs to be in that.)

IV

The Greek commentators discuss 1a24-5 by considering whether Aristotle's definition of 'in a subject' is either too broad or too narrow. They have the idea that the definition should apply to all accidents, and only to accidents. Furthermore, they think they know what ought to count as an accident. So if they can come up with something that the definition fits that ought not to count as an accident, that will show the definition to be too broad. Conversely, if they can come up with something that the definition fails to fit that ought to count as an accident, that will show the definition to be too narrow.

Their favorite example of an accident that seems not to fit the definition is fragrance. Here is the objection in Dexippus:

> And how is it not absurd to say that that which is in a subject cannot exist without that which it is in, when the fragrance can be separated from apples and roses? For often the qualities remain after those things which primarily possessed them no longer exist, as when the smell remains after wine has been drunk or garlic eaten?

Here is Dexippus's reply:

> But [Aristotle] did not say that it was impossible for what is in a subject to be separated from what it is in, but to exist apart. For the fragrance can be parted from the roses, but it cannot exist apart from them, but either perishes or transfers itself to other subjects. What he says next delineates the position still more accurately; for he did not just say of that alone that it cannot exist apart from that in which it was, but absolutely, apart from everything in which it is. The consequence of this is that even if the fragrance formerly in the apple changes its substrate by coming to be in the air, nevertheless it is in some substrate (subject), though in different ones at different times, and never in any way does anything escape the definition of accidents. (25, 8-22, Dillon's translation)

From this passage it is clear that Dexippus accepts Owen's Promiscuous-Parasite Interpretation of the final clause of 1a24-5. There need be nothing such that, for a given fragrance to exist, it has to be in that. Yet for a fragrance to exist, there must be something it is in. That is exactly what Owen thought Aristotle meant to require — no more and no less.

By the time we get to Ammonius, the picture has changed. For one thing, the standard example is now specifically the fragrance of an apple. Here is the way Ammonius presents the problem:

> Those, however, who say that it does not fit all accidents say that he has defined only the inseparable ones. Thus the fragrance in the apple is separable and comes to us at a distance from the apple, but is still an accident. If, then, it is separable from its subject, it would not be comprehended by the definition given. (28, 9-11)

To this alleged counterexample Ammonius offers two replies. The first reply sounds like garbled Dexippus: "Aristotle does not say in which it was but in which it is (therefore it is impossible for the fragrance to exist apart from the apple in which place it is; for either it is in the apple or it is in the air)." I confess I don't understand this reply. If, as we assume in the case of Ammonius's commentary, the text we have comes from student notes, it may well be that the students simply blew it.

The parallel passage in Philoponus (35, 22-6) — who is reported to have heard Ammonius's lectures — suggests that the second reply in what we have of Ammonius's commentary should be taken as a gloss on the first reply.[4]

The second reply which, in contrast to the mere three lines of the first reply, goes on for 23 lines, is much clearer. It begins this way:

> Further, not only does the fragrance of the apple come to us, but it comes with some substance of the apple. A sure sign of this is that after some time the apple will shrink and shrivel up, which shows that some substance of the apple in which the fragrance belongs is dissipated. (28, 15-18)

Here it seems pretty clear that Ammonius is relying on the Frede Primary-Host Interpretation of 1a24-5. His idea is that the apple fragrance rides to us through the air on minute apple-bits. That the

---

4 It should be noted, however, that Simplicius, who is also thought to have heard Ammonius's lectures on the *Categories*, repeats the line about Aristotle's not saying 'in which it was' but 'in which it is.' But he then goes on to draw a Dexippus-type moral (49, 14-18).

apple is constantly giving off minute apple-bits is shown, he thinks, by the fact that the apple eventually shrivels up.

Ammonius goes on to consider the objection that apples give off fragrance even when they are not shriveling —in fact, when they are still growing on the tree. He responds to this objection by claiming that during growth on the tree there is simply more substance being added through nutrition than bits being lost through effluence. The point of this long paragraph, as well as the point of the paragraph that follows it, is to defend the idea that the fragrance rides to us on a minute bit of whatever it is that has the fragrance. And the point in defending that claim seems to be to show that there is a primary host for a particular bit of fragrance, something it couldn't exist without being in. In the case of apple fragrance the primary host is apparently a minute apple bit.

The later commentaries of Philoponus (35, 17-36, 13) and Elias (152, 5-153, 2) follow Ammonius in giving prominence to the fragrance-of-the-apple example. Philoponus also seems to follow Ammonius in his solution. Thus Philoponus, too, seems to accept the Frede Primary-Host Interpretation of 1a24-5. Simplicius (49, 14-18) and Elias (152, 5-153, 2), like Dexippus, seem to affirm the Owen Promiscuous-Para-site Interpretation. 'Wherever the quality be,' Elias writes, 'it is in a subject' (153, 1-2). The context suggests he means: 'Wherever the quality goes, it will always be in some subject or other.' But none of these commentators takes Ackrill's line.

V

It is a consequence of Ackrill's Monogamous-Host Interpretation that things that are in a subject but not said of any subject — i.e., non-substantial individuals — turn out to be what Owen, following Bertrand Russell, called 'unit qualities.' Thus the color in my red balloon, since it cannot exist apart from my red balloon, is one of those unit qualities. Owen thought the doctrine of unit qualities was, at bottom, incoherent, and he wanted to save Aristotle from having an incoherent doctrine attributed to him.

It seemed to me when Owen's paper first came out — and it still seems to me today — that Owen picked the wrong place to draw the battle line. The most important thing at stake in the way we read 1a24-5 is not the doctrine of unit qualities. Commitment to unit qualities is compatible with Owen's reading of 1a24-5 anyway, though of course it is not required by it; and unit qualities can be given an independent motivation.[5] The most important thing that rides on 1a24-5 is not whether Aristotle countenanced unit qualities but whether Aristotle in the *Categories* is offering an entirely 'this-worldly,' Container Metaphysics.

Aristotle seems to be saying that the basic things that there are, are individual containers — little boxes. All other things besides the little boxes are either said of them as subjects — that is, they are specific or generic classifications of the little boxes — or else they are in the little boxes as subjects. Thus everything there is, is either an individual box, a species or a genus of individual box, or an item in the contents of an individual box.

It will follow, of course, that there are no species or genera that are not concretely exemplified, nor any items in other categories that are not concretely 'contained.' Rejecting Plato's story of the separate reality of the Forms, Aristotle tells a story that is strongly this-worldly. Concrete individuals in 'this world' are the primary realities (*ousiai*) because they are, literally, subjects for everything else.

Ackrill's interpretation of 1a24-5 ruins this story. On his interpretation, the only things present in the individual boxes will be nonsubstantial individuals — things that, though in a subject, are not said of a subject. The main reason to object to this result is not that it yields the embarrassing doctrine of unit qualities. The main reason to object is that it ruins Aristotle's boldly 'this-worldly' story. It will not be true that all other things are either said of primary substances as subjects or in them as subjects. Color, for example, will not be in them. Wisdom

---

5 Indeed, if we are to suppose that Aristotle countenanced them, we had better give them an independent motivation. Marc Cohen and I tried to do that in our paper, 'The One and the Many,' *Review of Metaphysics* **21** (1968) 630-55.

will not be in them. In-the-Lyceum will not be in them. Nor will is-sitting be in them. So individual substances will not be subjects for literally everything else.

Thus it will not be the case, on Ackrill's reading, that there exists such a thing as color if, and only if, color is in some individual box. Color can exist, on Ackrill's reading, by virtue of being in body — not in this particular body or that particular body, but just in body. But Aristotle says at 2b1-2, "Color is in body and *therefore* in an individual body" (emphasis mine). No doubt Ackrill is right to say that Aristotle is here being "compressed." But he is wrong to say that Aristotle is being "careless and compressed." Just the opposite.

On this point Aristotle's Greek commentators present us with a sweet irony. Their grand neo-Platonic sensibilities leave them unable to take with full seriousness the 'this-worldliness' of Aristotle's Categories. They can't suppose that Aristotle ever honestly considered individual organisms, like this human being and that horse, to be the primary realities. Yet they stand with Frede and Owen against the Ackrill reading of 1a24-5. Moreover, they suppose that the fourfold classification of 1a20ff. and the tenfold classification of Chapter 4ff. classify the very same items. In my view these two interpretive decisions together make the striking 'this-worldliness' of Aristotle's Container Metaphysics in the *Categories* not only possible, but also inescapable.

One could argue that the second interpretive decision by itself assures the denial of 'separated' realities. For if Aristotle really does mean "all the other things" when he says "all the other things are either said of the primary substances as subjects or in them as subjects," then not only will this grey and this color be in the old grey mare, but grey and color will be there, too. But, of course, if we decide the first question in Ackrill's way, we will be tempted to say, with him, that Aristotle's grand denial of separation (*chōrismos*) is careless and compressed. By going with Owen or Frede on 1a24-5 we remove that temptation. And that's exactly what the Greek commentators do. I say 'bully for them.'

CANADIAN JOURNAL OF PHILOSOPHY
Supplementary Volume 17

Aristotle's 'Peri hermeneias' in Medieval Latin and Arabic Philosophy: Logic and the Linguistic Arts

DEBORAH L. BLACK

In many fields within the history of medieval philosophy, the comparison of the Latin and Arabic Aristotelian commentary traditions must be concerned in large measure with the influence of Arabic authors, especially Avicenna and Averroes, upon their Latin successors. In the case of the commentary tradition on the *Peri hermeneias*, however, the question of influence plays little or no part in such comparative considerations.[1] Yet the absence of a direct influence of Arabic philosophers upon their Latin counterparts does have its own peculiar advantages, since it provides an opportunity to explore the effects upon Aristotelian exegesis of the different

---

1 With the exception of Averroes's brief *Middle Commentary*, which was translated by William of Luna sometime during the thirteenth century, none of the Arabic commentaries on the *Peri hermeneias* was translated into Latin, and even Averroes's work did not have a wide circulation. On the transmission, see R.-A. Gauthier's Introduction to the new Leonine edition of Thomas's commentary, *Expositio libri Peryermenias*, vol. 1.1 of *Opera Omnia*, Thomas Aquinas [1], 75-81. Perhaps this lacuna in the transmission of Arabic philosophy to the West is attributable to the long history of Latin philosophical commentary on the *logica vetus*, which made the aid of the Arabic commentators superfluous. The situation was far different from that pertaining to the assimilation of Aristotle's unfamiliar metaphysical and physical works, in which the help of Arabic authors was indispensable.

linguistic backgrounds of Arabic and Latin authors. This is especially evident in the discussions in *Peri hermeneias* commentaries
devoted to the relationship between logic and language, and to
the question of the differences between a logical and a grammatical
analysis of linguistic phenomena. While both Arabic and Latin
exegetes inherited, directly or indirectly, some of the same materials
of the late Greek commentary tradition, and of course, some of the
same issues inherent in Aristotle's own text, Arabic and Latin
authors filtered that same philosophical material through very different linguistic traditions, each with its own indigenous grammatical and linguistic theories. Given these circumstances, the very
linguistic gulf separating the Latin and Arabic authors, which in
many areas of philosophy remains merely incidental, becomes essential to the philosophical issues posed by certain parts of Aristotle's *Peri hermeneias*.

My aim in the present discussion is to explore a selection of the
standard passages in the medieval commentary tradition which give
rise to explicit considerations of logic's general status as a linguistic
art, and its special relationship to grammar. Amongst the Latin
commentators, I have confined my inquiry to authors whose commentaries were written in the thirteenth century, and with the
exception of Robert Kilwardby, to commentaries available in printed
editions.[2] Amongst Arabic authors, I have considered in the main
the writings of Al-Fārābī (ca. 870-950 AD) and Avicenna (Ibn Sīnā,

---

2 For an overview of the *Peri hermeneias* commentaries prior to the time of Aquinas,
see Gauthier's Introduction to Thomas Aquinas [1], 64-75. On the general subject
of the *Peri hermeneias* in the West see J. Isaac, *Le 'Peri hermeneias' en occident de
Boèce à saint Thomas* (Paris: Vrin 1953).

For the most part, I have confined my remarks on the Latin authors to direct
commentaries on the *Peri hermeneias*, and refrained from comparisons with more
general logical texts, both by these commentators and by other thirteenth-century authors. I suspect, however, that there are some tensions between the
approach to language and logic that is found in the commentary tradition, and
that found in independent logical treatises and in works on speculative grammar. But a full investigation of this topic is beyond the scope of the present
discussion.

980-1037 AD).[3] Since the question of Arabic influence on the Latin discussions of these topics is minimal, I propose to begin with the writings of Latin commentators, since the Latin discussions of the issues with which I am concerned are on the whole more thematic and homogeneous, and hence more approachable, than those of the Arabic authors.

I Logic and Grammar: The Latin Tradition

In the Latin commentaries on the *Peri hermeneias*, the question of the relationship between the logical and the grammatical study of language is treated thematically on both general and specific levels. On the general level, the question is addressed in the course of the standard introductory topoi regarding the subject-matter of the treatise, its place in logic, its purpose, and the significance of its title. These reflections provide, at least in theory, a set of canonical principles to which the more specific questions regarding the Aristotelian text can be referred and resolved. These specific questions occur primarily in the context of Aristotle's discussions of the noun and verb in chapters two and three of the text, and are generally concerned to explain the differences between Aristotle's perspective on linguistic topics and that of the standard grammatical authority, Priscian.

1. General Principles of the Logician's Treatment of Language

The Latin translation of the title of Aristotle's *Peri hermeneias*, *De interpretatione*, often served as an occasion for reflecting upon the linguistic content of the first four chapters of the text. Boethius's attempts to explain and justify the title provided the inspiration for many of the thirteenth-century explications, though there is consid-

---

3 I have omitted Averroes's *Middle Commentary*, even though it is the only Arabic text on the subject that was available in the West, since it is less concerned with the issues under consideration here than are the commentaries of Avicenna and Fārābī.

erable diversity in the individual commentators' interpretations of Boethius's remarks. Some commentators, in fact, appeal to Boethius as an authority, even though their explanation of the meaning of *interpretatio* in the title is not entirely compatible with Boethius's own view.

In the case of Martin of Dacia and Thomas Aquinas, this is done by bringing the logician's concern with the truth-value of statements directly into the meaning of *interpretatio*. In making this move, both authors are forced to claim that *interpretatio* is a synonym for *enuntiatio*, the Latin translation for Aristotle's *apophansis*, used to denote a complete statement which has a determinate truth-value. Martin, for example, replies affirmatively to the question of whether *enuntiatio* is the subject of the science treated in the *Peri hermeneias*, by citing Boethius's definition of interpretation: "For according to Boethius, interpretation, as it is used here, is nothing but vocal sound significant through itself, *in which there is either truth or falsity*" (my emphasis).[4] Now while the first part of Martin's citation is indeed from Boethius, the stipulation that an interpretation must possess a truth-value is explicitly rejected by Boethius, for Boethius denies that enunciation is the same as interpretation, and the possession of truth-values is the mark of an enunciation. For Boethius, then, nouns and verbs, as significant in themselves, *are* interpretations, although syncategorematic words are not.[5] Although Martin agrees with Boethius that syncategorematic terms are not encompassed by *interpretatio*, and hence are not discussed in Aristotle's text, he also argues that interpretation excludes the noun and the verb, that is, all non-complex vocal sounds, since complexity is a necessary condition for the assignment of a truth-value.[6] Aquinas, who offers essentially the same view

---

4 Martin of Dacia [1], q. 1, 236.1-3; see also 235.26-236.12.

5 For Boethius's discussion of the term *interpretatio*, see Boethius [1], prima editio (hereafter 1a), 32.8-34.28; secunda editio (hereafter 2a), 4.15-13.24. The passage cited by Martin is 1a:32.11-12: 'Interpretatio est vox significativa per se ipsam aliquid significans.'

6 Martin of Dacia [1], q. 1, 236.3-9

as Martin,[7] links his reading of the title explicitly to the identification of logic as a rational science, and to the need to justify the *Peri hermeneias* as concerned in some way with an operation of the intellect.[8] However, the inclusion of the noun and the verb in the text can be explained, according to Thomas, even though they do not fall under the proper meaning of interpretation, construed as enunciation. For they are the principles or parts of enunciations, and "it is proper to each science to treat the parts of its subject, just as it [treats] its properties."[9]

While neither Aquinas nor Martin makes any explicit attempt to link the definition of interpretation to the logic-grammar distinction, both seem to be concerned to modify Boethius's definition of *interpretatio* so that the consideration of the noun and the verb becomes a preliminary, not an essential, part of the science of interpretation. Their addition of truth-values to Boethius's definition of interpreta-

---

7 Unlike Martin, Aquinas does not add the difference "in which there is truth or falsity" to the Boethian definition of *interpretatio*. But he does argue that only "he who explains something to be true or false seems to interpret," and thereby ultimately accepts that "only enunciative speech, in which truth or falsity is found, is called interpretation" (Thomas Aquinas [1] 1.1, 6.48-52).

Regarding the interpretation of Boethius, Isaac and Gauthier have both argued that Aquinas only shows awareness of the *secunda editio* of his commentary. See Isaac, *Le 'Peri hermeneias' en occident*, 100 n. 1, and Gauthier's Introduction, 49. Thus, Gauthier cites the *secunda editio*'s definition of *interpretatio* as a *vox articulata per se ipsam significans* (2a:6.4-5) as Thomas's source for the definition of *interpretatio* as *uox significatiua que per se aliquid significat*, at 1.1, 6.35-37. However, Thomas's citation seems closer to the *prima editio*'s definition of *interpretatio* as a *vox significativa per se ipsam aliquid significans* (32.11-12). This calls into question Isaac's claim regarding the *prima editio* that Thomas "n'y a fait aucune allusion."

8 Thomas Aquinas [1], 1.1, 5.15-16: "Cum autem logica dicatur rationalis sciencia, necesse est quod eius consideratio uersetur circa ea que pertinent ad tres predictas operationes rationis." Aquinas is referring to the differences among the understanding of indivisibles, composition and division, and discursive reasoning; the *Peri hermeneias* is assigned to the second operation, composition and division.

9 Ibid., 1.1, 6, 59-61; see also 6.46-61.

Deborah L. Black

tion, contrary to Boethius's own express intentions, indicates a desire
to identify Aristotle's approach in the *Peri hermeneias* as unequivocally
logical, and worthy of the designation of *scientia rationalis*.[10]

In contrast to Martin and Thomas, Kilwardby and Albertus Magnus allude explicitly to the differences between logic and both grammar and rhetoric in their explanations of the meaning of
'interpretation.' Kilwardby, who prefers to base his explication on
Boethius's alternative definition of interpretation in the *secunda editio*
as *vox prolata cum imaginacione significandi*, remarks:[11]

> But here "interpretation" is to be understood according to Boethius, insofar as
> "interpretation" means "vocal sound uttered with an image of signifying." Nor
> should the book be placed under grammar or rhetoric for this reason, because
> "an image of signifying" adds something over and above "signifying," namely,
> to signify by presupposing becomingly and congruously, which are indeed
> intended by the grammarian and the orator, congruously by the grammarian,
> and becomingly by the orator. But [the *De interpretatione*] is placed under rational
> philosophy, as well as under linguistic philosophy, since rational philosophy

10 In the proemia to both his *Peri hermeneias* and *Posterior Analytics* commentaries,
    Aquinas limits his characterization of logic to that of a rational science, although
    he does not explicitly deny logic the status of a linguistic science. See *Expositio
    in libros Posteriorum analyticorum*, R.-A. Gauthier, ed., vol. 1.2 of Thomas Aquinas
    [1], Bk. 1, ch. 1 (Proemium), 3.1-5.50, for a more detailed version of the themes
    treated in the proemium to the *Peri hermeneias* commentary.

11 Robert Kilwardby, *Notule super Periarmenias Aristotilis*, P. Osmund Lewry, ed.,
    in Robert Kilwardby [1], 379.11-13. All citations of the introduction and first *lectio*
    of Kilwardby's commentary refer to the edition appended to Fr. Lewry's disser-
    tation. Before his untimely death in 1987, Fr. Lewry was preparing an edition of
    the entire commentary, and had provided a draft version of the text to members
    of his graduate seminar at the Pontifical Institute of Mediaeval Studies in
    Toronto in the spring of 1983. This draft translation forms the basis for my
    remarks on the remainder of Kilwardby's commentary, but references are also
    provided to one of the three manuscripts of the commentary, Venezia, Biblioteca
    Marciana lat. L.VI.66 [2528], fols. 1r-18v.
    For the reference to Boethius, see Boethius [1] 2a:4.27-8, where the phrase *sonum
    ... cum quaedam imaginatione significandi* is used as a definition of *vox*. At 5.22-6.3,
    it is used to distinguish *interpretatio* from *vox* and *locutio*.

30

does not altogether prescind from speech. And thus it is clear under what part of philosophy it belongs.[12]

In this passage, Kilwardby does not allude explicitly to truth-values, but the insistence that logic is a rational as well as a linguistic science fulfills a similar function, while allowing him to preserve Boethius's claim that the noun and the verb are in fact proper parts of the subject-matter of the text. Kilwardby, moreover, provides some explication of the relationship between linguistic and rational science: for according to the passage just cited, any rational science is by nature also linguistic, since it presupposes the fulfillment of grammatical and rhetorical well-formedness as a necessary condition. Rational sciences, however, add to their linguistic underpinnings an explicit reference to the conscious, signifying activity of a mind, the *imaginatio significandi* of Boethius.[13]

Among the Latin commentators, Kilwardby also provides one of the most direct formulations of the commonplace, encountered throughout the *Peri hermeneias* commentary tradition and in various other logical and grammatical texts, that logic considers language with a view to truth and falsehood, whereas grammar considers it with a view to congruity and incongruity. The occasion for his remarks is the observation that the definition of *oratio* (*logos*) given by Aristotle in the opening sentence of *Peri hermeneias* ch. 4 (16b26) differs from the definition of *oratio* given by Priscian:

> But one ought to say that the logician, in considering truth and falsity with regard to speech, defines speech through the things signified, since truth and

---

12 Robert Kilwardby [1], 379.11-22

13 None of the medieval commentators seems bothered by Boethius's explication of signification by reference to imagination rather than intellect. In her translation of Aquinas's commentary, Jean Oesterle suggests that the roots of this phrase are in Aristotle's distinction between mere physical sound (*psophos*) and voice (*phōnē*) at *De anima* 2.8.420b27-421a1, the latter requiring the presence of a soul capable of having *phantasia* of some sort. See *Aristotle: 'On Interpretation,' Commentary by St. Thomas and Cajetan (Peri Hermeneias)* (Milwaukee: Marquette University Press 1962), 17 n. 2.

> falsity are caused in speech by the things signified; so [Aristotle] says, "Speech is a significant vocal utterance...." But the grammarian, considering congruity and incongruity with regard to speech, defines speech through ordering, since congruity and incongruity are caused by the things consignified; but they [in turn] are consequences of the things, insofar as construction and ordering are owing to [the things], since [the things] are the media of constructing or ordering one word with another. So [Priscian] says, "Speech is a congruous ordering of words." And thus does the diverse intention of the authors make for diverse definitions.[14]

In this passage, Kilwardby is quite willing to tie the logician's concern with truth-values not merely to the formal structure of predication, but also to the fact that speech signifies and refers to the things which determine truth and falsity. In accordance with Aristotle's focus on significant vocal sounds, logical truth is construed by Kilwardby to be as much a semantic property as a formal one. Thus Kilwardby aligns the truth-congruity contrast between logic and grammar with the contrast between signification and consignification: logic attends directly to the signification of things, whereas grammar, while deriving its criteria of congruous construction from things, attends less directly to their representation as such. Now the distinction between signification and consignification is, of course, a common one in the logical and grammatical theory of the thirteenth century, and thus its employment as a solution to the doubt is not entirely unexpected. But Kilwardby uses the commonplace in a way that supplements his earlier suggestion regarding the relations between linguistic and rational sciences.

---

14 Robert Kilwardby [1], fol. 7v, lines 4-11:
   Sed dicendum quod logicus considerans ueritatem et falsitatem circa orationem, cum ueritas et falsitas causantur in oratione a rebus significatis, diffinit orationem per res significatas, dicens, *Oratio est uox significatiua*, etc.; set grammaticus, circa orationem considerans congruitatem et incongruitatem, cum congruitas et incongruitas causentur ab ipsis consignificatis, hec autem consequuntur res in quantum eis debetur constructio et ordinatio, quia sunt media construendi siue ordinandi dictionem cum dictione, diffinit orationem per ordinationem, dicens, *Oratio est congrua dictionum ordinatio*. Et sic diuersa intentio auctorum fecit diuersitatem diffinitionum.
   For the citation from Priscian, see Priscian [1] Bk. 2, 15, 1:53.28.

While he does not here mention the mediation of the mind, Kilwardby's claim that, like signification, consignification reflects the real ordering of things outside the mind, suggests that grammar too must in some sense be a rational science. For the ability of grammatical constructions to consignify extramental reality linguistically would seem to entail a corresponding conceptual grasp of the ordering. If logic is primarily a rational art that cannot be totally indifferent to the concerns of language, here grammar seems to be a linguistic art that must attend in part to the demands of reason.[15]

Albertus Magnus is closest to Kilwardby in his treatment of the preliminary issues, and provides what is clearly a Boethian construal of interpretation, as "a speech which is concerned with a thing as it is, spoken verbally for the purpose of explanation."[16] It is broader

---

15 In the *De ortu scientiarum*, Robert Kilwardby [2], ch. 49, §468, 160.19-161.2, Kilwardby treats signification as a property common to all the *sermocinales scientiae* included in the trivium, i.e., logic, grammar, and rhetoric. Arguing that every *sermo* is a *signum*, he claims that all the linguistic sciences must be concerned with *sermo significativus*. The difference between the three arts derives from the fact that grammar confines its consideration of language to the representation of what is already *nota*, whereas logic and rhetoric are *inquisitivus* of what is *ignota*. Cf. §474, 162.22-3, where grammar is said to be *[d]e sermone ... significativo per se*, rhetoric and logic *de [sermone] ratiocinativo per se*; and ch. 53, §493, where Kilwardby insists that logic is both rational and linguistic. This picture accords broadly with the suggestion in the *Peri hermeneias* commentary that both grammar and logic are rational as well as linguistic (for grammar's objects are *nota*), although it obviously suggests that the significative-consignificative distinction is rather arbitrary. But cf. §484, 165.12-15, where grammar is associated with both *modi significandi* and mental concepts: "Subiectum enim sermo significativus est secundum quod huiusmodi; finis, congruus, et aptus modus significandi omnem mentis conceptionem; definitio, scientia de sermone docens omnem animi conceptionem significare."
   The overall impression one gleans is that Kilwardby has a generally consistent approach to the question of the relations between logic and grammar, but is rather fluid in the terminology he uses to define their formal differences as distinct sciences.

16 Albertus Magnus, *Libri 2 Perihermeneias*, in Albertus Magnus [1] vol. 1, Bk. 1, tract. 1, ch. 1, 373b16-18.

than an enunciation, which requires that "something be said or predicated of something else (*aliquid de aliquo dici vel praedicari*)," although enunciation is "the most powerful interpretation (*potissima interpretatio*)." Still, Albert agrees that since the term 'interpretation' covers nouns and verbs as well as enunciations, the title handed down for the text is preferable to *De enunciatione*, even though it is conceded that enunciative statements are the work's proper subject-matter.[17] Unlike Kilwardby, however, Albert simply identifies rational and linguistic philosophy in this context. When addressing the traditional question, to which part of philosophy does the text belong, Albert assigns it to *scientia rationalis sive sermocinalis* as opposed to *realis*, since it considers 'being under the form of words (*ens stans sub sermone*).' Yet even this is not sufficient for Albert, and he goes on to bring the Avicennian conception of logic, as a method for reaching knowledge of the unknown, to bear upon interpretation: "[F]or interpretation is useful in order to have knowledge of complex, unknown things through complex, known things, because interpretation comes to be known in speech."[18] Albert also adds, in his discussion of the placement of the *Peri hermeneias* among the sciences, that it considers speech in terms of the accidents of subjectibility and predicability, and is thus ultimately ordained to the study of syllogistic.[19] Finally, in accepting the Boethian refutation of the claim that the work has *oratio* 'speech' as its proper subject,[20] Albert, like Kilwardby, explicitly

---

17 Ibid., 1.1.1, 374a3-27

18 Ibid., 1.1.1, 375b10-18; the text cited is ll. 15-18. For the Avicennian background, to which Aquinas also alludes, see below, n. 68.

19 Ibid., 1.1.1, 375b18-22.

20 Ibid., 1.1.1, 375b23-5. The Borgnet edition attributes this position to Andronicus, although Boethius mentions Alexander and Aspasius, as do other thirteenth-century commentators. It is not clear whether the mistake is Albert's or the editor's; it is obviously due to Boethius's discussion of Andronicus's misgivings about the authenticity of the text, which follows immediately after the discussion of the views of Alexander and Aspasius on *oratio*. For the controversy over *oratio*, see Boethius [1], 2a:10.4-11.11.

contrasts the logician with the grammarian (as well as the orator and poet), in terms of the nature of their respective concerns with speech. The basic point is that the genus of *oratio* is the common subject-matter of all the *artes sermocinales*, and thus proper to none. Rather, each art considers speech with a view to a different end: Albert does not mention the end of logic here, but he does concur with Kilwardby that the end of grammar is congruity, whereas that of rhetoric is agreeableness.[21]

While it is clear that the Latin commentators, in their explications of the title and subject-matter of Aristotle's *Peri hermeneias*, are all concerned in some way to delineate the relationship between reasoning and language within logic, there is considerable diversity in their approaches to this question. They agree that the principal concern of the text at hand is the enunciative statement and its parts, but there is no generally accepted basis for explaining the centrality of enunciation, nor the extent to which the treatment of such things as the noun and the verb is contained under the notion of interpretation. Certain formulaic distinctions between logic and grammar, rooted in the differences between the texts of Aristotle and Priscian, appear commonplace: grammar is concerned with congruity, consignification, and syntactical construction; logic is concerned with truth, signification, and subjectibility and predicability. But the divergences amongst the commentators' approaches to the preliminaries of exposition suggest that even these commonplace formulas were understood differently by the various authors who exploited them.

Ultimately, these divergences seem to stem from underlying differences in the commentators' views of the relation between the linguistic and rational orientations of logic. The acceptance of the traditional Boethian construal of the title seems to reinforce the harmony between logic and linguistic considerations, at the price of omitting to

---

21 Albertus Magnus [1], 1.1.1, 375b25-38. Martin of Dacia also uses the couplets of truth-falsehood and congruity-incongruity to contrast the logical and grammatical approaches to speech. See Martin of Dacia [1] q.14, 248.14-249.30, "utrum pertineat ad logicum considerare veritatem et falsitatem."

explain the underlying unity of the Aristotelian text. The attempt to bend Boethius's notion of interpretation to accommodate a fuller sense of logic's rational character and its peculiar concern with truth and falsity tends, for its part, to leave unexplained Aristotle's selective consideration of certain obviously linguistic topics, such as the nature of nouns and verbs, to the exclusion of others of at least equal logical interest, such as syncategoremata.[22] Yet even those who, like Martin of Dacia and Aquinas, depart from Boethius, and thus gravitate towards the simple identification of logic as the rational science and grammar as the linguistic science, are reluctant explicitly to sever logic from the linguistic arts. Rather, the logician, while focusing on the demands of logic as a rational science, is given license to include, as Aristotle does in chapters 2 and 3, a consideration of any linguistic phenomena that can be shown to have some bearing on, or participation in, his principal purpose.

2. Defenses of Aristotle's Treatment of the Noun

A more precise picture of how the Latin commentators view the respective approaches of logic and grammar to linguistic phenomena emerges from discussions devoted to Aristotle's treatment of the noun in chapter 2 and the verb in chapter 3. The most telling discussions are those that are concerned to justify the consideration of these apparently grammatical topics in a work of logic, and to explain why Aristotle, the foremost logical authority, does not concur with Priscian, the foremost grammatical authority, in his treatment of the same linguistic subjects.

Defining the Noun: The main focus of attention among the commentators, which will also provide the focal point of this second part of my consideration of the Latin logical tradition, is Aristotle's treatment of the noun in chapter 2. It is Martin of Dacia who addresses most directly the question of whether the noun is a proper subject of study

---

22 It is interesting to compare the Latin commentators with the Arabic philosophers on this point, for the latter always include particles in their discussions of the parts of speech in *Peri hermeneias* commentaries.

for the logician. Question 17 of his commentary openly challenges the logician on this point, objecting that since the noun is a grammatical object of knowledge (*scibile*), it does not "pertain to the logician to offer a determination of [it]."[23] In his reply, Martin does not take issue with the identification of the noun as a grammatical *scibile*, but he does argue that the grammatical characteristics of the noun do not exhaust its knowable properties. Martin constructs his positive case for the logician's right to determine the noun by appealing to the *ratio logica*, the formal perspective according to which logic studies its subjects. This *ratio* Martin identifies with the properties of subjectibility and predicability, that is, the properties that permit terms to form the subjects or predicates of an enunciative statement possessing a truth-value.[24] Thus, in his reply to the objection that the noun is a grammatical, not a logical, item of knowledge, Martin observes that there is nothing unwonted about diverse branches of philosophy considering the same thing from different perspectives, so long as each branch of philosophy remains within the confines determined by its own proper *ratio* or perspective. He parallels to the logical couplet of *subicibilis-praedicabilis* the familiar grammatical couplet of *congrua-incongrua*, here explicitly identified as the aim of the *modi significandi* insofar as they represent grammatical principles of construction.[25]

Martin's treatment of this question, in virtue of its specific appeal to the *modi significandi*, introduces further precision into the efforts to distinguish the grammatical and logical approaches to linguistic topics, by construing the commonplace points of contrast between the two arts as indicating the different formal perspectives of two distinct sciences. What is most noteworthy about this approach is Martin's insistence that the noun is not a distinctively grammatical *scibile*, but rather a linguistic object that becomes a grammatical *scibile* when viewed from one perspective, a logical *scibile* when viewed from

23 Martin of Dacia [1], q. 17, 253.14-17

24 Ibid., q. 20, 254.20-7. (Question 20 contains the replies to questions 17-20.)

25 Ibid., q. 20, 254.28-255.3

another. 'Noun,' then, is not an equivocal term used improperly in logic, and there is no suggestion that Aristotle would have done better to forget nouns and verbs entirely, and stick to the terminology of subjects and predicates.[26] For Martin, the overlapping of technical terms in logic and grammar serves to reinforce the underlying unity of the two sciences, which study two different sets of properties anchored in the same linguistic objects.

Kilwardby and Albertus Magnus seem to have in mind the same sort of justification as Martin, although they attempt to provide an account of the underlying causes of the logician's distinctive perspective on both the noun and the verb. According to Kilwardby, the grammarian begins his treatment of the noun by analyzing its embodiment in a vocal sound, and his analysis terminates in the intellect, that is, in the conceptual content to be signified by the imposition of the word as a linguistic sign. The grammarian is properly concerned with the actual vocal construction of a word in its own right. The logician, however, begins with the conceptual content that is to be signified, and terminates in its vocal sign.[27] Kilwardby does not mean, of course, that the logician's ultimate concern is with vocal expressions; rather, his claim reflects the order of sign-relations established by Aristotle at 16a3-8, in which vocal words are said to be signs of the *passiones animae*. Since the logician

---

26 One reason for this reluctance to import the unmistakably logical terms of subject and predicate may come from the need to distinguish the approach of the *Peri hermeneias* from that of the *Prior Analytics*. Aquinas, for example, argues that the designations of 'noun' and 'verb' apply to the signs of simple intelligibles insofar as they are considered as parts of enunciations; when treated as parts of a syllogism, these same signs are considered not as nouns and verbs, but as 'terms,' and they are treated under this formality in the *Prior Analytics* (Thomas Aquinas [1], 1.1, 6.80-7.97). Cf. Robert Kilwardby [1], 386.26-30. Albertus Magnus argues more generally that since the notions of subject and predicate depend upon the notion of enunciation, they cannot be determined until after Aristotle has determined the nature of the enunciation. See Albertus Magnus [1] 1.3.1, 400b34-401a14.

27 Robert Kilwardby [1], 386.9-26

is concerned with language principally as a sign of concepts, the concepts constitute the primary focus of logic, to which the study of their verbal embodiment is referred. Given this difference in the starting point of his investigation of language, then, the logician cannot simply take the grammatical definitions of nouns and verbs as ready-made principles. In explaining his rejection of this type of dependency of logic on grammar, Kilwardby further observes that the grammarian attends to those properties of nouns and verbs that render them *constructibilia*, and that these are not the same as the logically relevant properties which render them *subicibilia et predicabilia*.[28] Read in conjunction with the argument from their different starting-points, Kilwardby's claim would seem to be that words are constructibles insofar as they are considered qua vocal sounds, whereas they are subjects and predicates insofar as they are considered qua signs of concepts. Thus, given that the logician and the grammarian study their common objects from different starting points, and with a focus on different properties, the definitions of 'noun' and 'verb' offered by Priscian and Aristotle must differ.[29] As with Martin, Kilwardby accepts the claim that logical and grammatical nouns are essentially the same objects, understood in different ways; the divergence in their definitions is introduced, not by an equivocation, but by the diversity of Aristotle's and Priscian's ultimate intentions in their study of the noun.[30]

---

28 Ibid., 386.36-40

29 Ibid., fol. 4v, line 3: "Primum dubitabile est propter quid diffinitur hic aliter nomen quam a Prisciano, cum essentia uniuscuiusque sit semel."
Priscian offers more than one definition of the noun, but the medieval commentators take as canonical that of signifying substance with quality. See *Institutiones grammaticae*, 2.18 (Priscian [1], 1:55.6): "Proprium est nominis substantiam et qualitatem significare"; and 2.22 (Priscian [1], 1:56.29-57.4): "Nomen est pars orationis, quae unicuique subiectorum corporum seu rerum communem vel propriam qualitatem distribuit. dicitur autem nomen ... quasi notamen, quod hoc notamus uniuscuiusque substantiae qualitatem."

30 Robert Kilwardby [1], fol. 4v, ll. 4-7: "Set dicendum quod diuersa auctorum intentio fecit diuersitatem diffinitionum. Diffinitur ergo in grammaticis per

Deborah L. Black

Albert presents the most detailed consideration of why the logician cannot simply borrow his definitions from the grammarian, elaborating upon Kilwardby's claim that logic begins with the intellect and ends in speech. Albert explains that the logical definition of the noun as a conventionally significant vocal sound (*vox significativa ad placitum*) given by Aristotle takes the vocal utterance as a direct sign of the likeness of an object in the soul, as alluded to in the opening discussion of the *Peri hermemeias*. This in turn is the basis for the logician's appeal to truth and falsity as his primary principles, for truth and falsity properly speaking are only said to arise in relation to a knowing mind which composes and divides concepts in order to make them correspond with the things known. The grammarian's, that is, Priscian's, definition of the noun as 'substance with quality' completely overlooks the relation between language and mind, and hence the conceptual mediation that makes possible the assignment of a truth-value to the utterance, insofar as Priscian's definition refers directly to the substance and quality of the thing itself:[31]

> But for this reason, namely, that [vocal sounds] are signs of the passions which are caused in the soul by the intentions of things, it is held that they are not primarily signs of the things, but rather, they are primarily signs of the likenesses which are in the soul, and through these likenesses they are referred to things. And in this the signs considered here differ from the grammarian's consideration, for he considers those vocal sounds to the extent that they are signs of things immediately, and thus he says that the noun signifies substance with quality, whereas the logician says that it is a conventionally significant vocal sound.[32]

---

partes sui essentie in quantum est constructibile, quia per substantiam et qualitatem; hic autem per partes sue essentie in quantum est subicibile. Et est ista diffinitio magis formalis; illa autem magis materialis, cum fiat per partes essentiales."

The claim that the logical definition is more formal, the grammatical more material, reflects the view that the vocal sound, which is more central to grammar, functions as the matter of an utterance.

31 Albertus Magnus [1], 1.1.3, 379a19-b8

32 Ibid., 1.2.1, 381a27-39

Albert's solution here, conditioned as it is by the need to explain the texts of Priscian and Aristotle, seems sound: Priscian's reference to substance and quality in his definition of the noun appears to be founded upon the metaphysical structure of the external world, whereas Aristotle's definition of the noun, and the general approach of the *Peri hermeneias*, seems to be rooted more in the signification of reality as mediated by concepts. But viewed as part of the commentary tradition as a whole, Albert's remarks illustrate a pervasive feature of the approach of Latin authors to the linguistic aspects of logic. We have seen in our consideration of the introductory discussions of the commentators that Albert displays an approach to the general problem of distinguishing logic and grammar that is closest to that of Kilwardby. Yet Albert's comparison of Priscian and Aristotle in the present context has led him to claim that there is a stronger link between grammar and extramental reality than between logic and that same reality. By contrast, Kilwardby's comparison between Priscian's and Aristotle's definitions of *oratio* led to an emphasis on logic as more directly concerned with signifying things, although for Kilwardby grammar too ultimately takes the things as the measure of its study of consignification.[33] Yet when Kilwardby addressed the differences between the two authorities in their definitions of the noun, the relation to the intellect, as principle or as terminus, was a factor in *both* the logician's and the grammarian's perspectives on language. That two authors can begin from such similar perspectives on the general orientation of logic, and yet offer such varied explanations for the logician's concern with specific linguistic topics, is evidence of the general difficulties the commentators face in reconciling the goal of exegesis with the desire to offer a systematic account of logic's place amongst the linguistic arts.

Infinite Nouns: Aristotle's claim at 16a29 and following that terms such as 'non-man' (*ouk anthrōpos*) are not nouns, and have no proper label of their own, was a common locus for discussing the effects of

---

33 Cf. above, nn. 14-15.

the logician's purposes upon his account of linguistic phenomena. The Latin commentators — unlike their Arabic predecessors — accept the view of Boethius and Ammonius, stemming from Aristotle's remarks 16b15, that these terms, for which Aristotle coins the term *aorista* 'infinite' or 'indefinite,' are infinite in the sense that they signify pure negations rather than privations.[34] On this reading, the term 'non-X,' say, 'non-sighted,' can be applied to all things other than Xs, and even to non-existent subjects; it does not name a specific disposition that may be viewed as the privation of X, say, 'blindness,' which can be meaningfully predicated only with reference to things that have the potentiality to be Xs.[35] Thus, according to the Latin tradition, 'non-sighted' can meaningfully be said not only of blind humans and animals, but also of walls and stones. Against the background of this reading, the Latin commentators generally interpreted Aristotle's claims regarding infinite nouns not as a simple observation about the absence of a technical term for these kinds of negations in Greek grammar, but rather, as a claim excluding infinite nouns from the proper domain of logic.

On this reading, Aristotle is generally interpreted by the Latin philosophers to hold the view that infinite nouns *are* nouns in the grammatical sense. Martin of Dacia, as one would expect, addresses this area of concern by appealing directly to modistic doctrine. Thus,

---

34 These remarks in fact apply to the infinite verb, but the Latin commentators generally consider the logical status of infinite nouns and verbs to be equivalent. Ackrill translates the passage in question as follows: 'Let us call them indefinite verbs, because they hold indifferently of anything whether existent or non-existent'; see *The Complete Works of Aristotle: The Revised Oxford Translation*, 2 vols., Jonathan Barnes, ed. (Princeton: Princeton University Press 1984), 1:25-38.

For the Boethius text in question, see 1a:52.11-53.4; 2a:62.3-63.14. See also Ammonius [2], 41.16-42.8; medieval Latin translation, Ammonius [3], 79.62-80.88. It should be noted that I am using 'negation' very loosely here. The medieval commentators all deny that infinite nouns and verbs constitute negations in the sense of complex, negative, complete enunciations.

35 See for example Thomas Aquinas [1], 1.4, 23.223-27: 'Si autem imponeretur a priuatione, requireret subiectum ad minus existens; set quia imponitur a negatione, potest dici de ente et de non ente, ut Boetius et Ammonius dicunt.'

it is objected that the infinite noun must in fact be a noun, because it possesses the *modus significandi* of signifying substance with quality, which is proper to the noun. Martin concurs with this claim, but argues that it is logically irrelevant.[36] "Grammatically speaking," he says, the infinite noun does signify substance with quality; but its indeterminacy prevents it from signifying any 'nature' and thus it is excluded from the *ratio logica* of subjectibility and predicability.[37]

Similar reasoning is found in Simon of Faversham, where it is argued that infinite nouns cannot be parts of enunciative statements, since they signify no conceptual content, and hence, cannot be composed or divided by the mind:

> Note that the infinite noun and infinite verb are excluded from the consideration of the logician, because the noun and verb which the logician considers should be parts of enunciation; but infinite nouns are not parts of enunciation, because everything which can be a part of enunciation must signify some concept of the mind, for enunciation is principally for the sake of truth. But we cannot have truth except through that which expresses a determinate concept. For [the infinite noun and verb] are said indifferently of being and non-being, and therefore are neither verbs nor nouns for the logician, and thus are not his concern. However, they are not excluded from the grammarian's consideration, because they do possess those accidents of the noun and verb by means of which they can be composed with one another. And the Philosopher implies this when he says that the infinite verb is the sign of a saying about another.[38]

There is, of course, an obvious problem with Martin's and Simon's construal of Aristotle's remarks here. Although the application of the criteria for inclusion in logic seems unobjectionable, such an explication runs up against the realities of Aristotle's own text. While Aristotle does claim that infinite nouns and verbs are not fully nouns or verbs in the proper sense, the prominent place of infinite terms in the discussion of opposition in chapter 10 seems to belie the claim that it is *logice loquendo* that infinite nouns are not truly nouns. A more likely

---

36 Martin of Dacia [1], q. 22, 260.19-26

37 Ibid., q. 22, 260.28-261.3

38 Simon of Faversham [2], q. 4, 152.27-153.3

reading of Aristotle would be that he has introduced infinite terms into the text because of their logical importance to the theory of contraries and contradictories, recognizing nonetheless that traditional Greek grammar has no name for such terms.

Since both Martin and Simon wrote rather brief and selective question commentaries on the *Peri hermeneias*, which are generally confined to problems arising from the first three chapters of Aristotle's text, they give little indication of how they would respond to such a criticism. In the penultimate question of his commentary, question 10, Simon does, however, address the problem of whether an infinite verb, "while remaining infinite, can enter into an enunciation."[39] Simon answers the question affirmatively, on the grounds that even an infinite verb is a "sign of a saying about another (*nota dicendi de altero*),"[40] and so meets the conditions required for inclusion in an enunciative statement. While these verbs thus fail to meet the stipulated definition of verbs, they have the accidents of a verb, and so can perform its functions. Simon appeals further to the *modi significandi* of the verb, "through which it is capable of being ordered with something else in an enunciation."[41] Since the infinite verb retains this capacity, and since it does not possess the modes of signifying proper to any other part of speech, it can be included under the modes proper to the verb by default.

Simon's argument is clearly concerned to salvage the use of infinite terms within propositions, despite his denial of their logical status as verbs. Moreover, Simon explicitly mentions the square of opposition later in his reply. His justification, however, is quite unsatisfactory. The second argument seems circular: only if it is already assumed that the infinite verb *can* enter into an enunciation does it seem to follow that it must possess the *modi significandi* of the verb. Moreover, the appeal here to the grammatical notion of modes of signifying seems

---

39 Ibid., 165.11-12

40 Ibid., 165.31

41 Ibid., 165.34-166.1

inappropriate for establishing the logical legitimacy of infinite terms.[42] And the first argument seems incompatible with Simon's denial of the logical status of infinite terms:[43] if it has already been argued that infinite nouns and verbs do not meet the criteria by which they can be parts of enunciation, it is difficult to see how infinite verbs, whatever their affinity to true logical verbs, can then enter into enunciations. At the very least, this justification calls into question the meaningfulness of the earlier discussion. For Simon would seem to be in a position of holding that the failure to meet the logical definition of a part of enunciation is totally irrelevant to the ability of a term to enter into an enunciation.

Albert's treatment of infinite nouns shares with Simon's discussion of infinite verbs in question 10 the tendency to appeal to grammatical definitions and authorities to explain Aristotle's intention. Albert continually evokes Priscian's definition of 'signifying substance with quality' to defend the claim that the infinite noun is *not* properly a noun. While it might seem that Albert is using Priscian to prove that Aristotle held the infinite noun is not a *grammatical* noun, this is not in fact how Albert argues. Rather, he uses the grammatical definition of the noun to prove the logician's point, claiming that the failure to signify substance with quality prevents the infinite noun from being 'enunciated' of anything, and hence from participation in the end of logic.[44] Albert argues, like Simon, that since there is no other part of speech under which to classify such terms, they can be classed as nouns by default. While one might think that Albert is thus making a grammatical point, or more accurately, arguing, as did Kilwardby on a general level, that grammatical congruity or meaningfulness is a necessary but insufficient condition for logical consideration,[45] Albert manages to confuse matters in what follows. For despite the fact

---

42 Cf. Albertus Magnus's justification, discussed below at nn. 44-48.

43 See above at n. 38.

44 Albertus Magnus [1], 1.2.5.391a21-35

45 On Kilwardby see n. 12 above.

Deborah L. Black

that he has appealed to Priscian's definition of the noun, he concludes,
"Therefore, if you will, it shall be called an infinite noun, so that it will
have the definition of the noun (*ratio nominis*) with respect to the
method of grammar, and also be excluded from the perfect definition
of the noun with respect to logic."[46]

A later passage, in which the grammatical definition of the noun
is also used, seems to clarify matters somewhat, although Albert's
emphasis in the passage leads one to believe at first reading that it
is in blatant contradiction to the earlier passage. In this case, Albert
argues that the infinite noun does fulfill the grammatical definition
of the noun, since it signifies substance with quality in an attenuated
sense, for the quality that is signified is infinite and hence fails to
name a determinate substance.[47] This is, in fact, the reason why
Albert had earlier denied that the infinite noun could be used in
enunciations. But his failure to articulate explicitly the exact role that
the grammatical definition of the noun plays in the determination

---

46 Albertus Magnus [1], 1.2.5.391a41-5. Albert goes on to argue that the infinite
noun is not a negation simply, since a negation leaves nothing: *Non enim
simpliciter negatio est, quia negatio nihil relinquit* (391b1-2). Perhaps this is a
practical acknowledgement of the fact that infinite nouns are employed in
Aristotelian logic.

47 Albertus Magnus, [1] 2.1.1, 426b17-35:
In praecedentibus autem antecedentis libri dictum est quid est nomen, et quid
innominabile est: non homo enim secundum logici intentionem non dico nomen: nec tamen in aliam cadit partem orationis: sed dicitur nomen infinitum,
quod est nomen secundum aliquid, quia significat substantiam cum qualitate:
sed non habet nominis perfectionem, scilicet quod significet et interpretetur
quae sit illa qualitas qua substantia nominis habet determinari: et quia finitam
tollit qualitatem quae in homine est humanitas, et nullam ponit, ideo non
interpretatur et· significat substantiam nisi infinitam, cujus qualitas ipsa est
infinitas: sed talis qualitas sufficit ad hoc quod sit nomen secundum intentionem
grammatici, quae modos plusquam res attendit.
Note that the last clause of this passage identifies the grammarian's concern to
be with modes, presumably of signification, rather than with things. Yet earlier,
we saw Albert identifying grammar as concerned *principally* with the direct
signification of things, in contrast with logic's concern with things as signified
in the mind (see n. 32 above).

46

of its logical acceptance is frustrating, particularly since Albert seems to have found the grammatical reference to the ontology of substance and quality more suited to philosophical explication than Aristotle's own definition of the noun. It is not so much that what Albert says about the indeterminacy of the infinite noun does not adequately explain why he believes it should be excluded from logical consideration; it is simply that he has inadvertently suggested that the traditional delineations between the logical and grammatical approaches to language are rather arbitrary.[48]

Ironically, because of his general lack of concern with the grammar-logic distinction, it is Aquinas who gives the most satisfying explication of the status of the infinite noun. Since he accepts that the infinite noun expresses a negation, and not a privation, he agrees with the other commentators that the reason for Aristotle's remarks is that the indeterminacy of terms like 'non-man' allows them to signify being and non-being indiscriminately. However, Thomas does not read Aristotle as allowing infinite nouns to be grammatical nouns in some

---

48 As to Albert's position on the problem of the inclusion of infinite terms in the theory of opposition, the passage cited in the preceding note actually occurs in Albert's discussion of the theory of opposition. Albert has just distinguished (at Albertus Magnus [1] 2.1.1, 426a39-b16) affirmative enunciations with finite subjects from those with infinite nouns as their subjects. Although Albert reiterates that the infinite noun is *innominabile* because it is said of both being and non-being, he goes on to accept its inclusion as the subject of an enunciation, on the grounds that the infinite noun does signify something that is in some way one; he ends by declaring, *et talis unitas sufficit ad unitatem subjecti in propositione sive in enuntiatione una* (2.1.1, 426b37-9). In contrast to Simon, Albert argues the infinite verb cannot enter into an enunciation and retain its infinite status, since only the *radix* of the verb, the copula, remains in the infinite verb, while its predicative force is removed (2.1.1, 426b39-427b20).

Despite this difference, Albert seems to share with Simon a common desire to defend the use of infinite terms in enunciations, and thereby to defend Aristotle's practice in the later parts of the text. Yet despite this, both commentators are reluctant to reject the accepted interpretation of the alogical status of infinite terms. The result is that the *ex professo* discussions of questions regarding what makes a linguistic object logically interesting become almost irrelevant to determining specific points of logical doctrine and logical practice.

attenuated sense; rather, they are admissible in logic to the extent that some sort of underlying subject (*suppositum*) is presumed by the mind upon hearing them, thus allowing them to "signify according to the mode of the noun, so that they can be made subjects and predicates."[49] This explains Aristotle's ability to use infinite nouns in the central parts of the *Peri hermeneias*, and calls upon the extension of the logical criteria of subjection and predication as a vindication of that employment. Since Aristotle is not read as excluding infinite nouns from the logical definition of the noun in the first place, no violation of logical principles is required in order to explain logical practice.

II Logic and Grammar: The Arabic Tradition

Unlike their Latin counterparts, who take their cue from Boethius, the Arabic philosophers seldom offer detailed discussions of their views on the linguistic aspects of logical study in their *Peri hermeneias* commentaries. To discover the principles upon which their exegesis of that text is based, it is necessary to begin with more general works on logic and language.

1. General Views of the Logician's Treatment of Language in Arabic Philosophy

Of the principal Arabic Aristotelians, it is Fārābī who devotes the most attention to the philosophy of language.[50] His *Iḥṣā' al-'ulūm* (Catalogue of the Sciences)[51] devotes its first two chapters respec-

---

49 Thomas Aquinas [1], 1.4, 23.227-29, and in general, 23.207-39

50 Apart from his actual commentaries on the *Organon*, Fārābī's works dedicated to logic and language include the *Kitāb al-ḥurūf* (Book of Letters [or Particles]), *Kitāb al-alfāẓ al-musta'malah fi al-manṭiq* (Utterances Employed in Logic), and portions of the *Iḥṣā' al-'ulūm* (Catalogue of the Sciences) and *Kitāb al-tanbīh 'alā sabil al-sa'ādah* (Reminder of the Way to Happiness).

51 Arabic texts will be cited initially by their Arabic titles, with an English transla-

tively to the science of language (*'ilm al-lisān*), which is essentially grammar, and to the science of logic (*'ilm al-manṭiq*).[52] Fārābī uses the assumption that logic and grammar are two distinct rule-based arts or sciences to argue that each art must be autonomous in its own sphere, and that the two arts are directed towards different ends and concerned with different subjects. In this context, he offers what is perhaps the best-known formula for distinguishing logic and grammar in medieval philosophy: "And this art [of logic] is analogous to the art of grammar, in that the relation of the art of logic to the intellect and the intelligibles is like the relation of the art of grammar to language and expressions. That is, to every rule for expressions which the science of grammar provides us, there is a corresponding [rule] for intelligibles which the science of logic provides us."[53] Lest it should be thought that Fārābī has effected a simple correlation be-

----

tion of the title in parentheses. In subsequent citations, a shortened version of the English translation will be used. Where medieval Latin versions of the Arabic texts are available, I have in most cases provided references to these as well as to the Arabic original.

52 The term usually rendered as 'grammar,' *naḥw*, is, strictly speaking, narrower in range than its English counterpart, being closer to 'syntax.' See for example Fārābī, *Iḥṣā' al-'ulūm* (*Catalogue of the Sciences*), 3rd ed., Uthman Amin, ed. (Cairo: Librairie Anglo-Égyptienne 1968), 62.1, where grammar is said to concern itself with a particular part of the science of composite expressions, namely, the study of the proper endings to be used when forming complex expressions. For the medieval Latin translation of this work by Gerard of Cremona, see *Catálogo de las ciencias*, 2nd ed., A. G. Palencia, ed. (Madrid: Consego Superior de Investigaciones Cientificas 1953), 124.19-20. The subject-matter of grammar, then, is not language in general, but *'irāb*, inflection (62.5; Palencia, 124.24-125.1). On this point, cf. A. Elamrani-Jamal, *Logique aristotélicienne et grammaire arabe* (Paris: Vrin 1983), 98-101; G. Bohas, J.-P. Guillaume, and D.E. Kouloughli, *The Arabic Linguistic Tradition* (New York and London: Routledge 1990), 49-72.

53 *Catalogue of the Sciences*, 68.4-7; Palencia, 128.25-129.4. Fārābī also extends the analogy to include prosody at lines 8-10, Palencia lines 4-9. The Latin translator apparently did not know the Arabic term for prosody, *al-'arūḍ*, for he simply transliterates the Arabic. According to Palencia's apparatus, there is, however, a marginal gloss indicating that the Arabic term means *de ponderibus uersuum*.

tween logic and rational science on the one hand, and grammar and linguistic science on the other hand, his later consideration of the subject-matter of logic dispels any such view. While logic clearly has intelligibles as its principal focus, it is also concerned with language insofar as language embodies the intelligibles:

> And as for the subjects of logic, they are the things for which [logic] provides the rules, namely, intelligibles insofar as they are signified by expressions, and expressions insofar as they signify intelligibles. And this is because we only verify belief for ourselves by thinking, reflecting, and establishing in our souls facts and intelligibles whose role is to verify this belief; and we only verify [it] for someone else by communicating to him by means of statements by which we cause to be understood the facts and intelligibles whose role is to verify this belief.[54]

Fārābī clearly does not wish to relinquish all study of language to the realm of grammar, then, as his original formulation would suggest, but rather, he insists that the study of expressions, as signs of intelligibles, is an integral part of logic.

A more precise sense of the differences between a logical and a grammatical study of language is offered by Fārābī in terms of the contrast between universal and particular rules of language use. According to this formula, grammar and logic share a mutual concern with expressions, but whereas grammar provides rules pertinent to the correct use of expressions in a given language, logic provides rules encompassing all correct expression, insofar as it is significant of intelligibles. Thus, logic will have to concern itself with certain common features of all languages, on the assumption that common linguistic features are indicative of some fundamental intelligible content. While those features common to all languages will therefore

---

54 *Catalogue of the Sciences*, 74.10-15; Palencia, 133.23-134.1. Cf. *Al-Tawṭi'ah* (Introduction [to Logic]), Rafiq al-Ajam, ed., vol. 1 of *Al-Manṭiq 'inda al-Fārābī* (The Logic of al-Fārābī) (Beirut: Dar el-Mashreq 1985), 55.9-56.2; there is an English translation of this text, along with an earlier edition, in 'Al-Fārābī's Introductory "Risālah" on Logic,' D. M. Dunlop, ed. and trans., *Islamic Quarterly* 3 (1956-57) 224-35. The passage in question is translated in §1, 230.

fall under the scope of both logic and grammar, Fārābī claims that this does not blur the distinction between the two arts: each maintains its own proper perspective on these features, logic attending to them qua common, grammar qua idiomatic.[55]

An approach which is similar to Fārābī's occurs in a work by Abū Zakkarīyā Yaḥyā ibn 'Adī (d. 974), a Syriac Christian who was active in the translation movement, and reportedly a pupil of Fārābī.[56] In his treatise *Fī tabyīn al-faṣl bayna ṣinā'atay al-manṭiq al-falsafī wa-al-naḥw al-'arab* (*On the Difference Between the Arts of Philosophical Logic and Arabic Grammar*), he attempts to argue that there is no conflict between the philosopher's study of language within logic and the traditional study of Arabic grammar, appealing as did Fārābī to the notion of two distinct sciences, each defined by its own unique method, end (*gharaḍ*), and subject-matter (*mawḍū'*).[57] Like Fārābī, Yaḥyā is concerned with the differences between the grammar of a particular nation and the universal science of logic. He argues that the subject-matter of grammar is mere expressions (*al-alfāz*), and that it considers

---

55 *Catalogue of the Sciences*, 76.2-77.15; Palencia, 134.23-136.4. See esp. 77.5-7; Palencia, 135.24-28: "So the science of grammar in every language considers only what is specific to the language of that nation; and [it considers] what is common to [their language] and to other [languages], not insofar as it is common, but insofar as it is found in their language in particular."

56 On Yaḥyā see Nicholas Rescher, *The Development of Arabic Logic* (Pittsburgh: Pittsburgh University Press 1964), 130-4. The text I will be discussing is 'Yaḥyā ibn 'Adī's Treatise on the Difference between the Arts of Philosophical Logic and of Arabic Grammar (*Maqālah fī tabyīn al-faṣl bayna ṣinā'atay al-manṭiq al-falsafī wa-al-naḥw al-'arab*),' Gerhard Endress, ed., *Journal of the History of Arabic Science* 2 (1978) Arabic pagination 38-50/English pagination 192-81 (note that the English pagination is in inverse numerical order). There is a French translation in Elamrani-Jamal, *Logique aristotélicienne et grammaire arabe*, 187-97; a German translation is found in Gerhard Endress, 'Arabische Philologie und griechische Philosophie im Widerstreit,' in Burkhard Mojsisch, ed., *Sprachphilosophie in Antike und Mittelalter*, (Amsterdam: Verlag B. R. Grüner 1986), 163-299.

57 *Philosophical Logic and Arabic Grammar*, §3, E191/A40.1-4

those expressions with a view to their correct articulation and vocalization according to Arabic conventions. [58] The grammarian, then, is primarily concerned with the oral aspects of language, in particular with what vocal endings to use in what circumstances. What he is not concerned with, according to Yaḥyā, is the investigation of "expressions insofar as they signify meanings (*al-alfāẓ al-dāllah 'alā al-ma'ānī*)."[59] Nor is Yaḥya content simply to assert this as a bare fact; rather, he goes on to argue for this claim, on the grounds that grammatical operations upon words do not affect their basic significations. For example, in the sentence, "Amr hit Zayd (*ḍaraba 'Amrun Zaydan*),' the fact that in Arabic, "Amr' is given the ending 'un,' and 'Zayd' the ending 'an,' according to the norms for vocalizing the indefinite nominative and accusative, does not alter the significata of the words "Amr' and 'Zayd,' namely, the essences of these two individuals.[60]

These two defenses of the boundaries drawn by philosophers between logic and grammar contain a number of points noteworthy as background to the interpretation of the *Peri hermeneias*. Like their Latin counterparts, including the speculative grammarians, the Arabic philosophers construe the notion of signification quite narrowly: the signification of any expression corresponds solely to its bare lexical meaning.[61] Thus it can be said that changes in case, gender,

---

58 Ibid., §§6-9, E190-89/A41-42. Elamrani-Jamal has an excellent discussion of the implications of Yaḥyā's emphasis upon correct *'irāb* or vocalization. See the reference in n. 52 above.

59 *Philosophical Logic and Arabic Grammar*, §10, E188/A43.1. Yaḥyā notes in this passage that the grammarians claim that it is their intention to consider expressions as significant of meanings, a claim which Yaḥyā contends is misleading. See §10, E188/A43.1-5.

60 *Philosophical Logic and Arabic Grammar*, §§11-12, E188-E187/A43-44.

61 On this point in Latin speculative grammar, see Michael A. Covington, *Syntactic Theory in the High Middle Ages: Modistic Models of Sentence Structure* (Cambridge: Cambridge University Press 1984), 33-5; and Irène Rosier, *La grammaire spéculative de Modistes* (Lille: Presses Universitaires de Lille 1983), 45, 56-7, 212 n. 97. On

number, and so on do not affect the signification of a term at all, and the grammarian has no concern with language qua meaningful. Unlike their Latin counterparts, however, the Arabic philosophers do not appear to allow the grammarian anything analogous to meaning as part of his subject-matter, along the lines of the Latin *modi signifi-candi*.[62] Grammar is strictly limited to the conventional rules of articulation in a particular language group, and does not concern itself with whether or how such rules reflect universal linguistic structures, or relate to the semantic content contained within the utterances.

While it seems overly simplistic to claim on the basis of this survey of views that someone like Fārābī or Yaḥyā would simply identify logic as a universal grammar,[63] nonetheless I would argue that it is Fārābī's intention to subsume the study of universal grammar under logic as one of its principal parts. This cannot help but be significant for Fārābī's reading of the *Peri hermeneias*, especially when it is viewed in comparison with the readings of Latin authors. For where Latin authors will assign to grammar, i.e., speculative grammar, what they believe to be properly philosophical considerations of the nature of language and linguistic constructions, Fārābī would seem to be forced either to view those same considerations as essentially logical or, alternatively, to require the logician to transgress his proper bounds, and borrow certain distinctions from the grammarian.

this sense of meaning, *currens* and *currere* mean the same thing in Latin, just as do *Zaydun* and *Zaydan* in Arabic. An example of this view can be found in Boethius of Dacia [1], 55.60-56.71.

62 As I note below at nn. 100-2, there is an analogue to the notion of *modi significandi* in Avicenna's *Peri hermeneias* commentary, but it is not used to provide the basis for a universal science of *grammar*. Avicenna's remarks in this context do suggest, however, that he is willing to construe meaning more broadly than is Yaḥyā.

63 This view as it applies to Fārābī is upheld by F. W. Zimmermann, in his Introduction to *Al-Farabi's Commentary and Short Treatise on Aristotle's 'De inter-pretatione'* (Oxford: Oxford University Press and the British Academy 1981), esp. xli-lvii; cxviii-xxii; cxxxi, cxxxviii-ix. It is challenged by Elamrani-Jamal, *Logique aristotélicienne et grammaire arabe*, 77, 88.

Yet the Fārābīan model of logic as a science of reason which includes universal grammar as an essential part is not universally favoured in the Arabic tradition, at least not in theory. In the *Isagoge* of his *Shifā'* (Healing), Avicenna openly challenges the formulaic presentation of logic's relation to expressions that is found in Fārābī's *Catalogue of the Sciences*:

> There is no merit in what some say, that the subject-matter of logic is speculation concerning the expressions insofar as they signify meanings.... And since the subject-matter of logic is not in fact distinguished by these things, and there is no way in which they are its subject-matter, [such people] are only babbling and showing themselves to be stupid.[64]

Avicenna's critique is based upon the view that speech is entirely accidental to the activities of the intellect, and hence cannot properly be considered even part of the subject-matter of logic.[65] Avicenna invokes his doctrine of the so-called common nature, established in the previous chapter of the *Isagoge*, and its attendant claim that logic considers the quiddities of things insofar as they are subject to the accidents that accompany them as objects of conception (*taṣawwur*) by the mind.[66] The logician's need to refer to expressions at all is induced by pure necessity, and Avicenna goes so far as to argue that "if it were possible for logic to be learned through pure cogitation, so that meanings alone would be observed in it, then this would suffice.

---

64 Avicenna, *Al-Shifā'* (Healing), vol. 1, *Al-Mantiq* (Logic), part 1, *Al-Madkhal* (Isagoge), G. Anawati, M. El-Khodeiri, F. Al-Ahwani, and I. Madkour, eds. (Cairo: Al-Matba'ah al-Amiriyah 1952), Bk. 1, chap. 4, 23.5-6, 24.3-4. For the medieval Latin translation of this portion of Avicenna's logic, see *Opera philosophica*, 2 vols. (Venice 1508), 1:3rb19-21, 41-2. Avicenna's rather derisive description of the Fārābīan view is considerably toned down in the Latin, which simply reads *ideo deliquerunt*.

65 Avicenna does qualify this with respect to those logical arts whose function is essentially communicative, i.e., where discussion and debate are involved, as in dialectic, rhetoric, and poetics. See my *Logic and Aristotle's 'Rhetoric' and 'Poetics' in Medieval Arabic Philosophy* (Leiden: Brill 1990), 60-1.

66 *Isagoge*, 1.2, 15.1-8; Latin 1:2rb29-42

And if it were possible for the disputant to disclose what is in his soul through some other device, then he would dispense entirely with the expression."[67] Although the suggestion that language might be entirely dispensable under ideal conditions seems implausible, it is entirely consistent with Avicenna's epistemology, since he holds an extreme rationalist position on the origin of knowledge, and believes that in some rare cases (the paradigm case being prophecy) discursiveness, with its connection to imagination and cogitation, can indeed be dispensed with.[68] But given the adverse conditions under which human thought normally operates, logic is a necessary instrument of philosophy, and it must take into account the accidental properties that accrue to intelligibles via their sensual signification in speech:

> Thus the art of logic is compelled to have some of its parts come to consider the states of the expressions. And were it not for what we said, it would not also be required to have this part. And despite this necessity, the discourse concerning the expressions corresponding to their meanings is like the discourse concerning their meanings, except that the expressions are imposed as more fitting for actual practice.[69]

---

67 Ibid., 1.4, 22.14-17; Latin 1:3ra64-3rb4

68 Though one would presume that under these ideal conditions, the art of logic itself would be dispensable, since the circumstances rendering error possible would be entirely eliminated. For, in this case, no process would be needed to progress from the known to the unknown, whereas facilitating the acquisition of knowledge of the unknown is the purpose of logic according to Avicenna. On this last point see, for example, *Isagoge*, 1.3, 16.15-17.5.
   For Avicenna's departure from the Aristotelian theory of the dependence of thought upon imagination, the canonical text is Bk. 5, chap. 5 of the *De anima* part of the *Shifā'*. There Avicenna rejects the theory of abstraction from images for a theory of the direct emanation of intelligibles from the Agent Intellect; the images are thereby assigned a purely preparatory, rather than a specifying, function in intellection. See *Avicenna's 'De anima,' Being the Psychological Part of Kitāb al-Shifā'* F. Rahman, ed. (London: Oxford University Press 1959), 234.12-236.2; medieval Latin translation in Avicenna [1], 2:126.27-128.63.

69 *Isagoge*, 1.4, 23.1-4; Latin 1:3rb12-19. Despite the obvious critique of Fārābī in this passage, Avicenna may well have adapted this notion of the primacy of thought

In practice, then, Avicenna as much as Fārābī recognizes the linguistic component of logic: his disagreement is simply that, as a merely accidental condition of the intelligibles, it should not enter into the definition of the subject-matter of logic in any formal way. Avicenna thus differs with Fārābī in identifying logic solely as a rational art whose purpose is always to lead the mind from the known to the unknown. Logic ceases to be a linguistic art essentially, though it remains one accidentally. The gap between Avicenna and Fārābī is thus narrower than Avicenna's polemic might seem to indicate. And it becomes narrower still when the two men's commentaries on the opening sections of the *Peri hermeneias* are considered.

2. The Nature of the Logical Teaching of the 'Peri hermeneias'

Among the principal Arabic commentaries on the *Peri hermeneias*, only Fārābī's *Sharḥ* (Long Commentary) provides a consideration, parallel to the Latin discussions inspired by Boethius, of the meaning of 'interpretation' as it appears in the title of Aristotle's text. In that discussion, it becomes clear that despite his greater willingness to accept the linguistic character of logic, and to appropriate for logic many of the functions of a universal grammar, Fārābī generally concurs with the majority of medieval commentators, both Latin and Arabic, that the *Peri hermeneias* has the enunciative statement as its principal focus, and refers its treatment of all other topics to that end. Like Aquinas and Martin of Dacia in the West, Fārābī is forced to construe the meaning of 'interpretation' very narrowly in order to make it reflect the perceived aims of Aristotle's text.

Thus, Fārābī tells us that 'interpretation' means 'complete statement' (*al-qawl al-tāmm*), so that the title of the *Peri hermeneias* is meant to capture Aristotle's intention to examine the most perfect type of statement, namely, the one which is best able to cause a complete

---

over expression from Fārābī himself, who draws upon it in his *Sharḥ* (Long Commentary) on the *Peri hermeneias* and in the *Utterances Employed in Logic*. See below at n. 75; cf. also Zimmermann, Introduction to *Farabi's Commentary and Short Treatise*, xlii.

understanding in the mind, which Fārābī identifies as the simple, predicative, categorical enunciation (*al-qawl al-jāzim al-ḥamlī al-basīṭ*).[70] Although Fārābī does not have to deal with the precedent of the Boethian commentaries, which posed problems for the Latin authors who wished to offer a similar reading of the title, Fārābī's own remarks in other contexts highlight how strained is his repudiation here of the more natural reading of 'interpretation' as a reference to the interpretation of thought by language. When elaborating on the theme of inner and outer speech (*nuṭq*=Gr. *logos*) in his independent logical treatises, Fārābī is fond of the formula that external speech is "the *interpretation* through language of what is in the mind (*al-'ibārah bi-al-lisān 'an mā fī al-ḍamīr*),"[71] in which he uses the same term for 'interpretation' that is used as a translation for the title of the Arabic version of the *Peri hermeneias*.

Thus, despite Fārābī's own preoccupation with questions of language, and his staunch defense of significant language as principally the logician's concern, he opts for an identification of the subject-matter of Aristotle's *Peri hermeneias* that is biased in favor of the conception of logic as a purely rational science. In some ways, it is more difficult to justify this move in Fārābī's case than it is among the Latins, precisely because he has subsumed all consideration of language as interpretive of thought under the realm of logic. While the Latin philosophers were able, even forced, to assign some consideration of interpretive speech to the speculative grammarian, Fārābī's opting for this construal appears to leave him, at least in theory,

70 *Sharh al-Fārābī li-kitāb Arisṭūṭālīs fī al-'ibārah* (Long Commentary on 'Interpretation'), W. Kutsch and S. Marrow, eds. (Beirut: Imprimerie Catholique 1960), 19.16-18, 23.11-14; Zimmermann trans., 3, 8-9. I have used Zimmermann's translation throughout, with some modifications where indicated. On the construal of the title, see Zimmermann, 3-4 n. 5. It should be noted that Zimmermann discerns two different versions of Fārābī's proemium to the commentary (Introduction, cxliv, and 4 n. 3); my remarks are based on both versions.

71 *Introduction to Logic*, 59.14-15; Dunlop trans., 233. Cf. *Catalogue of the Sciences*, 78.3-4; Palencia, 134.15-16, where the same phrase is used in the same context.

Deborah L. Black

without a niche in the philosophical canon to which the consideration of language as significative can be properly assigned.[72] The imbalance in favour of logic's rational, as opposed to its linguistic, status is balanced somewhat in both Fārābī's and Avicenna's comments on the opening themes of the *Peri hermeneias*. Fārābī, for example, begins his commentary on the text by evokin g his general claim that logic must concern itself equally with both language and intelligibles:

> One of the first things anyone taking up logic must know is that there are sense-objects, or more generally, existents outside the soul; then intelligibles, conceptions, and images in the soul; and finally, expressions and script. We must know how they are related to one another; for the logician considers intelligibles insofar at they relate to both sides, namely, to the existents outside the soul and to expressions. He also studies expressions by themselves, but always in terms of their relation to intelligibles.[73]

At the end of his discussion of the nature of writing, Fārābī explains further that the *Peri hermeneias* studies significant statements "with respect to their imitation of the intelligibles, in the sense of taking their

---

72 Since grammar is not viewed as a truly universal, and hence truly philosophical, science by Fārābī, the philosophical study of language cannot be carried out by the grammarian.

73 *Long Commentary*, 24.2-7; Zimmermann trans., 10 (modified). The Arabic commentators all refer explicitly to sensibles when discussing what is outside the soul. This seems to stem from Aristotle's reference at 16a3-4 to 'passions' (*pathēmata*) in the soul, the phrase that reputedly caused Andronicus to dispute the authenticity of the text. The Arabic translation renders this as *āthār* 'traces,' the term commonly used for the forms found in the common sense and imagination insofar as they are remnants of sense perception. Thus, the Arabic translation has led the commentators to assume Aristotle is implicitly invoking the causal account of perception in the *De anima*, and through it alluding to the ultimate origin of intellectual thought in the senses. For the Arabic version of the text, see *Die Hermeneutik des Aristoteles in der arabischen Übersetzung des Isḥāk Ibn Ḥonain*, Isidor Pollak, ed. (Leipzig 1913; reprinted Nendeln, Liechtenstein: Kraus 1966), 1.4.

place and being substituted for them."[74] In the course of reaffirming the claim that logic gives equal consideration to both language and intelligibles, Fārābī has moved once again to a position asserting the priority of the rational to the linguistic within the logician's study of signification. In a move that evokes Avicenna's remarks on language in the *Isagoge*, Fārābī goes on to argue that the imitative relation between language and thought is in fact the principal reason why the logician can focus on the more perspicuous rules of linguistic composition, rather than directly upon the composition of the thoughts themselves:

> Complex expressions here take the place of complex intelligibles, since similar remarks attach to them. It makes no difference whether we discuss complex expressions or the compositions of the intelligibles signified by these expressions. Principally, the purpose is to explain the composition of intelligibles. But since intelligibles are difficult to grasp, Aristotle substitutes for them the expressions that signify them and studies their composition instead, with the result that it appears as though there were no difference between the composition of expressions and intelligibles.[75]

In order to complete the harmonization of the linguistic focus and rational aims of the text, Fārābī concludes his discussion of signification with an assertion of the parallelism between truth and falsity in language, and truth and falsity in intelligibles. The concern of the logician with the signification of truth and falsehood is, Fārābī argues, fully reflected in the logician's consideration of language as imitative of thought, for "combination in the soul parallels affirmation in speech; separation in the soul parallels negation in speech."[76]

---

74 *Long Commentary*, 25.22; Zimmermann trans., 13 (modified)

75 Ibid., 25.23-26.1; Zimmermann trans., 13-14 (modified). In his Introduction, xlii, Zimmermann draws attention to a parallel passage in the *Kitāb al-alfāẓ al-musta'malah fī al-manṭiq* (Utterances Employed in Logic), M. Mahdi, ed. (Beirut: Dar el-Mashreq 1968), 102.7-15, on the method of instruction known as the 'substitution of words' (scil. for thoughts), where the same theme of facilitating conceptual understanding through language is evoked, with somewhat pejorative overtones.

76 *Long Commentary*, 26.24-25; Zimmermann trans., 14-15

As for Avicenna, in the first chapter of the *'Ibārah* (Interpretation) of the *Shifā'*, he too echoes the general principles laid down in his *Isagoge*. Logic discusses expressions only accidentally, limiting itself to knowledge of the basic states of expressions that allow them to function as vehicles for arriving at knowledge of the unknown, these basic states being the signification of simple and complex meanings, with a view to their bearing upon truth and falsity:[77]

> Know too that among both the expressions and the traces which are in the soul there are some which are singular and some which are composite. And the nature of the two is parallel and corresponding. For just as the single intelligible is neither real nor vain, so too the single expression is neither true nor false. And in the same way that if another intelligible is combined in the mind with the single intelligible, and predicated of it so that there is a belief that this is or is not so, then that belief is either real or vain, so too when another expression is combined with the single expression, and predicated of it so that it is said to be so or not so, then it is true or false.[78]

The view expressed in this passage exactly parallels that expressed in Fārābī's consideration of the same Aristotelian passage: both men are concerned to defend the claim that the logician's prominent concern with questions of language can contribute to his ultimate goal of discerning truth from falsity in the realm of intelligibles. What is distinctive of Avicenna's presentation here, however, is the careful and deliberate manner in which he has chosen his terms for truth-values in the intelligible and linguistic realms. Perhaps in order to stress the difference between expressions and intelligibles, Avicenna deliberately uses different pairs of terms in each case: truth and falsity (*al-ṣidq/al-kidhb*) for language, real and vain (*ḥaqq/bāṭil*) for intelligibles. Now, if logic is primarily concerned with intelligibles, not expressions, we would expect the technical terminology of the logician to coincide with the terms applicable to intelligibles. But in fact,

---

77 Avicenna, *Al-Shifā'*, vol. 1, *Al-Manṭiq* (Logic), pt. 3, *Al-'Ibārah* (Interpretation), M. El-Khodeiri and I. Madkour, eds. (Cairo: Dar el-Katib al-'Arabi 1970), Bk. 1, ch. 1, 5.14-17

78 Ibid., 1.1, 6.1-6

Avicenna uses 'true' and 'false' as terms denoting the status of expressions, and 'real' and 'vain' as terms denoting intelligibles. The probable reason for this is to emphasize that the bond between intelligibles and reality is stronger and more direct than the bond between language and reality, since the terms chosen by Avicenna to designate the intelligibles suggest a concern with the ontological reality or fictiveness of what the intelligibles represent.[79] Yet its effect in this context is to suggest that even though the logician is primarily concerned with intelligibles, his substitution of the more perspicuous expressions corresponding to them is so deep-rooted that it determines the very import of his own technical language.

Their opening treatments of signification in their commentaries on the *Peri hermeneias* reinforce the impression that, despite the polemic directed by Avicenna against the Fārābīan presentation of the subject-matter of logic, both commentators agree essentially that Aristotle's initial consideration of signification serves to justify the discussion of linguistic topics in a logical text, given that logic is primarily interested in intelligibles. Both authors share the presumption that the ultimate goal of logic is the determination of truth and falsehood, and thus both relate their justification of the linguistic preoccupation of the text to the means whereby truth-values are assigned to enunciative statements. On the level of these general considerations of the scope and aims of the *Peri hermeneias*, neither Fārābī nor Avicenna has explicitly evoked a comparison of logic with grammar as a means of delineating more precisely the limits of the logician's focus upon language. But this is not unexpected, given the analysis of the relations between logic and grammar exemplified in such texts as Fārābī's *Catalogue of the Sciences* and Yaḥyā Ibn 'Adī's *Philosophical Logic and Arabic Grammar*. If grammar is viewed as an

---

79 The term *bāṭil*, for example, is used by Avicenna to describe fictional concepts like the phoenix. See, for example, '«Épître sur la disparition des formes vaines» d'Avicenne,' (French) J.R. Michot, ed. and trans., *Bulletin de philosophie médiévale* **29** (1987) 152-70, esp. 155.8; English translation in 'Avicenna's "Letter on the Disappearance of the Vain Intelligible Forms After Death",' J.R. Michot, trans., in *Bulletin de philosophie médiévale* **26-7** (1984-85) 94-103, esp. 98.

Deborah L. Black

idiomatic, particular, and non-philosophical science, it is less likely to be perceived as capable of providing much illumination of the methods and aims of a universal, philosophical science like logic, despite the accidental concern of both logic and grammar with linguistic phenomena. It is a general feature of the Arabic commentaries on the *Peri hermeneias* that the topos of logic versus grammar does not figure prominently in the discussion of the linguistic elements of the text, in the way it does amongst thirteenth-century Latin authors. But in their comments on Aristotle's consideration of the noun and the verb, Fārābī and Avicenna do provide important indications of their underlying presuppositions about the specific relations between logic and grammar.

3. Aristotle's Treatment of the Noun in the Arabic Tradition

Generally the Aristotelian definition of the noun as significant in isolation and prescinding from time caused no difficulty for Arabic authors. However, as with the Latin philosophers, both the infinite noun — which the Arabic philosophers called 'indefinite' (*ghayr muḥaṣṣal*)[80] — and the inflections of the noun were discussed in some detail.[81]

The Indefinite Noun: Unlike their Latin counterparts, the Arabic commentators generally accept the indefinite noun as properly logical, and thus they read Aristotle's remarks about the namelessness of indefinite nouns as a point about normal Greek usage. Fārābī, for

---

80 On the use of this term — which does not mean 'indefinite' except in logical contexts — see Zimmermann, Introduction to *Farabi's Commentary and Short Treatise*, cxx and n. 2.

81 The Latin commentators' discussions of the inflections of the noun were not included in the first part of this study in the interest of brevity, although this topic was also a common occasion for the Latin authors' presentation of their views on the relations between logic and grammar.

example, implies in his *Long Commentary* that the indefinite noun has essentially the same status as compound nouns which signify a single intentional object, such as the proper names Kallipos and 'Abd al-Malik,[82] since the indefinite noun is similarly composed of a negative particle and a noun "so that the complex of the two of them comes to be in the form of a single expression."[83] Fārābī also differs from both the Greek and Latin commentators in his interpretation of the signification of these nouns, which, he argues, is not infinite, nor of "any random thing, no matter whether existent or non-existent."[84] Fārābī suggests instead that Aristotle holds that both the indefinite noun and the indefinite verb signify something, either something existent, in the sense of something affirmed, or something non-existent, in the sense of something denied. That is, Aristotle is making the point that these terms have the force of a positive term, and so can be negated as well as affirmed, as in expressions of the form 'not non-P.' Thus, what is signified by indefinite terms is not non-being absolutely, but rather, the privation of a specific quality. The label 'indefinite,' therefore, simply indicates that no actual disposition or state (*malakah*=Gr. *hexis*) is signified by the term.[85] Fārābī also explicitly claims that his interpretation is justified by Aristotle's own practice in chapter 10, where statements with indefinite terms are interpreted by Aristotle as having the same force as 'plain' statements, i.e., those without any indefinite terms.[86]

82 A proper name in Arabic, literally meaning 'the king's servant.'

83 *Long Commentary*, 32.5, my translation (cf. Zimmermann trans., 20).

84 Ibid., 38.4; Zimmermann trans., 28. The topic here is not the indefinite noun, but the indefinite verb, and Aristotle's claim that it is said of both existent and non-existent things. Fārābī extends his comments here to cover all words of the form 'non-X,' be they nouns or verbs.

85 *Long Commentary*, 38.23-39.2; Zimmermann trans., 29. Cf. Fārābī's *'Ibārah* ([Short Treatise] on Interpretation) in vol. 1 of *Al-Manṭiq 'inda al-Fārābī*, 147.12-17; Zimmermann trans., 234. (Note that the page numbers in the margins of Zimmermann's translation refer to an earlier edition of Fārābī's *Short Treatise*.)

86 *Long Commentary*, 39.6-18; Zimmermann trans., 30.

Deborah L. Black

Clearly, then, Fārābī takes Aristotle's interest in the indefinite noun (and the indefinite verb as well) to be purely logical. Such terms are not being excluded from logic; rather, they are being added to it. If anything, it is *grammatically* that indefinite nouns are not properly considered nouns. Nonetheless, Fārābī appears to assume that Greek grammar reflects the logical status of indefinite nouns better than does Arabic. For he mentions several times the fact that indefinite nouns and verbs 'hardly exist' in Arabic, although they are quite

---

Fārābī's discussion of propositions with indefinite terms is complex and extended, and a full consideration of his views on the topic is beyond the scope of this paper. Zimmermann offers a brief discussion in his Introduction to *Farabi's Commentary and Short Treatise*, lxiii-lxvii. An extended consideration of indefinite terms in a variety of commentators is found in M. Soreth, 'Zum infiniten Prädikat im zehnten Kapitel der aristotelischen Hermeneutik,' in S. M. Stern et al., eds., *Islamic Philosophy and the Classical Tradition* (Columbia, SC: University of South Carolina Press 1972), 389-424. Averroes's views on indefinite terms have been discussed in two articles by H.A. Wolfson, 'Infinite and Privative Judgments in Aristotle, Averroes, and Kant,' *Philosophy and Phenomenological Research* 8 (1947) 173-87; and 'The Twice-Revealed Averroes,' in J. F. Ross, ed., *Inquiries into Medieval Philosophy: A Collection in Honor of Francis P. Clarke* (Westport, CT: Greenwood 1971), 211-41; both articles have been reprinted in Wolfson's *Studies in the History of Philosophy and Religion*, 2 vols., I. Twersky and G. H. Williams, eds. (Cambridge, MA: Harvard University Press 1973), 2:542-55 and 1:371-401, esp. 387-97. All subsequent citations refer to the reprinted versions of these two articles.

It ought to be noted that in the *Short Treatise*, Fārābī does allow that indefinite nouns can be extended from their proper signification of privation in two ways. First, they can be extended to allow their predication of all subjects which share a common genus or species with the subjects to which the privation properly applies, e.g., 'non-rational' as applied to horse, or 'non-bearded' to women. Second, they can be used in a still wider sense of all existent things, even those outside the genus to which their corresponding possession properly applies. Fārābī's example is the use of negative predications of God. But Fārābī insists that even in these extended uses, the subject of predication must be something existent. See *Short Treatise*, 153.10-155.6; Zimmermann trans., 238-40. On this extended and looser reading of indefinite terms, Fārābī's theory appears closest to that of Aquinas, who argued that the mind must presuppose some *suppositum* in order to use infinite terms. See above at n. 49.

common in other languages.[87] Indeed, Fārābī even appeals to conventional usage in languages other than Arabic to support his claim that indefinite nouns have the force of a simple noun and signify privations, noting that "the communities that use them do not count them as phrases" and give them an affirmative meaning. He even goes so far as to imply that other languages manage to reflect this logical point in the grammatical form of the words, claiming that for these other languages, "their shapes are the same as those of single expressions: for they behave like single expressions and they inflect like single expressions."[88]

Avicenna's explication of indefinite terms differs in certain details from that of Fārābī. Avicenna agrees with Fārābī on the fundamental point that terms of the form 'non-X' usually have the force of determinate privations, so that 'non-sighted,' for example, usually signifies that something which should be able to see is blind, and can only be

87 See, for example, *Short Treatise*, 135.17-136.1; Zimmermann trans., 222.

88 Ibid., 136.3-5; Zimmermann trans., 222. Cf. 138.6-9; Zimmermann trans., 225, on the indefinite verb.
   Fārābī's reference, in the parallel passages of the *Long Commentary* (39.11-13; Zimmermann trans., 30), to the discussion of privation in *Metaphysics* 5.22.1022b32-33, may explain his claim that indefinite terms in other languages than Arabic actually inflect like single terms. For Fārābī seems to think that Aristotle is talking about terms with a privative *alpha* in both the *Peri hermeneias* and the *Metaphysics*, and is unaware that the former text in fact discusses terms with the negative particle *ou* preceding them. This conflation of privative terms with indefinite ones may have been reinforced by the Arabic versions of the *Metaphysics*: the lemmata in Averroes's *Long Commentary* indicate that the privative *alpha* was rendered into Arabic by *lā*, the same term used to translate *ou* in Aristotle's discussion of indefinite nouns and verbs in the *Peri hermeneias*. See Averroes, *Tafsīr mā baʿd al-ṭabīʿah* (Great Commentary on the *Metaphysics*), 4 vols., 2nd ed., M. Bouyges, ed. (Beirut: Dar el-Machreq [Imprimerie Catholique] 1967, 1973), 2:647.5-6; and see the Arabic version of the *Peri hermeneias*, Pollak, ed. (cited in n. 73 above), 3.30 and 4.12. Averroes himself, it should be noted, also glosses Aristotle's remarks in the *Metaphysics* as referring to 'metathetic nouns' (*al-asmāʾ al-maʿdūlah*) (*Great Commentary*, 2:647.6-7).

applied to existent subjects.[89] But in the *Interpretation* of the *Shifā'*, Avicenna departs from Fārābī in his construal of the nature of the composition involved in indefinite nouns. Thus, in reply to the objection that the property, 'no part of which signifies in isolation' does not apply to all nouns, Avicenna argues that the indefinite noun is in some sense composite not only in its form but also in its signification.

The way in which Avicenna defends the Aristotelian definition of the noun against this objection also highlights the difference between his view of the interplay between logic and grammar in the Aristotelian text and the readings of the philosophers of the Latin tradition. The objection which Avicenna addresses naturally enough points to the fact that both the negative particle *lā* 'not'[90] and the noun with

---

89 *Al-Ishārāt wa-al-tanbīhāt*, J. Forget, ed., as *Le livre des théorèmes et des avertissements* (Leiden: Brill 1892), 27.9-11; 28.10-29.2; English translation, *Remarks and Admonitions, Part One: Logic*, S.C. Inati, trans. (Toronto: Pontifical Institute of Mediaeval Studies 1984), 83, 85-86.

Like Fārābī (see n. 86 above), Avicenna allows for a 'more general' use of indefinite terms, in which their meaning is taken to be broader than that of a privation. He is also insistent that, whether indefinite terms are taken in a broader or a narrower sense, their predication implies an existent subject. Avicenna admits in his *Interpretation*, 1.4, 27.9-28.6, that Aristotle's remarks on indefinite verbs could be taken to imply that they can be said of non-existent subjects, but he adds that Aristotle is wrong if this is what he meant. In the *Najāh* (Deliverance), M. Fakhry, ed. (Beirut: Dar al-Afaq al-Jadidah 1985), 54.19-26, Avicenna similarly allows the use of indefinite terms in broader and narrower senses, but prohibits their application to fictional entities like the phoenix. Thus, while it is proper to say, 'The phoenix is not sighted' (simple negation, 'Not [S is P]'), it is not proper to say, 'The phoenix is non-sighted' ('S is not-P'). In the *Remarks and Admonitions*, this same rule is applied to all affirmative statements. Only negative statements can be made about non-existent beings (28.16-29.1; Inati trans., 86). On this cf. Fārābī, *Short Treatise*, 155.2-4; Zimmermann trans., 240.

90 In the *Interpretation*, Avicenna presents indefinite nouns as compounds with the particle *lā*, reflecting the Arabic versions of the *Peri hermeneias*. In other works, he often reverts to the more natural Arabic construction with *ghayr* (literally, 'other than'). On the artificiality of the *lā* compounds with reference to Fārābī, cf. Zimmermann, Introduction to *Farabi's Comentary and Short Treatise*, cxxxiii-iv.

which it is combined are significant in separation. Hence, it seems unlikely that their combination into an indefinite noun can signify in the same way as simple nouns do, since in this sort of combination each part appears to retain the significance it would have had in isolation. In his reply, Avicenna claims that indefinite nouns are not in fact nouns in the full sense, and hence (as Aristotle observes) they do not have any proper grammatical label. They are not, Avicenna agrees, complete statements possessed of truth-values; rather, they are "composite expressions whose force is that of single [expressions], just like definitions."[91] Avicenna is implicitly evoking here his epistemological doctrine that some concepts, such as definitions and descriptions, while analyzable into parts and verbally complex, are nonetheless simple in meaning, and can, therefore, be signified as well by a corresponding simple expression. For example, the definition 'rational, mortal animal' signifies a single concept that can also be represented by the simple expression, 'human.'[92] What Avicenna means by simplicity here, is, therefore, the fact that such expressions, and their corresponding intelligibles, are merely objects of conception (*taṣawwur*), not of an assentive judgement (*taṣdīq*).[93] However, since their signification depends upon their autonomously significant parts retaining their significance even when composed, Avicenna likens them, not to names like 'Abd al-Malik, in which the literal meaning of the parts has no bearing on the noun's denomination of a particular individual, but rather, to expressions like 'shepherd,' 'marksperson,' and 'philosopher.' Of such phrases, Avicenna claims:

> And their correspondence to nouns does not indicate that they are in fact nouns. For the nature of both definition and description is like this. And despite this, there is no need for you to be deceived by the inclusion of the particle of negation

---

91 *Interpretation*, 1.2, 12.13

92 Ibid., 1.5, 32.18-33.3

93 For a discussion of this distinction in Arabic logic, see my *Logic and Aristotle's 'Rhetoric' and 'Poetics,'* 71-8.

in them, and thus for you to suppose that there is a negation in them. Not at all; rather there is neither affirmation nor negation in them, but instead, they are permitted to be affirmed, denied, or posited through affirmation and negation. But since they closely resemble nouns, let them be called indefinite nouns. And their judgement is like the judgement[94] of the predicate in our saying, "Zayd is in the house," for "Zayd" is a subject and "in the house" a predicate, while the latter is not in fact a noun, but rather, it is a composite. However, its composition is not like the unqualified statement, which is composed from two nouns, or from a noun and a verb, because it is composed from a particle and a noun. And it is neither a noun, nor is it an unqualified statement. And this is how you must understand this passage, nor should you pay any attention to the interpretations in which [others] are engaged.[95]

Avicenna's disagreement with Fārābī over the nature of the composition involved in indefinite terms seems to be a minor one from a logical perspective. Both philosophers agree that the significates of such terms are single concepts or intentions in the mind, and both seem ultimately concerned to argue the way they do for similar reasons — namely, to distinguish indefinite terms from negative statements, and thereby uphold their admissibility in both affirmative and negative enunciations. Where the two seem to differ is in their understanding of the *grammatical* underpinnings of Aristotle's dismissal of indefinite terms. Thus Fārābī, as already noted, upholds the parallel between compound proper names and indefinite terms because he believes that indefinite nouns assume the grammatical form and inflection of single expressions in all languages but Arabic, and have not only the signification of the noun but also the outward grammatical properties of the noun. Although Avicenna appears to be taking Aristotle's repudiation of the nominal status of indefinite terms more seriously than Fārābī, he too seems to be construing that repudiation as an assertion of the lack of *grammatical* simplicity in indefinite terms, not of their logical inadmissibility. This is shown by Avicenna's use of the complex predicate

---

94 The term 'judgement' (*ḥukm*) is used in a very broad sense in the Arabic commentary tradition on the *Peri hermeneias*, where it is roughly equivalent to 'meaning' or 'idea.' Its use does not imply composition, assent, or truth-value.

95 *Interpretation*, 1.2, 12.16-13.7

'in the house' to illustrate the tension between unity and complexity in these terms, as well as from his *purely* grammatical analysis of the composition of indefinite terms, i.e., as composed from a noun and a particle. Unlike his Latin counterparts, then, Avicenna does not hold that the ability to function as an independent subject or predicate term is at issue in this or parallel claims in the *Peri hermeneias*. Indefinite nouns are not fully nouns, as Avicenna himself has said, simply because they are the product of two independently significant elements, and so contravene the proper definition of the noun. There is, of course, one other consequence to be noted, if this is indeed how Avicenna's argument is to be construed. For it is *Aristotle* who has defined a noun as having no part significant in isolation: if such a definition cannot be met by expressions which are clearly able to function as the predicates and subjects of enunciative statements, then Aristotle's definition of the noun is not meant to be a uniquely logical definition, but rather, an element borrowed from grammar as a propaedeutic to purely logical considerations.

There is, in fact, independent confirmation that Avicenna regards these points, and parallel ones, to be properly grammatical theories imported by Aristotle into his logical texts. At the end of his discussion of propositions containing indefinite terms in *Al-Ishārāt wa-al-tanbīhāt* (Remarks and Admonitions), Avicenna explicitly distinguishes those characteristics of indefinite terms that are idiomatic to particular languages, and thus the concern of the linguist or grammarian (*al-lughawī*), from those characteristics that are logically significant. Amongst the former characteristics, Avicenna includes the determination of what indefinite terms signify, and whether their signification extends beyond privations. Only two considerations are mentioned as logically relevant: (1) The formal consideration of how the placement of the particle of negation affects the status of the statement as an affirmation or negation; and (2) the requirement that the subject of any affirmation, whether or not it contains an indefinite term, must be existent.[96] Both logically relevant properties are clearly

---

96 *Remarks and Admonitions*, 28.13-29.2; Inati trans., 85-6

tied directly to the process of assigning truth-values to enunciative statements, and to the ultimate ordination of the enunciative statement to syllogistic.[97] Except for the minimally necessary condition that positive predications require an existent subject, the question of the exact signification of indefinite terms is left to the determination of normal usage in each language group. In this respect, Avicenna's criteria for logical relevance are hardly distinguishable from those employed by his Latin counterparts; what separates his reading of the *Peri hermeneias* from theirs is the acceptance that many of Aristotle's remarks in the text have a grammatical, rather than a logical, import.

In many ways, Avicenna's perspective here seems more faithful to the Aristotelian text than does the Latin tradition's assumption that everything in the *Peri hermeneias* must have a logical significance. But when viewed in the broader context of the discussions in Islamic philosophy of the relation between logic and grammar, this attitude may seem problematic for a tradition that confines the grammatical study of language to the purely idiomatic, and eschews any claims that grammar considers language as significant of thought. While Avicenna's polemic against any essentially linguistic content in logic

---

97 The long discussion in Fārābī's *Short Treatise* of opposition in the metathetic proposition (*al-ma'dūl*, i.e., one containing an indefinite predicate) displays a similar concern with the applicability of the theory to syllogistic. Thus, Fārābī closes his discussion with a consideration of the logical equivalence of negations said of existent subjects and the corresponding metathetic affirmations, in which he focuses upon the problem of including negative predications as the minor premise of a first figure syllogism (154.16-155.4; Zimmermann trans., 239-40). Fārābī concludes by declaring that the extension of indefinite nouns to this wider meaning (i.e., as simply requiring an existent subject) is "of enormous benefit to the sciences" (155.4-5; Zimmermann trans., 240).

For discussions of the use of *al-ma'dūl* as a technical term for statements containing indefinite terms, see Zimmermann's Introduction to *Farabi's Commentary and Short Treatise*, lxiii n. 1; and Wolfson, 'Twice-Revealed,' 394; 'Infinite and Privative Judgments,' 545. Zimmermann and Wolfson argue convincingly that the use of *ma'dūl* and *'udūl* represents a translation of Theophrastus's Greek term *metathesis*, and thus reflects the secondary meaning of *'adala* 'to deviate,' not its meaning 'to be equal,' as Inati suggests (*Remarks and Admonitions*, 85 n. 28).

may make this problem less urgent than it might be for Fārābī or Yaḥyā Ibn 'Adī, in his *Remarks and Admonitions* Avicenna clearly shows that he accepts his predecessors' association of grammar with the study of the idiom of particular languages. But the linguistic properties that Avicenna mentions as idiomatic in his discussion of indefinite terms are clearly pertinent to the determination of the logical questions of whether an enunciation is affirmative or negative, and whether it predicates something of an existent subject. The grammarian's stipulation of where to place the negative particle in Arabic, and of what the scope of its negating force is, are at least partial determiners of the intended underlying logical structure embodied in an Arabic sentence. To make sense out of Avicenna's delineation of the concerns of logic and grammar, then, it cannot be assumed that the relegation of certain topics to the determination of the grammarian implies that they have no bearing upon logical concerns. Such remarks must rather be taken as indications of the pervasive, but accidental, determination of logical structure by its linguistic expression, and thus of the practical interdependence of logical and grammatical investigations. Unlike his Latin counterparts, Avicenna does not identify logical and grammatical concerns as parallel and mutually exclusive. While the delineations between logic and grammar remain formally as stringent for him, phenomena like indefinite nouns cannot be admitted in grammar and precluded from logic. Indefinite nouns must first be grammatical nouns before their logical status can be determined; if they do not exist in a particular grammar, they must be invented or imported from another language. But all linguistic phenomena must, from the Arabic philosophers' perspective, admit of grammatical analysis as a prelude to logical analysis.

The Inflected Noun: Like the indefinite noun, the oblique cases of the noun are denied the full status of nouns by Aristotle, on the grounds that the addition of the copula to them does not produce a complete enunciative statement which is true or false.[98] In their comments upon this exclusion, and upon the status of the oblique cases in general, the same interplay of logical and grammatical considerations that underlies the Arabic treatment of indefinite terms is evident.

Avicenna argues against the absolute nominal status of the inflections of the noun on much the same grounds as he disputes the status of the indefinite noun, namely, because both fail to have parts which do not signify in isolation. I use the term 'inflection' here rather than 'oblique cases' because Avicenna appears to include under inflection all vocalizations, and hence, all three cases of which Arabic admits, including the nominative. This, indeed, appears to be the key to his ability to read Aristotle's remarks regarding cases as simply another instance of the violation of the general condition of unity that both nouns and verbs must fulfill. His argument hinges on the fact that whenever a noun is pronounced with a determinate vowel-ending, there is signified, in addition to the basic lexical signification of the term, some further meaning:

> The state of the nouns which are called inflected is like this, for through them something additional to the denomination may be combined with the noun, which indicates a meaning other than what the bare noun indicates — this being one of the vowels and one of the inflections — so that a complex originating from the two parts is heard, one of which is the noun and the other that which attaches to it as a part of what is heard. So there is found here one part which signifies a meaning and another part which either signifies an absolute meaning, or signifies some signification, and through the complex necessitates a judgement which would not occur were it not for [the addition].[99]

---

98   *Peri hermeneias*, chap. 2, 16a32-b5

99   *Interpretation*, 1.2, 13.8-12

In these remarks, it is clear that Avicenna has Arabic grammar especially in mind: he focuses on the audible aspects of the utterance, and refers to the addition of one of the 'motions' to the base meaning, using the traditional Arabic grammatical term for the case endings.[100] While the overall tenor of Avicenna's remarks clearly suggests something akin to the Latin distinction between the signification of a word and the *modus significandi* of its grammatical form, the very conception of a noun's signification being altered by all of its cases, including the nominative, seems to stem from the general dispensability of case endings in much spoken and written Arabic. For my purposes, however, the most telling point in Avicenna's explication of the exclusion of the inflections of the noun is the way in which he must revise Aristotle's argument that the oblique cases are not fully nouns because they yield no truth-value when joined to the verb 'to be' — an argument ill-suited to Arabic at any rate. Avicenna substitutes as evidence for this exclusion the fact that the range of meanings implicit in the bare noun are considerably contracted when that noun is vocalized in any way: just as 'human being' can be white, black, or brown, but 'white human being' can only be white, so too the noun 'Zayd' can be the subject of a verb, its object, or the object of a preposition, but 'Zaydun' in the nominative case can only be a subject, 'Zaydan' in the accusative only an object, and so on.[101] In both cases, a new conceptual content is involved, which limits and restricts the possible uses and significations potentially present in the noun. Once again, then, Avicenna has read Aristotle, not as making a point about the conditions of logical predication, but rather, as making what is essentially a grammatical point in order to elucidate those basic grammatical features of a particular language which might be relevant to the expression of thought in language. For it is clear that Avicenna does not believe that nouns have one definition in logic, which excludes the inflections, and another in grammar, which encompasses them, as do his Latin successors. Rather, the grammarian

---

100 On grammar and vocalization, cf. n. 52 above.

101 *Interpretation*, 1.2, 13.16-14.14

defines the noun for his particular language, and the logician borrows this definition from the grammarian with a view to understanding its implications for his incidental need to embody meaning in a linguistic medium. That Avicenna views the entire Aristotelian discussion of the inflections of nouns as a grammatical exercise is, moreover, reinforced by the fact that he is conscious of having altered Aristotle's reference to the combination of inflected nouns with the copula in order to suit the needs of Arabic speakers. Despite Aristotle's reference to truth-values (which might be taken to indicate a point of logical doctrine), Avicenna here again assumes that Aristotle is simply drawing the reader's attention to a point of Greek grammar. At the end of his discussion of inflections in Arabic, Avicenna alludes to Aristotle's criterion for distinguishing the nominative and oblique cases, prefacing it with the observation that this is what the inflections of the noun are marked by in Greek: "As for the Greek language, the inflected noun in relation to it is that which, when temporal verbs like 'was,' 'will be,' and 'is now,' are added to it, is neither true nor false."[102]

Fārābī's discussions of inflected nouns in his commentaries on the *Peri hermeneias* do not give much attention to the question of whether the oblique cases have the full status of nouns, but his remarks on the

---

102 Ibid., 1.2, 14.14-16. As with the indefinite noun, it is again unclear whether Avicenna's remarks are fully compatible with the attitude expressed by Yaḥyā ibn 'Adī (nn. 56-60 above), in which all grammatical operations are said to be irrelevant to meaning. Since Avicenna accepts the confinement of grammar to what is idiomatic to a particular language, he would appear to accept the general outlines of Yaḥyā's argument. But he does seem to be more flexible than Yaḥyā in allowing that grammatical operations do affect meaning in some way, by contracting or restricting its extension. Thus, it is difficult to see how, given the passage under consideration, Avicenna could accept Yaḥyā's claim that the cases of the noun in no way affect its meaning. However, Avicenna's analogy with the addition of an accidental property to a definition may offer a means of reconciling his view with that of his predecessor. For Yaḥyā's basic point is that grammatical operations do. not affect the word's signification of one *essence* rather than another, a point which seems akin to Avicenna's claim that the word is altered by its cases only in the way that 'human being' is altered by the addition to it of the accident 'white.' The modification in both cases is an accidental, not an essential, one.

oblique cases in his *Short Treatise* do shed further light on his presuppositions concerning the relation between logic and grammar. In explaining how one differentiates the oblique from the upright case, Fārābī deliberately plays upon the ambiguity in Arabic of the term 'relation' (*iḍāfah*), which is used in logical contexts for the Aristotelian category, and also serves as the technical grammatical term for a genitival construction. Fārābī, however, extends the term 'relation' so that it applies to all the uses of all the oblique cases, not only to genitival constructs, but also to accusatives functioning as objects of verbs, and to genitives functioning as objects of prepositions: "[A noun] only becomes oblique whenever, given two related things, it is [the one which is] made a name for the thing which is the object of the relation essentially, whether it signifies it insofar as it is a correlate, or insofar as it belongs to some other [of the ten] categories."[103] In his further explication of this definition, Fārābī shows considerable interest in the interplay of logical and grammatical relations. For example, he tells us that in his definition he has stipulated "the thing which is the object of the relation *essentially*" for grammatical reasons, in order to indicate that the noun immediately governed by the construct may not denominate the subject of the relation directly, such as when the grammatically relative term is a relative pronoun referring back to a previous clause. For example, in Arabic one can correctly say, 'Zayd: his is the money (*Zaydun la-hu mālun*).' Here one might consider 'Zayd' to be the object to which the relation is made from a logical perspective, but grammatically, 'Zayd' is an 'object of relation' only mediately, and thus remains in the nominative case.[104] Along much the same lines, Fārābī observes that in general the terms of grammatical constructs (*alfāẓ al-iḍāfāt*) need not themselves be the logical relata (*al-muḍāfāt*). The former are merely whatever two terms happen to be

---

103 *Short Treatise*, 136.10-11, my translation (cf. Zimmermann trans., 222).

104 Ibid., 136.11-15. The translations of the technical terms coined by Fārābī are my own here; compare Zimmermann's translation, 222-3. For further remarks on Fārābī's deliberate conflation of all the oblique cases with the genitive, cf. Zimmermann, 222-3 n. 13, 224 nn. 1, 7.

combined with one another in the nominative and genitive cases; the latter, however, are "the things which come to be correlated because of these [grammatical relations]." Thus, if we say "Amr is the father of Zayd,' it is logically "Amr' and 'Zayd' who are correlated, but grammatically, only 'father' and 'Zayd' are parts of a relational construct.[105]

Fārābī's attempt here to make Arabic grammar more logically perspicuous, and more reflective of the basic Aristotelian dichotomy between upright and oblique cases, initially seems more akin to the Latin commentators' persistent distinction between the logician's and grammarian's definitions of linguistic phenomena than it does to Avicenna's general interpretation of Aristotle's remarks about language as allusions to common Greek usage. In collapsing both the accusative and genitive cases under a single notion of relation, Fārābī seems to be arguing that what counts as a grammatical distinction between cases need not be the basis for a corresponding logical distinction. But even after Fārābī has substituted the general notion of linguistic relata for the indigenous Arabic distinction between cases, he continues to differentiate between logical and grammatical relative terms. So he is not simply taking the upright-oblique distinction, construed in terms of relation, as a logical property of nouns that is absent from Arabic simply in virtue of its being a logical, rather than a grammatical, property. Rather, Fārābī's attempt to streamline Arabic grammar here reflects the same stance towards the logic-grammar relation that was manifested in his remarks regarding the grammatical form of indefinite nouns in languages other than Arabic. In both cases, Fārābī assumes that the grammatical form of a language can be assessed according to its capacity to fulfill more or less adequately the logician's needs, and in cases where the grammar of a particular language falls short of logical perspicacity, it can be modified accordingly. But even while modifying them, the logician remains dependent upon grammatical structures for that part of his art which pertains to the linguistic expression of meaning. He has no access to linguistic

---

105 *Short Treatise*, 137.3-7; Zimmermann trans., 223-4

topics that is entirely his own, or entirely free from determination by its underlying grammatical foundations.

III Concluding Remarks: A Comparison of Latin and Arabic Attitudes Towards the Problem of Logic and Language

Despite their acceptance of essentially the same theoretical view of the character of a logical study of language (and here we should not forget that the Latins did know both Fārābī's *Catalogue of the Sciences* and Avicenna's *Isagoge*), there seems to be a notable and fundamental difference between the Arabic and Latin exegetical approaches to the linguistic content of the *Peri hermeneias*. Nor is that difference simply attributable to diverse interpretations of the finer points of Aristotle's text, as in the case of infinite or indefinite nouns. Rather, the principal point of contrast seems to rest in two distinct construals of the nature of the logician's attention, or lack thereof, to the technicalities of grammar.

In the Latin tradition, the existence of a philosophically oriented theory of grammar, with its own set of definitions and its own proper method, tends to promote the view that philosophical grammar and philosophical logic are two autonomous sciences, each of which must establish its own unique approach to common linguistic phenomena. Thus, the grammarian does not 'lend' his definition of the noun or verb to the logician, since his definition attends to grammatically relevant properties, not logically relevant ones. And what may be a noun for the grammarian — such as the infinite noun or the oblique cases — need not be a noun for the logician.

In the Arabic tradition, however, this is not the case. Grammar and logic *are* autonomous, as we have seen, but *not* in the sense that the grammarian and the logician are free to determine their definitions of linguistic phenomena independently of one another. Rather, in the Islamic tradition, the logician is viewed as *borrowing* whatever he needs in the way of linguistic theory from the grammarian. Indeed, this point is made explicitly by Fārābī in his general treatment of the relation between logic and grammar:

> And in the case of what logic provides of the rules of expressions, it only provides those rules in which the expressions of [all] nations share, and it takes them insofar as they are common, and does not consider anything of that which is specific to any given nation, but rather decrees that what it needs of these things will be taken from the grammarians of this language.[106]

The point is repeated by Fārābī at the end of his *Reminder of the Way to Happiness*, and indeed provides the rationale underlying the opening grammatical discussions of the *Utterances Employed in Logic*, to which the *Reminder* serves as an introduction:

> And since it is the art of grammar which comprises the variety of significant expressions, the art of grammar must be indispensable for making known, and alerting us to, the principles of this art. So for this reason it is necessary for us to borrow from the art of grammar to the extent that is sufficient for alerting us to the first principles of this art [of logic]. Or [we must] undertake a fitting enumeration of the varieties of expressions which, in the custom of the users of this language, signify what this art comprises, if it should happen that the users of this language do not have an art in which the varieties of expressions which are in their language are enumerated. So for this reason, that which those of the past did in the way of including in logic things which belong to the art of language, borrowing from it to the extent that was sufficient, is explained. Or rather, the truth is that what was necessary for facilitating [logical] instruction was used. And whoever follows a path other than this path has neglected or overlooked the artistic order.[107]

Similarly, if one attends carefully to the remarks of both Fārābī and Avicenna on the differences between the linguistic terminology of the Arabic Aristotle and the normal usage of Arabic grammar, one notices that both assume that Aristotle's remarks on language in the *Peri hermeneias* are based upon the conventions of Greek *grammar*; neither of them entertains the possibility that the terms and definitions used

---

106 *Catalogue of the Sciences*, 77.12-15; Palencia, 135.28-136.4

107 *Kitāb al-tanbīh 'alā sabīl al-sa'ādah* (*Reminder of the Way to Happiness*), J.A. Yasin, ed. (Beirut: Dar al-Manahel 1987), §19, 83.7-84.4; medieval Latin translation, 'Le «Liber exercitationis ad viam felicitatis» d'Alfarabi,' H. Salman, ed., *Récherches de théologie ancienne et médiévale* **12** (1940) 33-48 (the translated passage is found at §40, 47.45-48.7).

in the text embody a purely logical perspective on language. The most obvious illustration of this approach occurs in the Arabic philosophers' discussions of the names for the parts of speech. For example, in the *Catalogue of the Sciences*, Fārābī remarks that what the Arabic grammarians call *ism, fi'l,* and *ḥarf,* the Greek *grammarians* call *ism, kalimah,* and *adāh,* that is, noun, verb, and particle.[108] And in his *Utterances Employed in Logic,* as a preface to a long consideration of the different types of particles, Fārābī openly proclaims that he will rely, not on Greek logic, but on Greek grammar: "And these particles (*ḥurūf*) are also of many kinds; however, it has not been the custom among the Arabic grammarians, up to our time, to isolate for each type of them a name that is proper to it. So it is necessary for us to use the names which have come down to us from the Greek grammarians in our enumeration of their varieties. For they singled out each variety of them with a proper name."[109]

None of this means, of course, that the logician cannot supplement the grammar he finds to suit his own needs, as Fārābī himself does in his theory of particles, or as we have seen him do when he collapses both oblique cases under the notion of relation proper in Arabic grammar to the genitive case alone. But none of the Arabic philosophers seems to have entertained the notion of beginning from scratch, from a philosophical perspective, in the field of universal grammar. For them, grammar and language mean fundamentally *particular* grammar, the language of this or that nation or people. The possibility of an independent study of universal grammar is a contradiction from the Islamic philosophers' perspective, not because the study of language cannot be universalized in some way, but simply because grammar is by definition not a truly universal science. That is, once one begins to do universal grammar, according to the Arabic tradition, one takes off the grammarian's hat, and dons that of the logician. I do not think the Arabic philosophers, and certainly not Fārābī, would reject the project of the Latin speculative grammarians per se,

---

108 *Catalogue of the Sciences*, 76.8-77.4; Palencia, 135.1-17

109 *Utterances Employed in Logic*, §2, 42.8-12

for they admit its fundamental tenet that there are universal features of linguistic expression shared by all nations. What they would do, however, is draw the boundary line somewhat differently.

But drawing the boundary line differently is not simply a matter of superficial taxonomy. For once logic is forced to assume both the role of providing a universal linguistic theory, and that of providing the rules for correct reasoning, sharp distinctions between these two spheres of investigation are no longer so easily made. And this, it would appear, accounts in large measure for the disparities between the Arabic and Latin philosophers' understanding of the linguistic content of the *Peri hermeneias*. The consequences, moreover, are para-doxical: for it is the Arabic philosophers, for whom grammar is an inferior, non-philosophical science, who are forced by their position to make the logician directly dependent upon the grammarian for the basic linguistic underpinnings of his discipline.

It is difficult to assess which approach to this Aristotelian text is preferable as a whole. As we have seen in our consideration of the Latin commentators, although there is not universal agreement over specific points of interpretation, there is a remarkable unity of ap-proach in terms of identifying which general principles are pertinent to the interpretation of the linguistic sections of the *Peri hermeneias*. Questions about the appropriateness of Aristotle's treatments of lin-guistic topics almost invariably take their inspiration from Priscian; and the apparent conflicts between logic and grammar can always be settled by some appeal to the twin criteria of truth and falsity on the one hand, congruity and incongruity on the other. Yet such a system-atic approach has its own pitfalls: there is a tendency to use formulas drawn from Priscian and Aristotle unreflectively, with little attention to overall context. But the Aristotelian text often remains intransigent, and efforts to show how Aristotle's views mirror the medieval divi-sion of labour between logic and speculative grammar often clash with Aristotle's obvious intent. This is evident, for example, in the treatment of the infinite noun, where the assumption that it is not a logically relevant item of study conflicts glaringly with the obvious fact that Aristotle considers it to be of interest because of its role in the theory of opposition.

In this respect, the Arabic approach to the specific teachings in the *Peri hermeneias*, though considerably less systematic, has a certain advantage. For the lack of a predefined notion of what is logically relevant and what is not gives the Arabic authors considerably more freedom in dealing with specific points of doctrine in the Aristotelian text. It also allows them to take Aristotle's remarks at their face value, and to accept that they may, at times, be grammatical rather than logical in character. In the case of the indefinite noun, this freedom from external constraint seems felicitous, for it allows both Fārābī and Avicenna to take into account the importance of Aristotle's discussion of indefinite terms for his views on the opposition of statements.

Yet despite these differences, fundamental as many of them are, what is in the end most striking about this sampling of discussions on logic, language, and grammar, in both the Arabic and Latin *Peri hermeneias* commentaries, is the overall similarity between the Latin and Arabic philosophers' *theoretical* positions on the character of logic as a linguistic science. Even Avicenna is not averse to the traditional metaphor of 'inner speech' as the subject-matter of logic, despite his polemic against the identification of logic as a linguistic science.[110] While Aquinas seems deliberately to avoid the label of *scientia sermocinalis* for logic, he seems to have few qualms about the appropriateness of Aristotle's discussion of linguistic topics in a logical text such as the *Peri hermeneias*. And in general, even given the existence of speculative grammar in the Latin tradition, which provided a convenient niche for the study of language in the philosophical canon, the ties between logic and language remained an underlying assumption of the Latin exegesis on the Aristotelian text. By the same token, all the philosophers whose commentaries we have considered avoid the opposite extreme of viewing the linguistic and rational characteristics of logic as essentially the same. Language and thought are kept

---

110 See *Isagoge*, 1.3, 20.14-15: "And the relation of this art to the internal reflection which is called 'inner speech' (*al-nuṭq al-dākhilī*) is like the relation of grammar to the external interpretation which is called 'external speech' (*al-nuṭq al-khārijī*)."

distinct; the metaphor of 'inner speech' remains a metaphor; and logic never becomes identified as simply a grammar of thought.

There are probably many factors that explain the medieval commentators' ability to preserve this balanced perspective on the rational and linguistic aspects of logic. The most obvious derives from the *Peri hermeneias* itself. For Aristotle's notion of *phōnē sēmantikē* precludes any pure separation between *artes sermocinales* and *artes rationales*, between the *'ilm al-lisān* and the *'ilm al-manṭiq*. To the extent that all significant speech is, for Aristotle and his commentators, essentially a sign of the *pathēmata tēs psychēs*, every linguistic art within the Aristotelian tradition must be grounded in a corresponding link to a signifying mind, and thus be, either explicitly or implicitly, a rational art as well. As to the other extreme of viewing logic as a purely linguistic science, the tendency amongst medieval philosophers in both traditions to associate language with the spoken, physically uttered word no doubt contributed to the reluctance to take the notion of 'inner speech' literally, and opt for the assimilation of the rational side of logic to its linguistic side. Conversely, the fact that logic in both the Latin West and the Islamic world was held to encompass the arts of dialectic, and even rhetoric and poetics, ensured that the concerns of oral discussion and communication remained prominent, though ancillary, and no doubt served to enhance the importance of language as an oral phenomenon for the practice of logic.

But perhaps the most deeply rooted explanation for the inseparability of the linguistic and rational aspects of logic derives, not from the medieval conception of logic itself, but rather, from the epistemological aims that logic, as an instrumental science, was meant to serve. For the assumption that logic must attend to the embodiment of concepts in language parallels the assumption, generally shared by these commentators and deriving from Aristotle's *De Anima*, that all intellectual cognition must be accompanied by a corresponding act of imagination.[111] From this perspective, it is no accident that the one

---

111 *De Anima* 3.7.431a16-17; 431b2; 3.8.432a3-10. Cf. *De Memoria* 1.449b3-450a1.

philosopher who comes closest to repudiating the linguistic conception of logic is Avicenna, who likewise repudiates the traditional
Aristotelian assumption of the essential link between images and
intelligibles.[112] And just as he admits the *practical* necessity for logic
to concern itself with language, so too in his epistemology does
Avicenna admit the *practical* dependence of most human knowledge
upon images, as preparations, and even substitutes, for purely intellectual conception.

The attempts of the commentators on the *Peri hermeneias* to preserve
both the rational and linguistic perspectives within logic can thus be
seen in part as reflecting the same attitude embodied in their acceptance of the interplay between concrete images and abstract intelligibles in human cognition. To the extent that the logical commentators
repudiated the notion of pure, disembodied intellection as a possible
human mode of cognition, to that same extent they repudiated the
possibility of a process of pure reasoning abstracted from all linguistic
embodiment, and subject to rules that are wholly other than the rules
governing vocal expressions.

---

112 For Avicenna's repudiation of the dependence of thought upon images even as
an efficient cause of thought, cf. n. 68 above.

CANADIAN JOURNAL OF PHILOSOPHY
Supplementary Volume 17

A Thirteenth-Century Interpretation of Aristotle on Equivocation and Analogy

E.J. ASHWORTH

This paper is a case study of how a few short lines in two of Aristotle's logical works were read in the thirteenth century.[1] I shall begin with a quick look at Aristotle's own remarks about equivocation in the *Categories* and the *Sophistical Refutations,* as they were transmitted to the West by Boethius's translations.[2] I shall continue with an analysis of the divisions of equivocation and analogy to be found in an anonymous commentary on the *Sophistical Refutations* written in Paris between 1270 and 1280.[3] I have chosen this author's work to focus on, because it offers a remarkably full account which brings together the elements found in many other logical works from the second half of the thirteenth century. In the course of my analysis I shall attempt to

---

1 For full bibliographies and more information on the matters touched on here, see E.J. Ashworth, 'Signification and Modes of Signifying in Thirteenth-Century Logic: A Preface to Aquinas on Analogy,' *Medieval Philosophy and Theology* 1 (1991) 39-67; E.J. Ashworth, 'Analogy and Equivocation in Thirteenth-Century Logic: Aquinas in Context,' *Mediaeval Studies* (forthcoming); E.J. Ashworth, 'Equivocation and Analogy in Fourteenth Century Logic: Ockham, Burley and Buridan,' *Historia Philosophiae Medii Aevi. Studien Zur Geschichte der Philosophie des Mittelalters,* B. Mojsisch and O. Pluta, eds. (Amsterdam: B.R. Gruner forthcoming).

2 Aristotle [2] and Aristotle [10]

3 Anonymous [1]. Of the two sets of questions edited by Ebbesen I shall use only the first (the SF commentary).

show the part played by four different sources: (1) the Greek commentators of late antiquity; (2) the new translations of Aristotle's *Physics* and *Metaphysics*; (3) the reception of Arabic works, particularly the commentaries of Averroes; and (4) new grammatical doctrines, notably that of *modi significandi*. At the same time, I hope to throw some light on the development of the doctrine of analogy as it was understood by late thirteenth-century logicians.

I shall begin, then, with the words of Aristotle himself. The first sentence of the *Categories* gives a definition of equivocals which, following Boethius's Latin translation,[4] goes as follows:

> Those that have only a name in common but a different analysis of their substance in accordance with that name are said to be equivocals, e.g. "animal" [in relation to] man and what is painted. These have only a name in common and the analysis of their substance in accordance with that name is different, for if one is to explain what it is for each of them to be an animal, one will give a distinct analysis for each.[5]

Before I turn to the *Sophistical Refutations*, I will make a few comments about the standard reading of this passage in the middle ages. First, as Boethius points out in his commentary,[6] Aristotle categorizes things as equivocal, but there is an obvious link with language: a thing is equivocal only as picked out by an equivocal term, just as a thing, perhaps the very same thing, is univocal only as picked out by a univocal term. Hence the important issue for the logician is the identification of equivocal terms, since it is only through them that we can pick out equivocal things. Second, the word '*nomen*,' which

---

4 Aristotle [1]. *Categories* 1a1-6 in Aristotle [2], 5: "Aequivoca dicuntur quorum nomen solum commune est, secundum nomen vero substantiae ratio diversa, ut animal homo et quod pingitur. Horum enim solum nomen commune est, secundum nomen vero substantiae ratio diversa; si enim quis assignet quid est utrique eorum quo sint animalia, propriam assignabit utriusque rationem."

5 I have borrowed much of this translation from the translation of Peter of Spain, N. Kretzmann and E. Stump, eds., *The Cambridge Translations of Medieval Philosophical Texts, Vol. I: Logic and the Philosophy of Language* (Cambridge: Cambridge University Press 1988), 89.

6 Boethius [2], col. 164

means both 'name' and 'noun,' should be taken here to refer to any part of speech.[7] Third, the presence of the word *'substantia,'* as Simplicius pointed out, is not intended to restrict the scope of discussion to substances.[8] Accidents too can be equivocals. Finally, people agreed that *ratio*, which I have translated as 'analysis,' had to cover not only definition in the strict sense[9] but also descriptions, which designate things by some property or other.[10] This is partly because the most general genera and individuals have no definitions,[11] but there are also epistemological implications. Even where a definition of an object is in principle possible, we may in fact know not its *quidditas*, but only some of its associated properties, and this limitation on our knowledge does not prevent us from using a word to pick out that object.

The second key passage from Aristotle's logic is in the *Sophistical Refutations*, where Aristotle writes:

> There are three modes of equivocation and amphiboly: one when either the phrase or the name primarily signifies more than one thing, e.g. *"piscis"* and *"canis"*; another when we are accustomed to speak in that way; a third when words put together signify more than one thing, but taken alone [signify] simply, e.g. *"scit saeculum."*[12]

---

7 Boethius [2] col. 164. See also the discussion by S. Ebbesen, *Commentators and Commentaries on Aristotle's Sophistici Elenchi: A Study of Post-Aristotelian Ancient and Medieval Writings on Fallacies* (Leiden: E.J. Brill 1981) vol. I, 181-2.

8 Simplicius [2], Vol. I, 39

9 See the frequently cited Aristotelian tag: "ratio quam significat nomen est definitio" (*Metaphysics* IV.1012a24-5). I take the Latin from Jacqueline Hamesse, *Les Auctoritates Aristotelis: Un florilège médiéval. Étude historique et édition critique. Philosophes médiévaux XVII* (Louvain: Publications Universitaires; Paris: Béatrice-Nauwelaerts 1974), 124 [116]. This florilegium (which dates from between November 22, 1267, and 1325) is an extremely useful guide to the commonplace tags picked up and used by almost all logical writers.

10 Boethius [2], col. 166; Simplicius [2], 39

11 Ibid.

12 Aristotle [9], *Sophistical Refutations* 166a15-20, quoted from Boethius's translation

Medieval authors took the passage as an implicit invitation to distinguish three varieties of equivocal term, and this approach was reinforced by a theory of language which privileged the individual term, as opposed to its propositional context. One of the challenges facing logicians was to provide a suitable spectrum of examples for the second mode;[13] another was to relate Aristotle's account of the third mode to contemporary theories of language.

Now let us look at our anonymous author. He began by pointing out that equivocation can arise in two ways, according to the different semantical and grammatical correlates of a word (*vox*).[14] A word can be equivocal either because it has more than one significate, as in the case of '*canis*,' which signifies a barking animal, a marine animal, and a star; or it can be equivocal because it has more than one *modus significandi*. Aristotle's modes one and two both deal with diversity of significates. In mode one, the significates are equally represented; in mode two, they are unequally represented. His mode three, on the other hand, involves a diversity of incompatible *modi significandi*. This classification, which is found in other authors, including Peter of Spain and Lambert of Auxerre,[15] immediately brings us to a consideration of one of my four sources, the new grammatical theories concerning *modi significandi*. There are two uses of the phrase '*modus significandi*.' There is a fuzzy use, employed by twelfth- and thirteenth-century theologians to indicate semantic constraints on the use

---

in Aristotle [10]: "Sunt autem tres modi secundum aequivocationem et amphiboliam: unus quidem quando vel oratio vel nomen principaliter significat plura, ut piscis et canis; alius autem quando soliti sumus sic dicere; tertius vero quando compositum plura significet, separatum vero simpliciter, ut 'scit saeculum' "(9).

13 Of course, some examples were drawn from *Sophistical Refutations* 165b30-166a15. Thus '*discere*' illustrated mode one, '*expediens*' mode two and both '*laborans*' and '*sedens*' mode three.

14 Anonymous [1], 116

15 Peter of Spain [1], 105; Lambert of Auxerre [1], 149. They both used the term '*consignificatio*,' but for a term to have *consignificatio* is for it to have *consignificata* or *modi significandi*.

of certain terms, such as abstract and concrete terms;[16] and there is a more precise grammatical notion, developed by grammarians in Paris at least from the 1240s on, in a movement which reached its peak in the treatises on speculative grammar written in the last three decades of the century. The effects of the nascent grammar are already to be found in Peter of Spain, who wrote in the 1230s; and both the fuzzy theological notion and the precise grammatical notion seem to be found in the writings of Aquinas. There were two main groups of grammatical *modi significandi*: essential and accidental. Essential *modi significandi* included word-class, such as being a noun, verb, or adjective. Accidental *modi significandi*, which included such features as case, gender, and number, were themselves divided into two subgroups, absolute and relational. Case was said to be relational or respective in thirteenth-century discussions, because it was obviously affected by sentential context; but time was said to be an absolute accidental mode, not affected by sentential context. The chief example used here was '*laborans*,' as it appears in Aristotle's paralogism: 'The person who was being cured is healthy, the sufferer [*laborans*] was being cured; therefore the same person is both a sufferer and healthy.'[17] Here the *modus significandi* of time was said to be at issue because '*laborans*' can signify either a present sufferer or one who suffered in the past. This account of '*laborans*' raised an important general question about Aristotle's description of the third mode, since the description seemed to allow for the effect of context. Although thirteenth-century logicians were generally willing to accept relational *modi significandi* as context-related, there was a strong belief that the essential and absolute accidental *modi significandi* of a word, as well as its signification, were fixed by their initial imposition, and that

---

16 See S. Ebbesen, 'The Semantics of the Trinity According to Stephen Langton and Andrew Sunesen,' in *Gilbert de Poitiers et ses contemporains. Aux origines de la 'Logica Modernorum.'* *Actes du septième symposium européen d'histoire de la logique et de sémantique médiévales. Centre d'études supérieures de civilisation médiévale de Poitiers* (Jean Jolivet and Alain de Libera, éds. (Napoli: Bibliopolis 1987), 426-7.

17 Aristotle [9]: *Sophistical Refutations*, 166a1-6

they could not be viewed as a product of sentential context or speaker intention.[18] Indeed, it was widely argued that no modification by context was possible unless through certain types of modifiers, called immediate adjuncts. Thus if one says '*Canis latrabilis currit*,' '*latrabilis*' is counted as an immediate adjunct and is allowed to restrict the reference of '*canis*' to four-legged animals, but if one says '*Canis currit*,' the verb is not counted as an immediate adjunct, and so cannot limit the reference of '*canis*.' Precisely the same type of argument applied to '*Laborans sanabatur*.' Since the verb is not an immediate adjunct, it is not the presence of a past-tense verb that causes '*laborans*' to refer to past sufferers. After all, as our anonymous author remarked, if the verb did have an effect, we would have to talk about the reference of '*laborans*' to future sufferers when we say '*Laborans sanabitur*' — 'The sufferer will be cured' — but nobody says this (*quod nemo dicat*).[19] So why did Aristotle define the third mode as he did? Here our author joins the earlier Peter of Spain and the later Duns Scotus in saying that there are indeed three modes of equivocation and three modes of amphiboly, but that the third mode described by Aristotle applied to amphiboly alone.[20] Peter of Spain modified this judgment by claiming that Aristotle seemed to want (*videtur velle Aristotiles*) an additional set of modes which was common to equivocation and amphiboly, and whose third mode applied to such composite equivocal terms as '*immortale*.'[21]

Now let us turn back to Aristotle's first two modes. The anonymous author tells us that, according to the Commentator (about whom I shall say more below), the first two modes relate to a further set of divisions.[22] First, there is a division into common and proper equivocation which is not found in the other logicians I have read. Common

18 For full details see the first paper cited above in n. 1.

19 Anonymous [1], 119

20 Ibid., 120; John Duns Scotus [2], 26B.

21 Peter of Spain [1], 99, 109-10

22 Anonymous [1], 117

equivocation is a characteristic of whole classes of words. Thus, the author claims, *'lectio'* is equivocal because all words ending in *'-tio'* are. The thought here may be that such a word can be taken in a more or less active sense, like words ending in '-ing' in English. For instance, one might say of a student, 'His reading of the first reading was perfunctory,' where 'reading' clearly has two different senses. However, the point about common equivocation is not further developed by our author.[23]

Proper equivocation belongs to words as individuals, and not just as representatives of a class. It too has two divisions: some words are equivocal by chance (*a casu*), and others are deliberately equivocal (*a consilio*). Chance equivocals include proper names, and in most authors they were also taken to include the standard example *'canis,'* though it is not given here. Deliberate equivocals are of four types. First, they may be *a simili*: for instance, 'man' can be said of a real man and of a painted man. Second, they may be *a proportione*: for instance, 'principle' (*principium*) can be used of both unity and point, for as unity is to number, so point is to line. Third, they can be *ab uno*, as when instruments and food are called 'medical' from their contribution to medicine. Fourth, they can be *ad unum*. Here our author gives two examples: 'healthy,' said of animal and urine, and *'ens,'* said of quality or quantity because it has attribution to one substance.

I shall leave the use of *'ens'* aside for the moment, and shall consider the general division into four types. To understand this, we need to talk about the second great influence: the Greek commentators of late antiquity, as transmitted by a small group of sources. For the *Sophistical Refutations* there is just one commentary, attributed to an otherwise unknown Alexander, who is always referred to as the Commentator.[24]

---

23 It may be related to the division between general and special signification found, for instance, in a commentary on *De Interpretatione* apparently written by Nicholas of Paris ca. 1250; see J. Pinborg, *Die Entwicklung der Sprachtheorie im Mittelalter, Beiträge zur Geschichte der Philosophie und Theologie des Mittelalters Band XLII, heft 2* (Münster: Aschendorff 1967), 27, n. 27.

24 For a discussion of Alexander, see Ebbesen, *Commentators and Commentaries on*

The commentary no longer exists, and is known only through a series of quotations in other commentaries. Ebbesen suggests that the author was either a Greek working between 850 and 1100, or the twelfth-century translator Jacobus Veneticus, using already extant Greek scholia. No other commentaries seem to have been available, even if any were written in late antiquity. For the *Categories* there were three sources. First there is the *Categoriae decem* of Pseudo-Augustine, which is in fact a fourth-century work by an unknown Themistian.[25] Second, there is the commentary by Boethius. Third, there is the Greek commentary of Simplicius, dating from the sixth century, which became known to the Latin-speaking West when William of Moerbeke translated it in 1266.[26] Simplicius made particularly extensive use of earlier Greek commentators, but Pseudo-Augustine and Boethius also made use of such sources as Porphyry,[27] as did the Commentator Alexander, judging by the references in our unknown author.

In particular, they took from Porphyry the division of equivocals into two main groups: chance equivocals (*fortuitu* in Pseudo-Augustine, *a casu* in Boethius) and deliberate equivocals (*voluntate* in Pseudo-Augustine, *a consilio* in Boethius, though Boethius also uses

Aristotle's Sophistici Elenchi, Vol. I, 286-9. Ebbesen has edited the fragments of the commentary in Vol. II, 331-555.

25 See Aristotle [2], LXXVII-LXXVIII. The text is reprinted as 'Paraphrasis Themistiana' in Aristotle [2], 133-75. It is copied by Alcuin: see *Excerpta ex Alcuini Dialectica*, Aristotle [2], 189-92.

26 For the date see Simplicius [2], xi.

27 For some discussion and references, see F. Desbordes, 'Homonymie et synonymie d'après les textes théoriques latins,' in *L'ambiguïté: cinq études historiques*, I. Rosier, ed. (Lille: Presses Universitaires de Lille 1988), 66; S. Ebbesen, 'Paris 4720A: A 12th Century Compendium of Aristotle's Sophistici Elenchi,' *Cahiers de l'institut du moyen-âge grec et latin* 10 (1973), 12-13; H. Lyttkens, *The Analogy between God and the World: An Investigation of its Background and Interpretation of its Use by Thomas of Aquino* (Uppsala: Almqvist and Wiksells 1953), 58-77. Greek commentators on the *Categories* (other than Simplicius), such as Ammonius, were not used until the Renaissance.

the word '*voluntas*').[28] In the first case the occurrences of the equivocal term were totally unconnected, as when both the son of Priam and Alexander the Great were called Alexander. In the second case, some intention on the part of the speakers was involved. This general division probably comes from Porphyry's reading of a text in the *Nicomachean Ethics* where Aristotle discusses the things to which the word 'good' is applied, and says, in Robert Grosseteste's translation, 'They are not like chance equivocals.'[29] This is a negative remark, as Pierre Aubenque has pointed out, and quite consistent with the claim that these things have the same name by necessity.[30] However, Porphyry turns the remark into the positive claim that some equivocal terms occur by intention or deliberation, thus giving us the division found both in the three early commentaries on the *Categories* which were available in Latin and in Alexander's commentary on the *Sophistical Refutations*.

Now let us turn to the subdivisions.[31] The first of these is similitude, whereby both a painted man and a real man can be called a man. This is interesting because it seems to be based on a transformation of Aristotle's example in the *Categories*, which had to do with 'animal,' applied both to a man and the image of a man. '*Zoon*' in Greek is polysemous, meaning both 'image' and 'animal,' and according to Aubenque, Aristotle clearly intended to emphasize the point that a living man and a painted image had nothing in common but their name. The Greek commentators, under the influence of Platonism, if Aubenque's suggestion is correct, ask us to focus instead on a simi-

---

28 Boethius [2], col. 166: "Consilio vero, quia ea quaecunque hominum voluntate sunt posita."

29 Aristotle [6], *Nicomachean Ethics*, 1096b26: "Non enim assimulantur a casu equivocis." I cite the translation of Grosseteste: Aristotle [7], 381.

30 P. Aubenque, "Sur la naissance de la doctrine pseudo-aristotélicienne de l'analogie de l'être," *Les études philosophiques* [special issue on analogy] 3/4 (1989), 298-9

31 For all the divisions, see Pseudo-Augustine, in Aristotle [2], 136-7; Boethius [2], col. 166; Simplicius [2], 42-4.

larity of form, and to suppose that the equivocation is in some way intended on account of that similarity.[32] This reading is strengthened in the hands of the Latin commentators by the fact that the Latin word *'animal'* is not polysemous, and hence Aristotle's example, which was translated literally by Boethius, makes sense only via a discussion of similarities.[33] The example is further transformed by the customary dropping of the word *'animal'* and the use of just *'homo'* and *'homo pictus,'* as we find in our author.[34] Only Duns Scotus expressed any skepticism about the example. He remarked that he (presumably Aristotle) did not understand *'animal'* to be an equivocal term, but merely argued that if it were, then it would be equivocal because there was a common term and no common *ratio*. Scotus added that he (again I assume Aristotle is meant) did not care much about examples, as long as they made a true point.[35]

The Greek commentators probably took the next three subdivisions from the passage in the *Nicomachean Ethics* where Aristotle asks whether goods are one by being derived from one good, or by being directed towards one good, or by analogy, and here Grosseteste does use the word *'analogia'* (1096b27-8). [36] The subdivision of *'analogia,'*

---

32 See discussion in Aubenque, 299-300.

33 Desbordes comments: "La traduction scrupuleuse de BOECE ... devait être passablement énigmatique pour un Latin, *animal* n'ayant jamais désigné en Latin la représentation graphique, ni même une classe de tableaux représentant des êtres animés quelconques" (64).

34 Cf. Boethius [2], col. 166: "Horum autem alia sunt secundum similitudinem, ut homo pictus et homo verus quo nunc utitur Aristoteles exemplo...." Perhaps Boethius did not mention the word *'animal'* here because he was listing equivocal things, but in medieval sources it is often clear that *'homo'* is being used as an equivocal term in the illustration of this case: see e.g. Aquinas in his commentary on *Physics* VII, lectio 8, number 947.

35 John Duns Scotus [3], 452A. He was dealing with the objection that if *'animal'* were equivocal, then all terms would be equivocal: see 450B.

36 "Non enim assimulantur a casu equivocis. Set certe ei quod est ab uno esse, vel ad unum omnia contendere, vel magis secundum analogiam..." (Aristotle [7],

called 'proportion' ('*proportio*') by Boethius, was placed second, after similitude. Pseudo-Augustine notes that it is called *analogia* in Greek, though he uses *pro parte* in place of *proportio*, as does Alcuin; and in William of Moerbeke's translation of Simplicius only the word *analogia* is used.[37] The explanation of the example '*principium*' clearly corresponds to Aristotle's use of the Greek term. However, two things should be noted. First, the passage in the *Nicomachean Ethics* where Aristotle defines *analogia* as an equality of ratios which involves at least four terms contains not the term '*analogia*' but the term '*proportionalitas*' in Grosseteste's translation.[38] Second, despite the obvious invitation to talk about what is later called the analogy of proportionality, no logician that I know of before Cajetan took it up.

The last two subdivisions of deliberate equivocation are from one (*ab uno*) (e.g. 'medical') and to one (*ad unum*) (e.g. 'healthy'). The two correspond to Aristotle's '*pros hen*' equivocation, assuming we follow the views of both Owens and Owen that Aristotle didn't really make a hard distinction between 'from one' and 'to one.'[39] We can note in passing that the examples 'healthy' and 'medical' are drawn from other places in Aristotle's works, such as *Metaphysics* 4.2, 1003a33-1003b3. These subdivisions were not much discussed in the thirteenth century, either by our anonymous author or by other logicians. What

381). Ebbesen argues that all four subdivisions are based on a theory of concept formation: see *Commentators and Commentaries on Aristotle's* Sophistici Elenchi Vol. I, 190-3.

37 Aristotle [2]: Pseudo-Augustine, 137; Alcuin, 190; Simplicius [2], 42

38 Aristotle [6], *Nicomachean Ethics* 1131a31-2. "Proporcionalitas enim equalitas est proporcionis, et in quatuor minimis" (Aristotle [7], 458). This is the version that Aquinas used for his commentary. Although it is sometimes attributed to William of Moerbeke, the identity of the man who revised Grosseteste's original text has not been established.

39 See J. Owens, *The Doctrine of Being in the Aristotelian* Metaphysics (Toronto: Pontifical Institute of Mediaeval Studies 1957), 117-18; G.E.L. Owen, 'Logic and Metaphysics in Some Earlier Works of Aristotle,' in G.E.L. Owen, *Logic, Science, and Dialectic: Collected Papers in Greek Philosophy* (London: Duckworth 1986), 182, n. 7.

E.J. Ashworth

we find most frequently is a discussion of *analogia*, in the new non-Greek sense of *pros hen* equivocation or focal meaning,[40] as either subsumed under, or simply identified with, the second mode of equivocation.[41] These discussions are noteworthy for two reasons: first, the presence of a special vocabulary, not just the word *'analogia'* itself, but also the word *'attributio'* and the phrase *'per prius et posterius'*; and second, the use of *'ens'* as an example. So far as the vocabulary is concerned, I shall content myself with noting briefly that it comes mainly from translations of Arabic sources,[42] including twelfth-century translations of Avicenna [43] and Algazel[44] and thirteenth-century translations of Averroes.[45] The word *'analogia'* seems to become estab-

40 The phrase 'focal meaning' was applied to Aristotle by Owen (see 184).

41 For details, see the second paper cited in n. 1. The classification of *analogia* in relation to mode two depended in part on the role assigned to metaphor (*translatio* or *transumptio*).

42 But for a discussion of the appearance of the word 'attribution' in philosophical vocabulary after 1220 and its relation to Latin translations of Aristotle's *Metaphysics*, see R. Andrews, 'Peter of Auvergne's Commentary on Aristotle's *Categories*: Edition, Translation, and Analysis,' 2 vols. (Diss., Cornell University 1988), vol. I, 15-16.

43 Avicenna [2]: "ens ... est intentio in qua conveniunt secundum prius et posterius ..." (f.72vb).

44 Algazali [1]: "Convenientia sunt media inter univoca et equivoca: ut ens quod dicitur de substantia et accidente ... esse vero prius habet substantia deinde accidens mediante alio: ergo est eis esse secundum prius et posterius..." (sig. a 3va). Albert the Great tells us that *convenientia* are what the Arabs called *analoga*: see the discussion in A. de Libera, "Les sources gréco-arabes de la théorie médiévale de l'analogie de l'être," *Les études philosophiques* [special issue on analogy] 3/4 (1989), 330-3.

45 Averroes [1]: "nomen entis non significat decem praedicamenta pura aequivocatione, neque univoce: non restat igitur quod significet ea, nisi aliquo modorum analogiae, et sunt scilicet significationes nominum significantium plures res, quae tamen referuntur ad unam rem secundum prius et posterius..." (Vol. VIII, f.364ra). As Lyttkens points out (77), he does not use the word *'analogia'* in the relevant section of his main commentary: "...nomen ens dicitur multis modis, &

96

is said of urine through attribution to an animal, which is healthy in the primary sense.

The first type of analogy occurs when we use genus terms, and is said to be equivalent to univocation. The author explained that of two species contained beneath one genus, one will be nobler than the other with respect to nature and perfection, because genus descends through contrary differences: one (e.g. rational in the genus of animal) involves possession; whereas the other (e.g. irrational) involves privation, which is less noble. On the other hand, if one considers mere aptitude to participate in a given genus, the different species are on an equal footing, which is why there is no full-fledged equivocation. This inclusion of genus as a type of analogy illustrates the effect of authority on logical discussion, even when the authoritative source lies outside the *Organon*. As translated into Latin, Aristotle's *Physics* contains a remark to the effect that equivocations are hidden in genera (*aequivocationes latent in generibus*);[54] and logicians found it necessary to fit this claim into the framework of equivocation and analogy, even if in the end the consensus was that the use of genus terms was univocal.

It is the second type of analogy which fails to fit into Aristotle's three modes, for it is said to fall between univocation and the second mode of equivocation. As in univocation, the characteristic picked out by the term is found in both analogates, but as in standard accounts of the second mode of equivocation, it is found in a prior and a posterior way: *secundum prius et posterius*. The example given is *'ens'*;[55] and our author explained that Avicenna had shown there must be a common characteristic for *'ens,'* because we know *ens* first, before we know substances and accidents. He also argued that the same point

---

54 Aristotle [8], *Physics* VII 249a22-5; Anonymous [1], 133; *Les Auctoritates Aristotelis*, 155 (193).

55 It will be noted that what the anonymous author says here is not entirely consistent with his earlier use of *'ens'* as an example of mode two equivocation (Anonymous [1], 117), unless the thought is that *'ens'* said of substance and accident is to be treated differently than when it is said of two kinds of accident.

could be established by reason, as opposed to authority, since *ens* in itself is neither determined to *ens per se* nor inconsistent with *ens in alio*.

With this introduction of a common characteristic for '*ens*,' we seem to have arrived at a point far removed from the brief Aristotelian texts with which we began. I hope that my study of one anonymous author has given you some idea of what happened along the road from ancient Greece to late thirteenth-century Paris.[56]

---

56 I would like to thank the Canada Council for the Killam Research Fellowship which enabled me to do the research for this paper, and Norman Kretzmann for his help and encouragement.

DIVISIONS OF EQUIVOCATION AND ANALOGY
FROM AN ANONYMOUS 13TH-CENTURY COMMENTARY
ON *SOPHISTICAL REFUTATIONS*

Univocatio	*Analogia*: type 1
Medium	*Analogia*: type 2

EQUIVOCATIO

    A.   From *modi significandi*

           (Aristotle's third mode)

    B.   From *significatio*

          I.   *communis*

          II.   *propria*

               1.   *a casu*

                     (Aristotle's first mode)

               2.   *a consilio*   *Analogia*: type 3

                     (Aristotle's second mode)

                     a)   *a simili*

                     b)   *a proportione*

                     c)   *ab uno*

                     d)   *ad unum*

CANADIAN JOURNAL OF PHILOSOPHY
Supplementary Volume 17

Aristotle and Aquinas on Cognition

JOSEPH OWENS, C.Ss.R.

I

There is little need today to be apologetic about making Aristotle the basis for a philosophical discussion on human cognition. Interest in the Stagirite is in fact on the upsurge: interest in Aristotle not merely as a great thinker who lived in a particular epoch of time, but more pointedly as a philosopher who has much to offer for the promotion of serious thinking in our own day. In this regard I might merely refer to some straws that are indicative of the direction in which the winds are blowing. One was a series of four lectures given by Richard Sorabji in the spring of 1990 at the University of Toronto, in which the relevance of Aristotle for understanding current philosophical problems became strikingly apparent to those who listened to or took part in the discussions. Another was the conference held at the University of Alberta the same year on Aristotle and his medieval commentators. A third is the reprinting of John Herman Randall's book *Aristotle*, which is scheduled to appear shortly in the collection entitled *The Easton Press Library of Great Lives*.

In 1960 Randall gave his reading public a thoroughly American Aristotle, geared to the pragmatic and progressivist philosophy of Randall's own milieu. If Aristotle had been writing now, Randall claimed, he would have directed all his philosophy to action and progress, instead of to contemplative thought.[1] You may retort that a more perverse misunderstanding of the general bearing in Aristotle's philosophy would be hard to imagine, especially if your ears are ringing with the almost oracular proclamation of Aristotle himself against people who thought that way: "Those who suppose, as the Pythagoreans and Speusippus do, that supreme beauty and goodness are not present in the beginning, because the beginnings of both plants and animals are *causes*, but beauty and completeness are in the *effects* of these, are wrong in their opinion. For ... the first thing is not seed but the complete being."[2] For Aristotle, perfection was already in the world from the start. To each of us and to every active being belonged the task of working out individual perfection by striving towards the perfection of the world's supreme final cause. From Randall's viewpoint, on the contrary, continued progress towards ever increasing perfection — perfection as yet nowhere found — was the norm of human endeavor. In this spirit of the then prevalent process philosophy, Randall maintained that if Aristotle were writing for modern Americans "he would not elevate knowing above practical action" (248).

Yet in spite of this bias of epoch and culture, Randall was able to find in Aristotle's thought a philosophy able to serve the needs of any age or culture whatever. Perhaps one might even say that *because* of this discrepancy between his own outlook and the quite apparent temper of the Aristotelian treatises, Randall was spurred on to envisage a depth in the *Stagirite's* thinking that lay below both modern and ancient Greek mentalities, a depth into which both those cultures sink their roots, thereby drawing rich life-giving nourishment into their bloodstreams. In regard to Aristotle's practical philosophy, Randall made that point explicit. He wrote glowingly of how Aristotle's thought "can be applied to *any* social and cultural materials ... to Soviet Russia, to medieval Christendom, to India, to New York City"

---

1 John Herman Randall, Jr., *Aristotle* (New York: Columbia University Press 1960), 300

2 Aristotle [4], *Metaphysics*, XII.7.1072b30-1073a1

(248). This was written long before *Glasnost* and *Perestroika* had been thought of. At the time, the iron curtain had already been erected. It appeared too deeply divisive for most people to allow any common ground for the two respective ways of thinking. But today the out-looks have changed, so much so that Randall's point can be applied to the whole of Aristotle's thought as well as to his ethics. The *Stagirite's* principles can in fact be brought to bear upon any culture and any age. They can be the means for deeper understanding of the thought and the reality of any epoch, not at all excluding our own.

In a word, the indications just mentioned suggest that present interest in Aristotle is located not basically in a revival or a develop-ment of his ancient Greek thought, but rather in taking Aristotle's philosophy at its face value and using it as a help for doing our own thinking. There is no question of necrophilia at issue.

It might be objected, however, that this way of viewing the situation does not fit into the currently accepted syndrome of western philoso-phy's historical development. We are now accustomed to look upon antiquity as having naïvely based philosophical thought upon real things, things known directly in themselves and taken uncritically as such. Next came the medieval period with corresponding uncritical acquiescence in real things existent in themselves, plus acceptance of other tenets of religious faith, as in Jewish, Muslim, and Christian circles. Then followed the Renaissance, with its backwards look to ancient culture, succeeded by the Enlightenment or modern period with its refined philosophical basis in human ideas. Finally, we are now in the postmodern period with its starting points in language and with the hermeneutical requirement of indefinitely recessive signifiers in any philosophical interpretation.

Into that syndrome, one has to admit immediately, the present interest in Aristotle does not fit at all. This interest is far from a further development along the lines indicated by postmodern thinking, and it is not appealed to by current hermeneutics for substantial help. But neither is it a backward plunge into the culture of a former epoch, like the activity of the Renaissance. It does not seek to make Aristotle's world live again in our own epoch. On the other hand, it does not look for new starting points in thought or language, as did the later philosophical trends. No, it leaves Aristotle's thought intact in the original setting. The thought it looks to for help remains that of the *Stagirite*. That thought is not adopted holus bolus as our own. But it does provide us with much appreciated assistance for our own thinking, and for understanding the thought of other philosophers both of past ages and of our own day. In this perspective one may probe the bearing and the value of Randall's conclusion incisively expressed at the end of his book: "Clearly, Aristotle did not say everything; though without what he first said, all words would be meaningless, and when it is forgotten they usually are" (300). At first hearing, this assertion may seem intolerably wide in its sweep, and irresponsible in its boldness. But it rings as a challenge to probe its import, and it is provocative enough to prompt and sustain the patience that is required to examine its meaning in depth.

II

In the contemporary philosophical forum, of course, a hearing may be asked for Aristotle in virtue of today's genial pluralism, just as it may be asked for any other philosophy. But something much more serious seems to be indicated by the reflections that have just been made. Those reflections tend to regard Aristotle's thought not merely as one philosophy alongside the others, but more importantly as a means for deeper understanding of those others and for working towards fresh and independent conclusions. In this way Aristotle's thought is envisaged not as a system fixed and closed in itself, but rather as a key that opens the doors for a more profound grasp of today's philosophical situation.

Against this background the first question that arises is about the way pluralistic thinking appears when it is assessed in the light of Aristotle's epistemological doctrines. In the *Peri hermeneias*, Aristotle described human thought as meant to represent things, while words and language express what is thought about those things.[3] Further,

---

3 Aristotle [1], *De interpretatione*, 1.16a3-8

in the *De anima* he showed that the human mind is entirely blank before it becomes sensible things in the actuality of cognition.[4] In cognition it *is* those things.[5] Of itself the human mind has no original content other than sensible things. The original content, then, will be the same in all three orders: namely reality, thought, and speech. The knowable content is what is present in the things, represented in thought, and conveyed in speech. With thought and language bearing on things, the content in all three orders is the same. There is no immediate reason why philosophies of things, philosophies of ideas, and philosophies of language should not be able to understand each other, to enter into dialogue with each other, and to profit each in its own realm by the insights of the others. Honest and appreciative acknowledgement of philosophical pluralism should be that simple an approach from the Aristotelian standpoint.

In this setting, moreover, things and thought and language are in themselves objects of immediate awareness. Accordingly, all three allow themselves, rightly or wrongly, to be used as starting points for philosophical thinking. The way is thereby open for understanding the pluralism that is so courteously accepted in present-day philo-sophical circles. But if this is actually the case, how could any trouble ever occur in the philosophical world? How is it that philosophers have been able to disagree so bitterly in the past, and to argue so acrimoniously against one another? Even today everyone seems to cling tenaciously to her or his own views, albeit under a polite smile of tolerance or even of pity when conversing with people of radically different opinions. And sometimes, tempers are still lost in animated philosophical discussion. How could this be possible if the philo-sophical situation is to be viewed from the Aristotelian perspective?

In the light of the history of western philosophy, the genesis of the discords becomes sharply apparent. For Aristotle himself, human thought conformed to external sensible things. In the ordinary course of nature it originated from no other object. Speech in its turn ex-

4 Aristotle [3], *De anima*, III.4.429a21-4

5 Ibid., III.2.425b25-426a19; 5.430a19-20; 7.431a1-2; 8.431b20-3

pressed thought about things. Language had no other content. Yet despite one's immediate awareness on each level, there was with Aristotle a definite epistemological order of each level to the others. Epistemologically, external things were basic. Thought was correct when it conformed to things. Speech was true when it conformed to what was correctly thought about things. Epistemologically, things just in themselves remained absolutely fundamental and regulative in this setting.

The attitude of grounding philosophy on things external to human thought remained unchallenged throughout antiquity and the middle ages, in spite of wide variations in the way those things were held to confront human knowledge. The Platonic Ideas, as Aristotle saw them, were reached from sensible things with the added note of eternal duration. For Plato himself they existed in natural reality and not just in human thought. Neo-Platonic commentators on Aristotle did distinguish intellectual knowledge as coming from within, in contrast to sensation, that came from without. But within the Plotinian framework the intelligibles as objects were prior to intellection. With Augustine, things themselves, spread before the mind in their primordial existence in the divine Word, were what confronted human intellection.[6] In one way or another, then, things external to human cognition were the basis upon which western philosophy was built throughout the centuries prior to Descartes.

With Descartes, however, the change in the epistemological viewpoint was drastic. Philosophy before his time, Descartes claimed, had been a victim of the childish propensity to think in terms of sensible objects, instead of through clear and distinct ideas in the manner of mature mathematicians. A severe intellectual asceticism — comparable to the spiritual asceticism that Descartes knew from Lafleche as the means of training for religious life — was required to rid the mind of its childhood tendencies and accustom it to think in terms of ideas only. Malebranche spelled this out graphically in saying that for acquaintance with the sun and the stars you do not go for a walk

---

6 Augustine [2], *De magistro*, 12.40; 48.23-49.5

around the heavens. Rather, you look at the ideas you have about them in your own mind. It is these ideas that you first know, and you base the rest of your philosophical thinking upon them. Subsequent philosophers, such as Locke, Hume, and Condillac, made sensations function in this epistemological role of starting points for human cognition. But with them the cleavage from the Aristotelian stand remained just as drastic. For Aristotle, external sensible *things* were epistemologically the basic starting point. For the empiricists of the seventeenth and eighteenth centuries, the starting points were located in internal *sensations*, not in external things. Locke's stand that all our knowledge comes from sensations is just as radically distinct from Aristotle as is Descartes's, for the Aristotelian tenet is that sensible things, not internal sensations, are the starting points for all naturally acquired knowledge.

But Aristotle's overall view, diverse as it is from that of the seventeenth and eighteenth centuries, provides the means for seeing how this new way of starting philosophy could attain acceptance with these later thinkers. We are in fact immediately aware of our cognition. With a bit of Cartesian asceticism — the kind still practised on first year philosophy students to make them doubt the beliefs they bring with them — one can easily come to disregard the problem of the order that the sensation or the thought has to the thing. Sensations or ideas are then used as absolute starting points. The obvious consideration that what is sensed or known is something other than the sensation or the thought, is easily neglected. Refusal to probe in the starting points themselves the order of cognition to things, entailed the consequences brought out in the repeated failures of the Cartesians to demonstrate the real existence of things outside cognition, or of the American Neo-Realists and Critical Realists to account for errors in the perception of external things.

A parallel situation holds likewise in regard to philosophies based on language. We are immediately aware of what we say, and accordingly can take speech as a starting point for philosophizing. But again, the order of speech to thought and things, as noted by Aristotle, is neglected. And again, the consequences have to be faced. Instead of bearing on the great realities of life, as western philosophy has traditionally claimed to be doing, the object of philosophy becomes restricted to the intricacies of language, leaving reality to the natural sciences and other disciplines, and leaving itself open to Bertrand Russell's biting sarcasm that linguistic analysis becomes silly talk about silly statements.[7] Where historicity is made basic, as in postmodern hermeneutics, the thrust is to weave a web of words that will catch as best it can the "quivering elements of reality itself."[8] The starting point is still language, involving an endless chain of signifiers. The origins of philosophical statements are traced to the historical and linguistic conditions that make them possible. These origins in their turn require corresponding explanation in terms of their own historical and linguistic conditions, and so on in infinite regress. The pursuit has been very interesting, but hardly satisfactory.

In regard to contemporary pluralism, however, the issue here is obvious enough. By reason of their radically diverse starting points, philosophies that spring ultimately from thought or language are immune from attack by philosophies based upon external things. Other philosophies cannot be *refuted* on Aristotelian grounds. On the basis of their own chosen starting points they reject, either offhand or with reasoning cogently grounded on those accepted starting points, the very notion of things in themselves as an immediate object of human cognition. Reasoning based on external things in themselves, consequently, does not make contact with them. They are not open to argument based ultimately upon what is existent in itself and in that way outside human cognition. Hence one cannot use Aristotle to refute Enlightenment or postmodern philosophies. The stand that something outside cognition can be functioning as the basis of all philosophical demonstration is in fact given short shrift. If the thing is outside cognition, it is thereby unknown just in itself. At best it can be reasoned to or inferred from something already inside cognition. From this perspective the starting point for philosophical reasoning cannot be

---

7 Russell, *My Philosophical Development* (London: George Allen & Unwin 1959), 230

8 Gary Brent Madison, 'Hermeneutics and (the) Tradition,' *Proceedings of the American Catholic Philosophical Association* **62** (1988), 169

external to cognition itself. The Aristotelian way of thinking is historically outmoded for people who take their starting points from thought or language. It does not have the conventionally accepted weapons for engaging in Enlightenment or postmodern controversy.

For the same reason, modern and postmodern philosophies do not have the means for coming to grips with Aristotelian arguments. There is no question of refuting Aristotelian positions on the strength of their own radically different starting points. But the task of the philosopher is to understand. His objective does not consist in refuting, as may sometimes be the case with a theologian. In this respect Aristotle's tenets do show us how to understand today's pluralistic situation in philosophy. They explain how other philosophies are able to develop their divergent views. We are immediately aware of external sensible things, and immediately aware of our own perception and knowledge of them, though with epistemological priority for the sensible things. What is expressed in language is our thought about the things, and we are immediately aware of our words and sentences. Things, thought, and language offer innumerable different starting points, starting points immediately known and able to be chosen deliberately as the principles of a distinct philosophy. In this way philosophical pluralism is given a rational explanation. One is able to acknowledge sincerely and appreciatively the insights and worth of philosophies with which one radically disagrees, and draw genuine profit from the wide range of thought displayed in the panorama of western reasoning. The innate pluralism of philosophical thought, in the innumerable varieties that confront us today, is thereby understood in depth and made use of in one's own thinking.

Finally, one sees how the same person can at various stages in a career change her or his philosophy. Starting points in any of the three orders — reality, thought, and language — are immediately known and can be used at any time to start a new and different way of thinking. A change of starting points means in this way a different philosophy. A person who becomes dissatisfied with her or his present philosophy, or comes to reject the consequences to which it leads, is free to start all over again on different immediately evident principles. Aristotle's tenets make this all very clear. They enable us to *understand* our present-day philosophical pluralism.

III

By the same token, however, a philosophy based on things in themselves cannot look for support from philosophies grounded on thought or language, when it seeks to vindicate its own starting points. It itself has to substantiate its own procedure, and answer on its own grounds the objections brought by others against it. When, for instance, it is accused of naïvely assuming that known things exist in themselves outside human thought, it can only ask that the accusers take a closer look at their own thought and see if the situation is actually as simple as they have presumed. In this perspective Aristotle's philosophy is able to offer a thoroughgoing defense of its own procedure. It can be elaborately apologetic (in the ancient sense of 'apology' as a rational defense of one's own tenets), but not at all in today's use of the term. Anyone who reads carefully Aristotle's *De Anima* can hardly be tempted to regard its elaborate account of human cognition as at all naïve. One may disagree with it because of one's own philosophical starting points, but one can hardly accuse it of superficiality in its procedure.

In confronting the problem of cognition, the Aristotelian account calls attention to the fact that every thought and every sensation is of something other than itself.[9] What you see or know directly is the desk or the table, and not the act of seeing or of knowing it. You are, of course, concomitantly aware of your own cognitive acts, but only in the course of attaining something else. What you see is something else, and not directly the act of seeing. What you know directly is likewise something other than the act of knowing, even though awareness of the act itself is always concomitant. This tenet, however, is not a conclusion that can be reached from the nature or idea of cognition itself. As far as the notion of cognition goes, cognition can be either directly of itself, as in the case of the Aristotelian separate substances, or of something else, as in human cognition. Aristotle faced this question in justifying his conclusion that a separate sub-

---

9 Aristotle [4], *Metaphysics*, XII.9.1074b35-6

stance is the knowing of itself, even though in all cognition of which we are immediately aware the knowledge is of something other than the concomitantly known act. Aristotle's stand on this question, therefore, is based not on the essence or nature or idea of cognition, but on the fact of what is directly known in sensation or in any other act of human cognition. The object is in fact something other than the act itself, and in the case of sensation, cognition bears directly on something extended and sensibly qualified: for instance, on a table or a chair. It does not bear directly on the cognition. You can only reflect closely on your own awareness and see if this is not the case.

But, the objector will urge, all this goes on within the awareness itself. The notion of something other than the cognition arises within the cognition only. It does not take you outside the cognition. It is something that springs up within your own cognitive activity. You are merely assuming that there is something outside that corresponds to it.

This is the standard objection that has had to be faced from the time of Descartes on. The objection is based upon the dogmatic assumption that what we are aware of is our own cognition, instead of something other than the cognition. Aristotle's stand, in facing the aporia to which I have just referred, is that in the ordinary way of knowing with which we are immediately acquainted, the cognition is always of something other than itself. Aristotle has to argue very elaborately for a different situation in the case of separate substances. He means accordingly that what we first know directly is a thing in itself, a thing other than the cognitive act and cognitive agent.

There is no attempt to argue from the thought or perception to the thing. External things have epistemological priority. One's thought and oneself are known only through concomitance to this basic object.

What does this mean? How can what is acknowledged to be originally outside cognition get within cognition? With the basis of reasoning located firmly in the thing that is other than the cognitive act, Aristotle is able to offer his explanation of what knowing or perceiving a thing means. It means that the percipient or knower becomes and is that thing in the actuality of the cognition. This is not a case of having a thing in a material way. In material possession the possessor remains distinct from the thing he has, in the way you possess a house or a car. On the other hand, cognition means thoroughgoing identity with the thing insofar as it is perceived or known. Aristotle repeats this assertion of identity of knower and known too often to leave any doubt about its important role. To know a thing is to *be* it in a distinctive way of being. Obviously, on account of this thoroughgoing identity of knower and things known, the one cannot be cognitively grasped without concomitant awareness of the other, for they are the same in the actuality of the cognition. In this way the concomitant awareness of the cognition is present in every cognitive act that bears directly on something else. You cannot be aware of the thing perceived or known without thereby being aware of yourself as knower, and vice versa.

On this account cognition is something very different from photography or recording. Cognition is not like *having* a picture or sounds. The camera does not *see* the landscape. The recording machine does not *hear* the sounds. They have the impressions, but they are not aware of them. As something essentially different, the cognitive activity has to be explained in terms of being rather than of having. You *have* the sensations and the concepts, quite as the machines have the impressions, but you *are* the things perceived or known. Knower and thing known do not produce a third thing in the cognitive activity, as is the case in material production. Rather, the two become one and the same in the actuality of the cognition.

From the strictly epistemological standpoint, this thoroughgoing identity of knower and thing known is the most important and most fundamental tenet in the Aristotelian conception of knowledge. Yet it is the tenet that evokes the hardest sales resistance in students, and is the last Aristotelian dictum to which they come to assent. They instinctively revolt against the prospect of *being* the things they know. They do not like the idea of being a brown cow or a big bad wolf just because they are seeing those animals or thinking about them. They can be shown that the tenet is explicit in Aristotle, but they recoil at accepting it for themselves. All one can say to them is to continue to think it over. It is a profound insight that has to be absorbed very gradually. It can be approached in various ways, but ultimately it itself is what has to provide the basis for the legitimacy of the approaches themselves.

The overall difficulty here lies in a failure to grasp the full import of Aristotle's frequently repeated norm that being is meant in various ways. A thing can be in a material or an immaterial way, a substantial or an accidental way, a physical or a cognitional way. To be a brown cow cognitionally does not at all mean to be a brown cow physically. Likewise, you are a brown cow only accidentally in your contingent act of cognition, while you remain your own self substantially. Further, you are not changed into a cow in a material way when you receive its form in cognition. All-pervasive for Aristotle is the meta-physical insight that form is the cause of being. Form makes a thing be, be what it is, and be a unit. In any physical change, the form is received materially, insofar as physical matter takes on a new form in generation or in perishing or in alteration. Physical matter receives a new form in procreation, and loses that form in death or in altera-tion. In every case of physical change a matter loses one form and takes on another, under the influx of an efficient cause, as when wood is reduced to ashes by fire. But when a form is received in immaterial fashion, there is no loss of form in either the knower or the thing known. The immaterially received form becomes in cognition the form of the recipient in the actuality of the awareness. It makes both be one and the same thing in the cognitive order. It makes them be cognitively a unit, though in physical being each retains its own distinctive result of the causality.

That is what cognition means for Aristotle. His explanation shows in its own terms how something external to cognition can be episte-mologically prior to the cognitive act, and how all our cognition originates in sensible things rather than directly in the sensations themselves. It shows how there can be no question of a sensible replica leaving a distant thing and traveling through the media to the sense organ. It lets us understand how an astronomer can literally *see* today a cosmic event that took place millions of years ago in physical being. It allows no ground for the objection that as we do not know what happens to the sensible stimulus in its journey along the nerves from sense organ to cortex, we have no guarantee that the external thing may not have changed or may have vanished completely in that infinitesimally short time. In these and similar cases there is no insuperable difficulty in explaining how the form is impressed physically and cognitively by its efficient causes through the appropriate media upon a distant thing. The form is thereby able to make the knower be the things or events as they are at the time the efficient causality originates.

As an illustration, a form may be worked into marble by a sculptor, or into lines and colors on a canvas by a painter. The artistic form originates in the mind of the sculptor or painter. There is no question of a facsimile or image of it traveling down through the nerves and muscles of the artist, and then through the chisel or brush to the surface of the marble or canvas. No, the image or form exists only in the mind of the artist and in the finished product. It does not exist in the media. The late Marshall McLuhan's dictum that the medium is the message holds only in a causal sense, though with very important bearing. The medium, rather, is the means by which the efficient cause acts upon a subject. Through nerves and hands and tools the artist is exerting her or his efficient causality upon the subject that is spatially distant from the agent, and is thereby bringing about the form in the new instance. The form is existent as such only in the efficient cause and in the ultimate effect. In the image on the television screen the color and pattern are present solely in the real game being played in the Skydome, and on the television screens throughout the country. In the miles of transmitting media there is neither color nor image, but simply the electronic signals that cause the television set to reproduce the images on the screen.

The case of television is of course material reception. The television set itself does not see or hear or know what is going on in the Skydome. The apparatus is not cognitive. But there is neither more nor less difficulty here in understanding how the colors and pattern of a distant object are transmitted in immaterial as well as material fashion to the retina without coloring the air. It is the same overall problem of how an efficient cause can transmit form through media without affecting the media in the same way it affects the ultimate subject upon which it is working.

In sensation, then, the external thing impresses through the media its own form in immaterial fashion upon the percipient, and thereby makes the percipient be one with the thing itself in the actuality of the cognition. In this way Aristotle's philosophy is within its own procedure fully capable of justifying its basis in external things themselves, rather than in sensations concerning them. It is not acquiescing to the existence of external things naïvely. It is offering an elaborate and penetrating explanation of how it can regard all human thought as based epistemologically upon things external to the thought. Their real existence in themselves is known in epistemological priority to our sensations and thought about them. Aristotle's explanation shows how real things, existent in themselves, speak to us immediately in our thought, since they are identical with us in complete fashion in our cognition. It is reality itself that is talking to us. There is no room here for the caricature of a 'hot line' to the external world. The real external things come first in our cognition. Ourselves and our cognition are known only by reason of our concomitant identity with them in the actuality of the awareness. If the notion of a 'hot line' could at all be introduced into the problem, it would be rather from the external things to our sensations and thoughts.

In that way the Aristotelian explanation allows each individual thing to stand in its own right absolutely, as an independent starting point for philosophical thinking. It is there, in itself, and is known as such. It does not have to be explained hermeneutically by something preceding it, in infinite regress. Aristotle allows eternal succession of cosmic changes, and the recurrent rise and fall of civilizations, but he does not make truth and certainty the victim of our inability to encompass in our knowledge this infinite regression of causes. Each existent thing is an absolute on which one can base philosophic reasoning.

But all this is within Aristotle's own philosophical territory. If others — and they are legion — wish to say 'No, we cannot see our way clear to basing our philosophy on external sensible things as absolute starting points,' Aristotle has no philosophical means to refute them. He has to let them go their own way, but with the understanding that they have to accept the consequences of their own thinking. He gives us the means to see in his own context what they are doing, and thereby leaves us fully at home in today's pluralistic world, a philosophic democracy that permits each citizen to think in her or his chosen way.

IV

Aristotle, then, enables us to understand in depth the widely pluralistic thinking that the western world has produced in the course of its long and varied history. His philosophy also offers leads and means for pursuing one's personal thought in new directions and to new heights. Here fresh inspiration comes from other sources, and may in turn throw new light on the original Aristotelian conclusions. This will not result exactly in a further development of Aristotle. Rather, it will give rise to authentically new philosophy within the Aristotelian tradition. The point may be aptly illustrated by an instance from the philosophical thought of Thomas Aquinas in the thirteenth century of our era, on the topic of existence.

For Aristotle, quiddity and existence were melded together. One might distinguish the two logically, in one's mind or in definition. But for practical purposes it was better not to do even that.[10] However, Aquinas, like other theologians of the middle ages, was approaching the theme against the Biblical background of creation. The things that come under our experience did not have their being from themselves but from an omnipotent creator. Created things were decidedly not their own being. In that setting it was imperative to concentrate more intensely on the things immediately known, and look in them for some kind of distinction between themselves and the existence they had acquired through creation. Various kinds of distinction were seen by different thinkers. The impulse for this could not come from Aristotle, or be looked upon as a development of his thought. It was new philosophy, and had to be established on new and further grounds, even though it still worked on real things in themselves, as had been the case with the *Stagirite*.

Aquinas, working in this new perspective, saw that the nature of things was known in intellectual abstraction while their existence was grasped through judgment. From that philosophically new starting point he demonstrated that every created thing was really distinct

---

10 Ibid., IV.2.1003b22-30

from its existence. The identically same thing could thereby have different ways of existing, while remaining exactly the same thing in nature and individuality. Every finite thing had existence primarily in the divine creative essence, where Augustine, as did Malebranche centuries later with great flourish, made the things the immediate object of human intellection. In that existence, as Aquinas repeated from Anselm, the creature was really identical with the divine creative essence.[11] Second, the thing could exist in itself, in the world of perishable objects, and there function as the subsequently notorious 'thing in itself.' Also it could exist in cognition, angelic or human.[12]

This explanation involved three different modes of existence: namely, divine existence, real finite existence, and cognitional existence. It permitted one to see how something could remain identically the same thing under the three different ways of existing. In the epistemological context it allowed a much sharper vision and a much neater way of expression than with Aristotle. It permitted one to see and to say that external things come to *exist* in one's cognition, in addition to the Aristotelian formula that knower and thing known are identical in the actuality of the awareness. Aristotle eschewed the expression that the things themselves are in the mind, on account of his explicitly cited Empedoclean setting in which cognition of like by like would have to mean that earth in reality as an object was known through earth really present in the mind.[13] But Aquinas in his new approach could say without hesitation that the whole universe can exist in the mind of an individual person.[14] This is definitely not a development of Aristotle. Rather, it goes against Aristotle's way of developing the theme. It is a different philosophy, proceeding from new philosophical principles, but spurred on and guided by the

---

11 Aquinas, *Scriptum super Sententiis*, 1.36.1.3 ad lm; Thomas Aquinas [2], I, 836

12 Aquinas, *Quaestiones quodlibetales*, 8.1.1. Resp.; Thomas Aquinas [10], 159-60

13 Aristotle [3], *De Anima*, III.8.431b28-432a3; cf. I.5.410a1-12

14 Thomas Aquinas [8], *De veritate*, 2.2.Solut.; Thomas Aquinas [1] vol. XXII, 44.118-33

Aristotelian principles of actuality and potentiality, substance and accident, the four types of causality, and the origin of human cognition in external sensible things. It shows that the nature of a finite thing, though known in abstraction, can be an object of cognition only as existent in one of the three ways just mentioned. Only as an existent, and never as just an Avicennian nature, can a thing be perceived or known. What receives no satisfactory explanation in the Aristotelian text thereby finds an answer in the approach of Aquinas.

The same point could likewise be illustrated by Thomistic contributions on topics such as free-will, the moral order, and the temporal beginning and end of the cosmic processes. On those questions Aristotle goes just so far, and then remains silent. This is what seems to lie behind the Renaissance dictum *sine Thoma mutus esset Aristoteles* — 'without Thomas Aristotle would stay silent.' What other medieval thinkers have to say, for instance in their doctrines on the common nature, may similarly be of help.

V

One may now ask whether this investigation substantiates Randall's irritating claim that even though Aristotle did not say everything, "without what he first said all words would be meaningless, and when it is forgotten they usually are." The assertion that "Aristotle did not say everything" holds even within the strictly philosophical realm, insofar as history shows definitely that Aristotelianism is not the only profitable way in which one may philosophize. The widely varied pluralism in the history of western thought, and the wisdom one may absorb by osmosis by reading types of philosophy other than one's own, are obvious facts. But for a satisfactory explanation of how all this intellectual ferment takes place, the account given by Aristotle is unmatched.

The reason, I would suggest, is that Aristotle is able to let reality itself do the talking. He shows how real things in themselves can be accorded epistemological priority. Things are able to be acknowledged as final arbiter without sacrifice of respectability for a philosopher. Aristotle makes clear how one can honestly and consistently meld one's philosophic life with the real life one is daily living in common with the non-philosophical public. There seems to be something not right in situations like the Cartesian insistence that the reality of the external world must be demonstrated even though no one could really doubt the fact; or in Locke's refusal to have controversy with any person who questions Locke's real existence outside that person's thought; or in Hume's recourse to a really good dinner and real game of backgammon when philosophical speculating became too dejecting. Aristotle shows how the ultimate recourse to real things is philosophically correct, and is not to be looked upon as a bow to human weakness. In that perspective he enables us to see how the real has philosophically the last word.

Without the backing by reality, words and thoughts do lose their meaning. So applied, Randall's assertion may come to appear as an understatement rather than as an irresponsible exaggeration. Instead of claiming that when in philosophy Aristotle is forgotten, words are *usually* meaningless, one is tempted to say, with appropriate reservations, that they *always* are. But in any case, this conscious and justified and all-pervasive grounding in reality merits in full the niche traditionally accorded to Aristotle as *the* philosopher *par excellence*, and, in Dante's words, "the teacher of those who know." Yet quite often Aristotle may pursue a line of thought only to a certain limit. He is conscientious in not pushing his conclusions further than his premises allow. In this way he seems to become silent for a listener of a later era. It is here that a radically different notion of existence enabled Aquinas to interpret the Aristotelian texts in a manner well beyond their original implications. In cases of this kind, study of Aquinas may aid us in breaking through the Aristotelian silence, and thereby in enhancing our own work upon the topics at issue.

This conclusion is well illustrated in the difficulties about the nature of human knowledge, difficulties that in the minds of some contemporary writers have borne epistemology to the brink of the grave.[15] Locke had called for examination of our own abilities before

---

15 For a discussion of this topic, see Susan Haack, 'Recent Obituaries of Epistemology,' *American Philosophical Quarterly* **27** (1990), 199-212.

approaching other philosophical problems.[16] In the wake of that appeal there has been an almost universal tendency in subsequent epistemology to base the reliability of human knowledge upon the reliability of our cognitive faculties. In the light of Aristotle's explanation of cognition, the circularity of this procedure becomes apparent. One sees why it can lead to frustration in epistemology. Our intellect is pure potentiality in the cognitive order. What we can know about our intellect actually, including its reliability, comes from real sensible objects and our concomitant awareness of them. We know that these things cannot be and not be at the same time in the same respects, that each of them is something that is extended and existent, and that two and two of them are four. We can find on deliberate examination that this knowledge is certain. In that way the reliability of our actual knowledge itself, checked against the epistemologically prior existents, is the basis for reasoning to the reliability of our cognitive powers, and not vice versa.

On the one hand, this Aristotelian epistemology has to face a charge of extreme dogmatism. It makes every particular instance of existence an absolute. Each instance stands epistemologically in its own right, and in itself offers a solid basis for philosophical reasoning. Philosophies that have their starting points in human thought or language, moreover, are from the Aristotelian viewpoint absolutely wrong from start to finish, even though their treatment of details may be of outstanding aid in the philosophical enterprise. These stands can hardly help but have a savor of unacceptable dogmatism when they are assessed in modern or postmodern circles.

On the other hand, a charge of extreme relativism has to be faced by the notion that philosophies are as individually distinctive as are fingerprints. Yet the Aristotelian conception provides a single absolute and mandatory standard by which all philosophies are to be judged. The standard is the one real world in which we all live and think and act. The one standard is the same for all. Human thought

---

16 Locke, *An Essay Concerning Human Understanding*, 1.1.4; John Locke [1], 44-5. Cf. ibid., 'Epistle to the Reader,' 7.

and language about that real world can offer innumerably different sets of starting points upon which philosophies may be built. In this respect the Aristotelian conception of human knowledge, with the relation of that knowledge to thought and things, shows how pluralism in philosophy comes about, and why none of the philosophies can be refuted by any other even though in details all may receive inspiration and guidance from others. But in no way do the conceptions of knowledge in Aristotle and Aquinas dispense from a single absolute standard by which all philosophies can be judged. This norm cannot be demonstrated to anyone looking for proof on the basis of modern or postmodern starting points. It itself remains true to the explanation of pluralism in which no philosophy can refute any other. It has to wait till the opponent is no longer able to accept the notion that one's knowing can add anything to the thing itself.[17]

---

17 Cf. Bertrand Russell: "I could no longer believe that knowing makes any difference to what is known" (*Contemporary British Philosophy* [First Series], J.H. Muirhead, ed. [London: George Allen & Unwin 1924], 360). This was in reaction to the argument previously accepted from Bradley that a thing may be altered in the process of being known: "And you cannot ever get your product standing apart from its process" (Francis Herbert Bradley, *Appearance and Reality*, 9th imp. [Oxford: Clarendon 1930], 23).

CANADIAN JOURNAL OF PHILOSOPHY
Supplementary Volume 17

Aquinas on the Foundations of Knowledge

ELEONORE STUMP

I Introduction

Aquinas is sometimes taken to hold a foundationalist theory of knowledge. So, for example, Nicholas Wolterstorff says, "Foundationalism has been the reigning theory of theories in the West since the high Middle Ages. It can be traced back as far as Aristotle, and since the Middle Ages vast amounts of philosophical thought have been devoted to elaborating and defending it.... Aquinas offers one classic version of foundationalism."[1] And Alvin Plantinga says, "we can get a better understanding of Aquinas ... if we see [him] as accepting some version of *classical foundationalism*. This is a *picture* or total way of looking at faith, knowledge, justified belief, rationality, and allied topics. This picture has been enormously popular in Western thought; and despite a substantial opposing ground-

---

1 *Reason Within the Bounds of Religion* (Grand Rapids, MI: Eerdmans 1984) 2nd ed., 30. Wolterstorff has since altered his view; see 'The Migration of the Theistic Arguments: From Natural Theology to Evidentialist Apologetics,' in *Rationality and Religious Belief*, Robert Audi and William Wainwright, eds. (Ithaca, NY: Cornell University Press 1986) 38-81.

swell, I think it remains the dominant way of thinking about these topics."[2]

Foundationalism is most frequently associated with Descartes, and the sort of foundationalism ascribed to Aquinas is sometimes distinguished from that attributed to Descartes. Plantinga, for example, distinguishes what he calls 'ancient and medieval foundationalism' from the modern foundationalism found in Descartes, Locke, and Leibniz, among others, but he thinks Aquinas's brand of foundationalism has enough in common with the foundationalism of Descartes and other early modern philosophers that they can all be conflated under the heading 'classical foundationalism.'

This sort of foundationalism is currently thought to be in trouble; various philosophers, including Plantinga himself, have raised serious objections to it. In the first place, this brand of foundationalism gives the counter-intuitive result that much of what we think we know is not to be counted as knowledge. The propositions we can take to be properly basic don't entail or even render probable many of the apparently nonbasic propositions we ordinarily claim to know. Plantinga's examples include "all those propositions that entail ... that there are persons distinct from myself, or that the world has existed for more than five minutes." In the second place, there are reasons for doubting whether foundationalism is right in confining the set of properly basic beliefs to those which are self-evident and evident to the senses. Memory beliefs, Plantinga argues, are neither self-evident nor evident to the senses, but they certainly seem to be properly basic. The belief that I walked to school this morning, rather than driving or bicycling, is a belief I hold without basing it on other beliefs; and since it seems perfectly rational for me to take this belief as basic, this memory belief and others like it also seem to be properly basic beliefs. Finally, Plantinga has argued that the central claims of this sort of foundationalism cannot meet foundationalist criteria, because these

---

2 'Reason and Belief in God,' in *Faith and Rationality: Reason and Belief in God*, Alvin Plantinga and Nicholas Wolterstorff, eds. (Notre Dame, IN: University of Notre Dame Press 1983), 48

central claims can't be held as properly basic beliefs — they aren't self-evident or evident to the senses — and it's very difficult to see how they could be traced back to properly basic beliefs. Plantinga concludes his case against the theory with the announcement that "classical foundationalism is bankrupt" (62). And in a recent book designed to acquaint students with current thinking about theories of knowledge, Lehrer ends his examination of foundationalism by claiming that as a theory of knowledge it "is a failure."[3]

So if the theory of knowledge held by Aquinas is foundationalism of this kind, then there are some good arguments for rejecting his views.

Of course, neither Wolterstorff nor Plantinga is an historian of philosophy, and I began with their views for just that reason: to show that contemporary philosophers engaged in epistemology accept this view of Aquinas's theory of knowledge as just what would be expected. One highly regarded historian of philosophy, however, who has expressly addressed the issue of foundationalism in the history of Western philosophy is T.H. Irwin. In his recent book *Aristotle's First Principles*,[4] Irwin argues that at least in the *Posterior Analytics* Aristotle himself is a foundationalist. "Aristotle therefore recognizes first principles with no further justification; but he denies that his view makes knowledge impossible, because he denies that demonstration requires demonstrable first principles. In denying this, he implies that in some cases complete justification is non-inferential, since it does not require derivation from other propositions. Non-inferentially justified first principles allow us to claim knowledge without facing an infinite regress or a circle. Aristotle's conclusion implies a foundationalist doctrine, requiring true and non-inferentially justified beliefs as the basis of knowledge and justification" (130-1).

And Irwin takes the *Posterior Analytics* as an epistemological treatise in which Aristotle develops his foundationalism:

---

3 *Theory of Knowledge* (Boulder, CO: Westview Press 1990), 62

4 Oxford: Clarendon Press 1988

Aristotle's account of scientific knowledge develops from his metaphysical realism and his epistemological foundationalism;

[in the *Analytics*] he treated foundationalism as the only alternative to skepticism. (134; 197)[5]

Irwin himself takes a rather negative attitude towards this side of Aristotle's philosophy: "we must say that Aristotle's foundationalism in the *Analytics* results from a one-sided view of science and objectivity, and that this view needs considerable modification in the light of Aristotle's views on first philosophy" (473). Irwin's views, of course, are not the only available interpretation of the *Posterior Analytics*.[6] Nonetheless, if his account of Aristotle is correct, it provides some confirmation for the common view of Aquinas as a foundationalist, since it would not be unreasonable to suppose that Aquinas simply accepted and developed the theory of knowledge he found in Aristotle.

In this paper I want to reexamine this picture of Aquinas's epistemology.

II Foundationalism

It will be helpful in this enterprise to be clear about what is being attributed to Aquinas. Here is Plantinga's description of classical foundationalism:

Foundationalism is best construed ... as a thesis about rational noetic structures.... According to the foundationalist a rational noetic structure will have a foundation — a set of beliefs not accepted on the basis of others; in a rational noetic structure some beliefs will be basic. Non-basic beliefs, of course, will be

---

5 See also 139-41, 148-50, 315, 318, 326, 482-3.

6 For a different interpretation of the nature and purpose of the *Posterior Analytics*, see, for example, Jonathan Barnes, 'Aristotle's Theory of Demonstration,' in *Articles on Aristotle*, Jonathan Barnes, Malcolm Schofield, and Richard Sorabji, eds. (London: Duckworth 1975) 65-87.

accepted on the basis of other beliefs, which may be accepted on the basis of still other beliefs, and so on until the foundations are reached. In a rational noetic structure, therefore, every non-basic belief is ultimately accepted on the basis of basic beliefs. (52)

A further and fundamental feature of classic varieties of foundationalism [is that] they all lay down certain conditions of proper basicality.... [A] belief to be properly basic (that is, basic in a rational noetic structure) must meet certain conditions.... Thomas Aquinas ... holds that a proposition is properly basic for a person only if it is self-evident to him or "evident to the senses." ... [T]he outstanding characteristic of a self-evident proposition is that one simply sees it to be true upon grasping or understanding it ... Aquinas and Locke ... held that a person, or at any rate a normal, well-formed human being, finds it impossible to withhold assent when considering a self-evident proposition.... [P]ropositions "evident to the senses" are also properly basic. By this latter term ... [Aquinas] means to refer to perceptual propositions — propositions whose truth or false-hood we can determine by looking or employing some other sense. (55-7)

So, on Plantinga's description of the type of foundationalist theory of knowledge he attributes to Aquinas, it consists in the following claims:

1. Some propositions are properly basic in the sense that it is rational to accept them without basing them on other proposi-tions.

2. Properly basic propositions include only propositions which are self-evident or evident to the senses, that is, propositions which can be known to be true either just by understanding their terms or by employing one or more of the senses.

3. All non-basic propositions must be accepted, directly or indi-rectly, on the basis of properly basic propositions.

It is common to add one more set of conditions to this list. Wolter-storff stipulates that

4. the properly basic propositions can be known with certitude,

and that consequently

5. the propositions known on the basis of properly basic propositions can be known with certitude (Wolterstorff, 29; cf. also 36).

And Lehrer emphasizes the search for a guarantee of truth, or for
certainty, as the hallmark of foundationalism:

> [A] central thesis of the traditional foundation theory was that basic beliefs are
> immune from error and refutation; (42)

> [S]ome beliefs *guarantee* their own truth. If my accepting something guarantees
> the truth of what I accept, then I am completely justified in accepting it for the
> purpose of obtaining truth and avoiding error. We are guaranteed success in
> our quest for truth and cannot fail. (40)

Finally, although it need not be, foundationalism has often been
taken as a species of internalism: the view that knowledge is constituted by certain states internal to the knower and accessible to him.
And although it is possible to combine features of both foundationalism and reliabilism, foundationalism has sometimes been distinguished from reliabilism, put forward as a species of externalism —
the view that knowledge is constituted largely or entirely by states or
processes external to the knower, or at any rate not internally accessible to him. Plantinga's own favored theory of knowledge has certain
features in common with reliabilism. On Plantinga's account,[7] when
a person has enough warrant for a true belief, the belief counts as
knowledge. His complicated explanation of warrant includes these
claims: in order to have warrant, a person must hold true beliefs
acquired by a reliable process, when his cognitive faculties function
as they were designed to function (by evolution, for example, or by
God) in an environment in which they were designed to function; and
beliefs with sufficient warrant constitute knowledge. This account is
avowedly externalistic. One can't tell just by looking within oneself
and reflecting on the results of introspection whether one's faculties

---

7 I am grateful to Alvin Plantinga for giving me access to his forthcoming work
on epistemology.

are functioning as they were designed to function or whether the environment in which they are functioning is the appropriate one.

Although both Plantinga and Wolterstorff freely speak of Aquinas as a foundationalist, or classical foundationalist, I want to avoid the sort of controversy which can be raised by epistemological taxonomy. Rather than attempting to determine precisely which species of foundationalism Aquinas is supposed to have held, a task that would require an exegesis of Plantinga and Wolterstorff as well as Aquinas, I propose to try eschewing such taxonomy altogether. So, for the sake of brevity and clarity, instead of asking whether Plantinga and Wolterstorff are right to present and repudiate Aquinas as a classical foundationalist, I want to prescind from their terminology and focus just on internalism and the claims in (1)-(5) above. The idea of a theory of knowledge characterized by (1)-(5) is that there is a small set of propositions which we can know with certainty to be true without inferring them from anything else that we know, and that our non-basic beliefs will also be known with certainty if we base them on that small set of certainly true propositions. In Aquinas's case, the propositions which properly serve as the foundation for the non-basic beliefs are supposed to include just two groups: those whose truth is seen as soon as they are understood, and those whose truth is evident to the senses. As we examine Aquinas's views, I will be concerned to ask just whether he holds an epistemological theory which is internalist and which can be characterized by (1)-(5). It will, of course, be helpful to have a noun by which to refer to this position rather than referring to it always by some clumsy circumlocution. So for ease of exposition I will refer to this theory as 'Foundationalism,' capitalizing the term to remind the reader that it does not refer to foundationalism as a whole or to some commonly discussed species of foundationalism, but picks out instead only an epistemological position which is internalist and which is characterized by (1)-(5).

III Evidence for and against Foundationalism in Aquinas

Why would anyone suppose Aquinas is a Foundationalist? One of the main reasons is that the Latin term for the subject of Aquinas's commentary on the *Post. An.* — namely, '*scientia*' — has often enough been translated as 'knowledge' and his commentary has consequently been taken to consist in an exposition of his theory of knowledge. Understood in this way, the treatise can give an appearance of Foundationalism.

There is a process of reasoning, Aquinas says, which yields its results necessarily, and in this process the certitude of *scientia* is acquired. (I will leave '*scientia*' untranslated, so as not to make any assumptions at the outset about the appropriate English equivalent for it.) This process of reasoning consists in demonstrative syllogisms.[8] Each demonstrative syllogism has two premises, and these premises must be better known and prior to the conclusion (Ibid., I lectio 4). But demonstration does not give rise to an infinite regress. There are first principles of demonstration, and these are themselves indemonstrable (Ibid., I lectio 35).

> It is not possible to acquire *scientia* of (*scire*) anything by demonstration unless there is prior cognition of the first, immediate principles. (Ibid., II lectio 20)

And so, Aquinas says,

> *scientia* ... which is acquired by demonstration, proceeds from propositions which are true, first, and immediate, that is, which are not demonstrated by any intermediate but are evident by means of themselves (*per seipsas*). They are called "immediate" because they lack an intermediate demonstrating them, and "first" in relation to other propositions which are proved by means of them.[9]

There is no cognition that has more certitude than the cognition of such first principles, and they are the cause of certitude in one's cognition of other propositions (Ibid., II lectio 20). They are not only necessary but known per se (cf., e.g., ibid., proemium; lectio 9), and

---

8 Thomas Aquinas [17], *Super Post An., proemium*

9 Ibid., I lectio 4: "scientia ... quae per demonstrationem acquiritur, procedat ex propositionibus veris, primis et immediatis, id est quae non per aliquod medium demonstrantur, sed per seipsas sunt manifestae (quae quidem immediatae dicuntur, in quantum carent medio demonstrante; primae autem in ordine ad alias propositiones, quae per eas probantur)."

any *scientia* takes its certitude from them (Ibid., I lectio 42). There are different sorts of *scientia*, but one of his paradigms is mathematics (Ibid., I lectio 1).

What sorts of propositions are first principles? On the one hand, Aquinas says that the first of all the principles are the law of noncontradiction and the law of excluded middle. But definitions, too, are principles of demonstration (Ibid., I lectio 20; II lectio 2). In fact, every proposition in which the predicate is in the definition of the subject is known per se (Ibid., I lectio 5; lectio 9). On the other hand, he says that propositions accepted by the senses, such as that the sun is now eclipsed, are the most known (*notissima*) (Ibid., I lectio 16).

These remarks and others like them can certainly give rise to the impression of Foundationalism. In fact, it looks as if Aquinas is committed to just those Foundationalist claims listed above. Propositions which we know in virtue of understanding their terms — that is, self-evident propositions — and propositions evident to the senses are properly accepted as basic. All other propositions which form part of our knowledge must be accepted on the basis of these properly basic propositions. So we begin with properly basic propositions and proceed by means of demonstrative syllogisms to non-basic propositions. In this way, we begin with what can be known with certainty — the properly basic propositions — and move to non-basic propositions, which are deduced from the properly basic ones and so also count as knowledge known with certainty.

But just a little further exploration of his views shows that this picture of Aquinas's theory of knowledge is irremediably inaccurate.

In the first place, there is ample evidence that Aquinas's notion of *scientia* is not equivalent to our notion of knowledge. *Scientia* isn't of contingent or corruptible things.[10] In fact, there is no *scientia* of individual things; demonstration always has to do with universals.

---

10 Thomas Aquinas [3], ST Ia q.79 a.9; Thomas Aquinas [17], *Super Post. An.* I lectio 4, lectio 16: "neque demonstratio, neque scientia est corruptibilium." Aquinas does think that we have *scientia* of the natural world, but we have it in virtue of the fact that we have *scientia* of the universal causes which operate in nature. See, for example, *Super Post. An.* I lectio 42.

Demonstration must always be on the basis of universals. (*Super Post. An.* I lectio 16)

Universals are the objects of our inquiry, just as they are the things of which we have *scientia*.[11]

"Universal" is taken here as a certain suitability or adequation of a predicate to a subject, as when the predicate isn't found apart from the subject or the subject without the predicate.... Demonstration is properly speaking of a universal of this sort. (Ibid., I lectio 11)

[Aristotle] asserts that two things pertain to *scientia*. One of them is that it is universal, for there is no *scientia* of individual things susceptible to sense.

Besides things which are true and necessary and which cannot be otherwise, there are things which are true but not necessary, which can be otherwise; but it is evident ... that there is no *scientia* of such things.[12]

If 'scientia' were Aquinas's term for knowledge, then we would have to attribute to him the view that we can have no knowledge of contingent, corruptible, or singular things; and that would be a very odd view of knowledge. Furthermore, it would be hard to square with Aquinas's own claim, presented above, that propositions accepted on the basis of the senses, such as that the sun is now eclipsed, are most known (*notissima*).

But there is further evidence which suggests not only that *scientia* isn't Aquinas's equivalent of 'knowledge' but in fact that *scientia* should be understood as a special species of the broader genus *cognitio*, which looks like a much better candidate for an equivalent to our notion of knowledge.[13]

---

11 Ibid., II lectio 1: "ea quae quaeruntur sunt universalia, sicut et ea quae sciuntur."

12 Ibid., I lectio 44: "ponit duo ad eam pertinere: quorum unum est quod sit universalis. Non enim scientia est de singularibus sub sensu cadentibus"; "praeter vera necessaria, quae non contingunt aliter se habere, sunt quaedam vera non necessaria, quae contingit aliter se habere. Manifestum est autem ex praedictis, quod circa huiusmodi non est scientia."

13 In fact, there are some passages in which Aquinas uses '*cognitio*' in a way that

If he has a word which expresses what the English term 'knowledge' does, it is probably *'notitia,'* although that Latin term doesn't seem to have the range the English term does; where we would expect to use the verb 'know,' Aquinas uses not the verb cognate with *'notitia'* but rather *'cognosco,'* 'cognize.'

Aquinas explains *'scire,'* the verb cognate with *'scientia,'* in this way:

> To have *scientia* ("*scire*") of something is to cognize it perfectly ("*perfecte*");[14]

> *Scientia* is cognition acquired through demonstration. (Ibid., II lectio 1)

And he defines *'scire'* as Aristotle does:

> To have *scientia* [of a thing] is to cognize the cause of the thing;[15]

> a cause is the intermediate in a demonstration which brings it about that we have *scientia* (*facit scire*).[16]

In fact, Aquinas explains *scientia* in a way which suggests that he has in mind a Porphyrian tree of cognition, with *scientia* occupying one of the branches of the tree, along with other species of cognition. *Scientia*, he says, is one of several dispositions (*habitus*) which are related to what is true. There are five such dispositions, and they all are types of cognition. Following Aristotle, he lists the five as art, wisdom, prudence, understanding, and *scientia* (Ibid., I lectio 44).

Both *scientia* and wisdom are virtues of the speculative intellect, he says in another place. As for understanding, a person is said to have understanding or *scientia* insofar as his intellect is perfect in cognizing

---

wouldn't allow *'cognitio'* to be translated 'knowledge': as, for example, when he occasionally talks of a false cognition.

14 Thomas Aquinas [17], *Super Post. An.* I lectio 4: "scire aliquid est perfecte cognoscere ipsum."

15 Ibid., I lectio 13: "scire est causam rei cognoscere"; see also lectio 4 and lectio 42.

16 Ibid., II lectio 1: "causa est medium in demonstratione, quae facit scire."

truth.[17] Prudence and art have to do with the practical part of the soul, which reasons about things that can be done by us; prudence is right reason about things to be done, and art is right reason about things to be made. But wisdom, understanding, and *scientia* have to do with the speculative part of the soul. Understanding is a disposition regarding first principles of demonstration. Wisdom considers first causes (that is, higher or divine causes), and *scientia* has to do with conclusions based on lower causes.[18]

So for all these reasons it seems clearly a mistake to render '*scientia*' as 'knowledge' and therefore even more of a mistake to interpret Aquinas's theory of *scientia* as a theory of knowledge. What he has to say about *scientia* cannot consequently be taken to express his views about the nature or structure of knowledge. (What his account of *scientia* comes to and how it should be interpreted will be discussed below.)

But what about the appearance of Foundationalism presented just above? What about Aquinas's apparent adherence to the view that there are properly basic beliefs, which ground all other propositions believed and which are known with certainty?

Properly basic beliefs for Aquinas are supposed to consist in propositions evident to the senses and self-evident propositions or propositions known with certainty to be true as soon as their terms are understood. Let's consider these two groups in turn.

It is true that Aquinas thinks the senses cannot be deceived as regards their proper objects;[19] but the proper objects of the senses are something below the propositional level. Any belief about the world of physical objects based on the senses, such as the belief that there is

---

17 Thomas Aquinas [9], q. un., a. 7

18 Thomas Aquinas [15], L I, l 1, 34; cf. also Thomas Aquinas [14], L VI l 1-6.

19 Thomas Aquinas [3], ST Ia q.17 a.3: "circa propria sensibilia sensus non habet falsam cognitionem nisi per accidens et ut in paucioribus, ex eo scilicet quod propter indispositionem organi non convenienter recipit formam sensibilem"; "falsitas dicitur non esse propria sensui, quia non decipitur circa proprium objectum."

a coffee cup in front of me or that there is a tree outside the window, is a belief with regard to which we may be mistaken, on Aquinas's view. Aquinas quotes with approval Augustine's dictum that we can make mistakes with respect to any of our senses, and he gives an affirmative answer to the question whether there is falsity in the senses.

> We are not deceived in the judgment by which we judge that we sense something. But from the fact that a sense is sometimes affected otherwise than as things are, it follows that that sense sometimes reports things to us otherwise than they are. And therefore by means of sense we make a mistake with regard to things, though not with regard to sensing itself.[20]

These claims on Aquinas's part, of course, don't show that it's wrong to attribute to him the view that propositions evident to the senses are properly basic beliefs. He surely does think that propositions evident to the senses are accepted without being based on other beliefs, and he also clearly thinks that, most of the time at any rate, we are rational in accepting such beliefs as basic. What Aquinas's claims about the fallibility of the senses do show, however, is that propositions evident to the senses may be false and that therefore they don't constitute a class of propositions known with certainty. Consequently, the noetic structure in which the non-basic beliefs of a person are based on propositions evident to his senses may or may not constitute a set of beliefs known with certainty. On Aquinas's view, if the foundation includes propositions evident to the senses, there is no guarantee that the resulting structure comprises knowledge; it might consist in error instead.

Should we then understand Aquinas as a Foundationalist who restricts the foundations of knowledge to self-evident propositions? The evidence here too is against Foundationalist interpretations of Aquinas.

---

20 Ibid., q.17 a.3 ad 1: "non decipiamur in judicio quo judicamus nos sentire aliquid. Sed ex eo quod sensus aliter afficitur interdum quam res sit, sequitur quod nuntiet nobis rem aliter quam sit aliquando. Et ex hoc fallimur per sensum circa rem, non circa ipsum sentire."

The candidates for self-evident propositions in Aquinas are the first principles of a *scientia*. Now these come in two sorts, what Aquinas (following Aristotle) calls the common principles, such as the law of noncontradiction, and what he labels the proper principles, such as that every man is an animal.[21]

Common principles, unlike proper principles, are common to every *scientia*. They are not only true, indemonstrable, and known per se, but, in fact, Aquinas says, a common principle can't be confirmed by an argument. It is known by the light of natural reason, and no one can form an opinion which is the contrary of a common principle.

Common principles, then, clearly look like candidates for the properly basic foundation of certain knowledge. There are problems here, too, however. It's obvious that common principles are basic; not only are they not derived from other propositions, but they can't be. Furthermore, there is no possibility here of falsity, as there was in the case of propositions evident to the senses; common principles are not only true but known by the light of natural reason itself. So common principles seem manifestly properly basic. The problems arise from our cognition of common principles. To say that they are known per se is not the same as saying that they are known per se *by us*.[22] We can think something isn't a common principle when in fact it is. We can also deny common principles, out of obstinacy, for example (Ibid., I lectio 27). We cannot *really* deny common principles, in the sense that we believe the opposite of a common principle to be true; but we can deny common principles orally (*'ore'*) (Ibid., I lectio 19) and verbally (*'secundum vocem'*), in accordance with a false opinion or imagination (Ibid., I lectio 27).

---

21 For the distinction between common principles and proper principles, see, e.g., Thomas Aquinas [17], *Super Post. An.* I lectio 17, lectio 18, lectio 43.

22 For this distinction, see, e.g., *Super Post. An.* I lectio 4, lectio 5.

> Nothing is so true that it cannot be denied verbally. For some people have denied orally even this most known principle, "The same thing cannot both be and not be."[23]

A common principle is known per se in the sense that if a person really understands the terms of the principle, he will see that it must be true; but he might not understand the terms of the principle even though he can use those terms adequately in ordinary discourse. The proposition that God exists is known per se, on Aquinas's view. If a person understands the term 'God,' he will also understand that God is simple and that therefore God's essence includes his existence; but, of course, it is possible for a person to be able to use the term 'God' adequately in ordinary discourse and not understand the term in such a way as to see that the proposition 'God exists' is necessarily true.[24]

In the case in which a person denies a common principle, Aquinas will want to say both that the denier doesn't *really* understand the principle and that in any case what the denier takes to be the case does not constitute the opposite of the principle he is denying. But the interesting point for our purposes is that even though common principles are known by the light of natural reason, it is perfectly possible that what is in fact a common principle be rejected by someone as false (or at any rate possible that he should reject the common principle as he understands it), and therefore it is also possible for a person to take what is in fact false as true and use it as a common principle. Consequently, there is no guarantee that when a person begins with propositions which function as common princi-

---

23 Ibid., I lectio 19: "nihil est adeo verum, quin voce possit negari. Nam et hoc principium notissimum, quod non contingat idem esse et non esse, quidam ore negaverunt."

24 Thomas Aquinas [4], SCG I c.11: "simpliciter quidem Deum esse per se notum est: cum hoc ipsum quod Deus est, sit suum esse. Sed quia hoc ipsum quod Deus est mente concipere non possumus, remanet ignotum quoad nos. Sicut omne totum sua parte maius esse, per se notum est simpliciter: ei autem qui rationem totius mente non conciperet, oporteret esse ignotum. Et sic fit ut ad ea quae sunt notissima rerum, noster intellectus se habeat ut oculus noctuae ad solem...."

ples for him, the resulting noetic structure will comprise knowledge; just as in the case of propositions evident to the senses, the result might be error instead. Of course, in this case whatever is based on propositions that really are common principles will unquestionably be *true*; the problem is that a cognizer might be deceived and in the place of genuine common principles might instead have false propositions. If he is deceived, he isn't really understanding the common principles at issue; but the salient point is that for all he knows he might be in the state of not really understanding the relevant common principles. Therefore, if he begins with propositions which function for him as common principles, the cognizer has no guarantee that what he builds on that foundation will even be true, let alone constitute something known with certainty.

What about proper principles, then? It seems even less likely that proper principles can serve as the foundations of knowledge.

No *scientia* can reach its conclusions on the basis of common principles alone; proper principles are always required also.[25]

There are very many proper principles; in fact, Aquinas says, following Aristotle, the number of principles isn't much less than the number of conclusions (Ibid.: "principia non sunt multum pauciora conclusionibus"). These principles are universals and describe a cause (or sometimes an effect) of something[26] (that is, a material, formal, efficient, or final cause or effect).[27] And these principles are always established by means of induction.

---

25 Thomas Aquinas [17], *Super Post. An.* I lectio 43: "non possunt esse aliqua principia communia, ex quibus solum omnia syllogizentur ... quia genera entium sunt diversa, et diversa sunt principia quae sunt solum quantitatum principia, ab his quae solum sunt principia qualitatum: quae oportet coassumere principiis communibus ad concludendum in qualibet materia."

26 Cf., e.g., Ibid., I lectio 4: "demonstrationis propositiones sint causae conclusionis. quia tunc scimus, cum causas cognoscimus." "Ex singularibus autem quae sunt in sensu, non sunt demonstrationes, sed ex universalibus tantum, quae sunt in intellectu."

27 Cf., e.g., Ibid., I lectio 10; II lectio 9.

Demonstration proceeds from universals, but induction proceeds from particulars. Therefore, if universals, from which demonstration proceeds, could be cognized apart from induction, it would follow that a person could acquire *scientia* of things of which he didn't have any sense perception. But it is impossible that universals be comprehended without induction.[28]

Universals, from which demonstration proceeds, don't become known (*nota*) to us except by induction.[29]

It is necessary to cognize the first, universal principles by means of induction.[30]

For this reason, Aquinas says that there is a sense in which there are two roads to *scientia*; one is demonstration and the other is induction.[31] Proper first principles, then, which are necessary to any *scientia*, aren't basic at all, let alone properly basic. And what they are based on is induction. But, of course, induction is a notoriously uncertain mode of inference, as Aquinas himself recognizes: "a person who makes an induction by means of singulars to a universal doesn't demonstrate or syllogize with necessity."[32] And he draws an analogy between induction and the method of analysis he calls 'division': "the method of division is analogous to the method of induction.... When something is proved syllogistically ... it is necessary that

---

28 Ibid., I lectio 30: "demonstratio procedit ex universalibus; inductio autem procedit ex particularibus. Si ergo universalia, ex quibus procedit demonstratio, cognosci possent absque inductione, sequeretur quod homo posset accipere scientiam eorum, quorum non habet sensum. Sed impossibile est universalia speculari absque inductione." Cf. also, e.g., Thomas Aquinas [15], L I, l 1.

29 Thomas Aquinas [17], *Super Post. An.* I lectio 30: "universalia, ex quibus demonstratio procedit, non fiunt nobis nota, nisi per inductionem."

30 Ibid., II lectio 20: "necesse est prima universalia cognoscere per inductionem."

31 Ibid., I lectio 30: "duplex est modus acquirendi scientiam. Unus quidem per demonstrationem, alius autem per inductionem."

32 Ibid., II lectio 4: "Ille enim qui inducit per singularia ad universale, non demonstrat neque syllogizat ex necessitate."

the conclusion be true if the premisses are true. But this is not the case in the method of division....''[34]

So not only is there no guarantee that what a cognizer uses as a proper first principle of *scientia* will be something known with certainty, there isn't even a guarantee that what the cognizer starts with as a first principle will be *true*, since it is the result of induction. Of course, since first principles are *defined* as true, if a cognizer begins with first principles, he will begin with something true. But since what we use as a first principle has to be the result of induction, what we use as first principles might very well not be genuine first principles at all, and there is no simple formal procedure for telling the genuine from the counterfeit. Even when a cognizer does begin with a genuine first principle, however, he will not be starting with a properly basic proposition, since the genuine first principle he begins with will be derived by induction.

Finally, a word should be said about Aquinas's term 'certitudo,' generally translated as 'certainty.' Very little of Aquinas's commentary on the *Posterior Analytics* is devoted to an explanation of *certitudo*, but in the small space he gives to an exposition of the notion, he says these sorts of things about it:

> *Scientia* is also certain cognition of a thing, but a person cannot cognize with *certitudo* anything which can be otherwise. And so it must also be the case that what we have *scientia* of cannot be otherwise than it is.[35]

Furthermore, he compares one *scientia* to another in order to determine which has more *certitudo* (or is *certior*) than the other. Geometry, for example, has less *certitudo* than arithmetic. Finally, a cause is *certior* than its effect; a form is *certior* than matter (Ibid., I lectio 41).

---

34 Ibid., "ita se habet in via divisionis, sicut et in via inductionis.... C\um enim aliquid syllogistice probatur ... necesse est quod conclusio sit vera, praemissis existentibus veris. Hoc autem non accidit in via divisionis...."

35 Ibid., I lectio 4: "scientia est etiam certa cognitio rei; quod autem contingit aliter se habere, non potest aliquis per certitudinèm cognoscere; ideo ulterius oportet quod id quod scitur non possit aliter se habere."

What exactly he has in mind with *'certitudo'* or *'certior'* isn't clear. But clearly it would be a mistake to translate *'certitudo'* in such contexts as 'certainty.' Certainty, as we understand it, seems to be a relation between a knower and what is known, but it's difficult to see why anyone would suppose that such a relation couldn't obtain between a knower and a contingent state of affairs. And in the comparison of one *scientia* to another or of a form to matter, questions of the relation between knower and what is known don't seem to come into the discussion at all. For these reasons, we should be cautious about how we render Aquinas's term *'certitudo'*; it is undoubtedly misleading simply to take it as equivalent to our term 'certainty.' In fact, although demonstration produces "the *certitudo* of *scientia*,"[36] Aquinas is perfectly willing to talk about the possibility of error arising in demonstration. For example, following Aristotle, he says "in order not to fall into mistakes in demonstration, one must be aware of the fact that often a universal seems to be demonstrated but in fact is not."[37]

So, to summarize, then, on the view which takes Aquinas to be a Foundationalist, what constitutes the foundation for knowledge for him are propositions evident to the senses and the first principles of *scientia*; these will be the properly basic propositions which are known with certainty and from which all other non-basic propositions known with certainty are derived. But, in fact, the evidence that Aquinas is a Foundationalist depends on interpreting *'scientia'* as equivalent to 'knowledge,' and we have seen good reasons for supposing that such an interpretation is decidedly mistaken. Furthermore, on Aquinas's view, in one way or another, a person can be deceived as regards all the propositions which are supposed to

---

36 Ibid., proemium: "Est enim aliquis rationis processus necessitatem inducens, in quo non est possibile veritatis defectum; et per huiusmodi rationis processum scientiae certitudo acquiritur."

37 Ibid., I lectio 12: "quod non accidat in demonstratione peccatum, oportet non latere quod multoties videtur demonstrari universale, non autem demonstratur."

ground knowledge for him, so that the propositions which are supposed to be known with certainty according to Foundationalism aren't even guaranteed to be true on Aquinas's account and therefore obviously can't provide a guarantee of the certain truth of other, non-basic propositions derived from them. Finally, among the first principles of any *scientia*, on Aquinas's account, are proper principles, and these are propositions which aren't even basic, let alone properly basic, since they are derived from induction.

These considerations by themselves seem to me enough to undermine the claim that Aquinas must be taken to be a Foundationalist. In what follows I want to consider what theory of knowledge Aquinas does hold. The evidence adduced there seems to me to constitute further reason, if any is needed, for rejecting the view of Aquinas as a Foundationalist.

IV Reliabilism in Aquinas's Theory of Knowledge

If Aquinas isn't a Foundationalist, what view of knowledge does he take? Like Aristotle, Aquinas is a metaphysical realist. That is, he assumes that there is an external world around us and that it has certain features independently of the operation of any created intellect, so that it is up to our minds to discover truths about the world, rather than simply inventing or creating them. On Aquinas's account, the human intellect was created by God for the purpose of discovering such truths about the world.

> All natural things are the product of divine art.... And so God gives to everything the best disposition, not best *simpliciter* but best as ordered to its proper end.... The proximate end of the human body is the rational soul and its activities.... Therefore, I say that God constituted (*instituit*) the human body in the best disposition appropriate to such a form [i.e., the soul] and its activities;[38]

---

38 Thomas Aquinas [3], ST Ia q.91 a.3: "omnes res naturales productae sunt ab arte divina.... Sic igitur Deus unicuique rei naturali dedit optimam dispositionem, non quidem simpliciter, sed secundum ordinem ad proprium finem.... Finis autem proximus humani corporis est anima rationalis et operationes ipsius....

A soul is united to a body in order to understand, which is [its] proper and principal activity. And consequently it is necessary that the body united to a rational soul be best suited to serve the soul in those things which are needed for understanding;[39]

A person is said to have understanding or *scientia* insofar as his intellect is perfected to cognize what is true, which is the good of the intellect.[40]

Not only did God make human beings in such a way as to be optimally suited for the rational soul's cognition of what is true, but the fact that human beings are made in the image of God consists just in their being cognizers of this sort.

Only creatures that have intellects are strictly speaking in the image of God.[41]

Since human beings are said to be in the image of God in virtue of their having a nature that includes an intellect, such a nature is most in the image of God in virtue of being most able to imitate God.[42]

Being in the image of God pertains to the mind alone.... Only in rational creatures is there found a likeness of God which counts as an image ... as far as a likeness of the divine nature is concerned, rational creatures seem somehow to attain a

---

Dico ergo quod Deus instituit corpus humanum in optima dispositione secundum convenientiam ad talem formam et ad tales operationes." Cf. also ST Ia q.76 a.5.

39 Thomas Aquinas [5], q.8, ad 15: "anima unitur corpori propter intelligere, quae est propria et principalis operatio. Et ideo requiritur quod corpus unitum animae rationali sit optime dispositum ad serviendum animae in his quae sunt necessaria ad intelligendum."

40 Thomas Aquinas [9], q.un., a.7: "Dicitur enim aliquis intelligens vel sciens secundum quod eius intellectus perfectus est ad cognoscendum verum; quod quidem est bonum intellectus."

41 Thomas Aquinas [3], ST Ia q.93 a.2: "solae intellectuales creaturae, proprie loquendo, sunt ad imaginem Dei."

42 Ibid., q.93 a.4: "cum homo secundum intellectualem naturam ad imaginem Dei esse dicatur, secundum hoc est maxime ad imaginem Dei, secundum quod intellectualis natura Deum maxime imitari potest."

representation of [that] type in virtue of imitating God not only in this, that he is and lives, but especially in this, that he understands.[43]

So God has made human beings in his own image, and they are made in his image in virtue of the fact that, like him, they are cognizers; they can understand and know themselves, the world, and the world's creator. And human beings can accomplish this feat because God has constructed them to be cognizers and attainers of truth. How God has done so is a story Aquinas tells more of elsewhere than in his commentary on *Posterior Analytics*; I will content myself with just a word or two about it here.

Human cognizing, on Aquinas's view, is a process which depends primarily on two cognitive capacities (or sets of capacities): sense and intellect. Aquinas's account of sense is based on this view:

With regard to its proper object sense is not deceived ... (unless perhaps by accident as a result of some impediment which happens as regards the [physical] organ);[44]

With regard to its proper sensibles, sense does not have false cognition, except by accident, and in only relatively few cases, because it doesn't receive the sensible form properly on account of some indisposition of the [physical] organ....[45]

And this astonishing optimism as regards sense perception is echoed by his view of the intellect:

---

43 Ibid., q.93 a.6: "Esse ergo ad imaginem Dei pertinet solum ad mentem ... in sola creatura rationali invenitur similitudo Dei per modum imaginis.... Nam quantum ad similitudinem divinae naturae pertinet, creaturae rationales videntur quodammodo ad repraesentationem speciei pertingere, inquantum imitantur Deum non solum in hoc quod est et vivit, sed etiam in hoc quod intelligit...."

44 Ibid., q.85 a.6: "Sensus enim circa proprium objectum non decipitur... nisi forte per accidens, ex impedimento circa organum contingente."

45 Ibid., q.17 a.2: "circa propria sensibilia sensus non habet falsam cognitionem, nisi per accidens, et ut in paucioribus: ex eo scilict quod, propter indispositionem organi, non convenienter recipit formam sensibilem."

The proper object of the intellect is the quiddity of a thing. And so as regards the quiddity of a thing, considered just as such, the intellect is not mistaken;[46]

in a simple consideration of the quiddity of a thing and of things cognized by means of it, the intellect is never deceived.[47]

As sense gets its form directly by a likeness of [its] proper sensibles, so intellect gets its form by a likeness of the quiddity of a thing. And so regarding the quiddity [of a thing] (*quod quid est*), intellect is not deceived, just as sense is not deceived regarding [its] proper sensibles.[48]

For my purposes here what is important about these implausible sounding claims is just the attitude Aquinas takes towards our cognitive capacities. On Aquinas's view, our cognitive capacities are designed by God for the express purpose of enabling us to be cognizers of the truth, as God himself is. In particular, when we use sense and intellect as God designed them to be used in the environment suited to them, that is, in the world for which God designed human beings, then those faculties are absolutely reliable. In fact, not only are they reliable but as regards their proper objects it is even the case that neither sense nor intellect can be deceived or mistaken. The nature of Aquinas's account of our cognitive capacities can be shown most graphically by considering what he has to say about Adam.

It could not be the case that, while innocence remained, a human intellect accepted anything false as true.... The rectitude of the original condition is not compatible with any deception on the part of the intellect.[49]

---

46 Ibid., q.85 a.6: "Obiectum autem proprium intellectus est quidditas rei. Unde circa quidditatem rei, per se loquendo, intellectus non fallitur."

47 Ibid., q.85 a.6 ad 1: "in absoluta consideratione quidditatis rei, et eorum quae per eam cognoscuntur, intellectus nunquam decipitur."

48 Ibid., q.17 a.3: "Sicut autem sensus informatur directe similitudine propriorum sensibilium, ita intellectus informatur similitudine quidditatis rei. Unde circa quod quid est intellectus non decipitur: sicut neque sensus circa sensibilia propria."

49 Ibid., q.94 a.4: "non poterat esse quod, innocentia manente, intellectus hominis

Every error is either guilt or punishment, and neither of these could be in the state of innocence; therefore, neither could error.[50]

As the true is the good of the intellect, so the false is its evil.... If an opinion is false, it is a certain evil act on the part of the intellect. And so since in the state of innocence there was no corruption or evil, there could not be in the state of nature any false opinion.... And in this way in the intellect [of human beings in the state of nature] there could be no falsity.[51]

In a way, then, what has to be explained on Aquinas's views is not so much what accounts for our ability to know as what accounts for the fact that we are sometimes in error. And, in fact, it turns out that for Aquinas, because God has designed our cognitive capacities in such a way as to make us cognizers of the truth, it is only in our post-fall condition that error, deception, mistake, or even false opinion is a possibility at all. Error has to be explained as either guilt or punishment, on Aquinas's account. For my purposes here, we can consider this account of Aquinas's just as a source of information about his theory of knowledge. And in light of these views of his, it seems reasonable to take his theory of knowledge as a species of externalism, with reliabilist elements. On Aquinas's account, the reliable method or process whose functioning constitutes our knowing is just the natural operation of our cognitive capacities. For Aquinas, then, human knowledge is a function of our using the cognitive capacities God created in us as God designed them to be used in the world God created them to be used in. It is, on reflection, not at all surprising to find a theory of knowledge of this sort in a

---

alicui falso acquiesceret quasi vero ... rectitudo primi status non compatiebatur aliquam deceptionem circa intellectum."

50 Thomas Aquinas [8], q.18 a.6 s.c.: "omnis error vel est culpa, vel poena: quorum neutrum in statu innocentiae esse poterat. Ergo nec error."

51 Ibid., q.18 a.6: "sicut verum est bonum intellectus, ita falsum malum ipsius ... si ipsa opinio falsa, sit quidam malus actus intellectus. Unde cum in statu innocentiae non fuerit aliqua corruptio vel aliquod malum, non potuit esse in statu innocentiae aliqua falsa opinio ... ita in intellectu eius nulla falsitas esse potuisset."

theist, which may help to explain why Aquinas's approach to knowledge bears a strong resemblance to the theory of knowledge Plantinga develops after rejecting the views he mistakenly attributes to
Aquinas.

V Aquinas's Approach to Epistemology

It might occur to someone to object that if my interpretation of
Aquinas's approach to epistemology is correct, we should expect to
find some explicit statement of it somewhere in his works. In fact,
what we have is a discussion of the way in which the mind acquires
true beliefs — for example, in the commentary on *De Anima* — and
exposition of *scientia*, which turns out to be only a species of cognition
— for example, in the commentary on the *Posterior Analytics*. If Aquinas is an externalist, why isn't there in his works some straightforward presentation and analysis of externalism as a theory of
knowledge?

To see the answer to this question, it helps to consider theories of
knowledge in terms of an analogy. Suppose we were reflecting not
on our cognitive capacities and theories of knowledge, but rather on
race cars and theories of excellence in race car driving. Any good,
complete manual presenting a theory of excellence in race car driving
ought to include at least three parts. There might or might not be (I)
an introduction in which the manual explains what no one really
needs to be told, that excellence in race car driving is a matter of
winning as many races as possible. But there needs to be (1) a section
on race tracks, saying something about the environment in which the
race car is designed to be driven. Then there should be (2) a section
on race cars themselves, and it should be divided into two parts. (2a)
Information about the general mechanics of race cars would comprise
one part; it would explain in general how such cars are built and how
they are designed to work. (2b) The other part would consist in
evaluation of different sorts of companies or mechanics which build
such cars and would explain the extent to which various firms or
individuals could be trusted to turn out excellent machinery. Finally,
there ought to be (3) a section on race car drivers and what they need

to do to drive well. This section will also be divided into two. (3a) One part will present general advice on how to avoid crashes; (3b) the other will give information on what drivers can do to make the car go as fast and as far as possible.

These parts of a theory of excellence in race car driving correspond to elements in a complete theory of knowledge. Which of the three parts of such a theory one emphasizes is a function of one's whole worldview and values.

Given Aquinas's robust faith in a provident creator of the world who has made human beings in his image and, like himself, cognizers of the truth, it is not surprising that some elements of the theory don't get much explicit development or analysis. He takes for granted that (1') the goal aimed at in the use of human intellect is the acquisition of truth about the world and its creator and the avoidance of falsehood. And as for (1') the track on which human cognitive equipment operates, Aquinas, like Aristotle, is clearly a realist; he thinks that there are truths about the world which the human mind must discover, rather than invent. This view flows from his theological commitments and therefore doesn't need or get lengthy argumentation. For these same reasons, it would be a mistake to look for explicit consideration of knowledge as a function of the reliable operation of human cognitive capacities. Given Aquinas's beliefs about God, it isn't likely that (2b') the part of epistemological theory corresponding to the section on car makers in the theory of race car driving will be well developed. The maker of human cognitive equipment is God, and his purpose in making that equipment is to enable human intellects to imitate him in his activity as a knower. This view, which Aquinas takes to be revealed by Scripture, is so fundamental to his beliefs that it gets little explicit attention. (That worries about the nature and possibility of knowledge raised, for example, by skepticism should loom much larger in a theory of knowledge which isn't embedded in a theistic worldview or which is an accompaniment to an atheistic outlook is certainly understandable. It is plausible to suppose, however, that a theory of knowledge at least similar to Aquinas's can form part of a non-theistic worldview. For God as the guarantor of the reliability of human cognitive equipment, it is possible to substitute evolution and to suppose that the theory of evolution provides roughly the same support for such a theory of knowledge that Aquinas's theism does.)

What is of far more interest to Aquinas than these issues are those parts of a complete theory of knowledge corresponding to the remaining parts of a thorough theory of race car driving — (2a'), (3a'), and (3b'). The epistemological equivalent of an account of the mechanics of race cars is comprised in Aquinas's commentary on *De anima* and his other discussions of the way in which the human mind works. (There is, of course, no reason why this part of Aquinas's philosophy can't also be understood as part of his philosophy of mind. But insofar as his theory of knowledge takes knowledge to be a function of human cognitive capacities' operating as they were designed to operate, the story of how the mind operates will also be part of a complete theory of knowledge.) This part of the story is the subject for another paper, and so I leave it aside here.

What is left is the equivalent of that part of a treatise on race car driving that we might think of as the driver's manual: (3a) how to avoid crashes and (3b) how to get the most out of the car — how (3a') to avoid falsehood and (3b') acquire truth, perhaps even truths of a deep, significant, or far-ranging character. Here, too, which of these two parts of the enterprise of knowledge one emphasizes is a function of one's values and worldview. Aquinas does discuss, for example, the nature and detection of fallacies in reasoning or the way in which the mind can be deceived. But a driver who thought her car was built by God and she herself was under the direct providential care of God, who supposed that God himself wanted her to win races, might be less worried about the possibility of crashing and more concerned with doing her part to make the car go as far and as fast as possible. Similarly, Aquinas, who thinks in general that everything happens under God's providential control, supposes in particular both that God is the maker of human cognitive equipment and that God designed that equipment for the purpose of acquiring truth. Consequently, it isn't surprising to find him paying less attention to how we know we're not mistaken or deceived or how we keep from being in those undesirable states and more attention to how we use our cognitive capacities in gaining truth. Of course, this story will be considerably complicated if we add to it Aquinas's views concerning the effects of sin on the will and his account of the relations between intellect and will, but these additional considerations will only complicate and not undermine the epistemological story I have argued for here. At any rate, the method for acquiring significant and far-ranging truth is, in my view, the object of Aquinas's work on *scientia*, especially in his commentary on the *Posterior Analytics*, as I hope to show in what follows.

VI Aquinas's Commentary on the *Posterior Analytics*

As we have seen, *scientia*, on Aquinas's view, is the cognition of the causes of things, where the causes in question aren't divine causes but belong to a lower order. "A cause," he says, "is what is sought in all ... inquiries [in which demonstration plays a part]."[52]

In retrospect, it seems clear that this description by itself should have given us pause about adopting the view of Aquinas as a Foundationalist whose theory of *scientia* is a theory of knowledge. A Foundationalist theory of knowledge is a theory which explains what counts as knowledge and what does not and which accounts for the trustworthiness of what counts as knowledge. But the theory of *scientia* is a different enterprise; *scientia* is a matter of cognizing causes of things, of finding causal explanations for currently accepted claims.

So, for example, Aquinas says that

> There are certain things which we would not ask about with [any] doubt if we were to see them, not because *scientia* consists in seeing but because the universal, with which *scientia* is concerned, would be obtained by means of experience, on the basis of the things seen. For instance, if we were to see glass as porous and see how the light is transmitted through the openings of the glass, we would have *scientia* (*sciremus*) of why the glass is transparent.[53]

---

52 Thomas Aquinas [17], *Super Post. An.* II lectio 1: "Causa autem est quod quaeritur in omnibus praedictis quaestionibus."

53 Ibid., I lectio 42: "Quaedam enim sunt de quibus non quaereremus dubitando, si ea vidissemus; non quidem eo quod scientia consistat in videndo, sed in

Similarly, he says,

> Suppose ... that someone were on the moon itself and by sense perceived the interposition of the earth by its shadow. He would perceive by sense that the moon was then eclipsed by the shadow of the earth, but he would not for that reason have full *scientia* of the cause of the eclipse. For what causes an eclipse in general (*universaliter*) is the proper (*per se*) cause of the eclipse.[54]

> *Scientia* is superior to sense. For it is clear that cognition which is through a cause is nobler, but a proper (*per se*) cause is a universal cause ... and therefore cognition through a universal cause, which is the character of *scientia*, is more honorable. And because it is impossible to apprehend a universal cause by means of sense, it follows that *scientia*, which shows the universal cause, is not only more honorable than all sensory cognition but also than all other intellective cognition, when it is of things which have a cause.[55]

Descriptions of these causes serve as the *premisses*, rather than the conclusions, of demonstrative arguments.

> The middle of a demonstration is a cause;

> quantum ex rebus visis per viam experimenti accipitur universale, de quo est scientia. Puta si videremus vitrum perforatum, et quomodo lumen pertransit per foramina vitri, sciremus propter quid vitrum est transparens."

54 Ibid., I lectio 42: "Ponamus ergo quod aliquis esset in ipsa luna, et sensu perciperet interpositionem terrae per umbram ipsius: sensu quidem perciperet quod luna tunc deficeret ex umbra terrae, sed non propter hoc sciret totaliter causam eclipsis. Illud enim est per se causa eclipsis, quod causat universaliter eclipsim."

55 Ibid., I lectio 42: "scientia est potior quam sensus. Manifestum est enim quod cognitio quae est per causam, nobilior est: causa autem per se est universalis causa, ut iam dictum est; et ideo cognitio per universalem causam, qualis est scientia, est honorabilis. Et quia huiusmodi universalem causam impossibile est apprehendere per sensum, ideo consequens est quod scientia, quae ostendit causam universalem, non solum sit honorabilior omni sensitiva cognitione, sed etiam omni alia intellectiva cognitione, dummodo sit de rebus quae habent causam." See also Thomas Aquinas [15], L 1 lectio 1.

> by the middle of a demonstration all the [four] causes are manifested, because any of these [four] causes can be taken as the middle of a demonstration.[56]

So, on Aquinas's views, demonstration isn't a matter of starting with epistemically certain propositions and deducing conclusions which are consequently equally certain, in order to have knowledge of a particularly rigorous sort. Rather, on his account, in order to find a demonstration we need to look for causes of what is described in the claim that is to be the conclusion of the demonstration. Once we have the demonstration, we have *scientia* of the subject matter presented in that claim in virtue of having a causal explanation of the state of affairs described in the demonstration's conclusion. And what demonstration confers is not so much epistemic certainty as it is depth of understanding. Because Aquinas is often misunderstood on this score, Paul Durbin, in commenting on Aquinas's understanding of demonstration, says

> After Descartes it has become necessary to distinguish Aristotelean "syllogismus" and "demonstratio" from a Cartesian, rationalist "deduction." Aristotle and St Thomas do not begin with self-evident principles and derive conclusions therefrom in a rationalist-deductive mode (even though *Posterior Analytics* is often interpreted this way); rather, they begin with a statement to be justified (it will become the "conclusion" only in a formal restatement of the argument) and "reduce" it back to its ultimate explanatory principles.[57]

When Aquinas himself describes what he is doing in his commentary on the *Posterior Analytics*, he describes his project in this way. There are two different processes human reason engages in; one is discovery or invention, and the other is judgment.

> Following the path of inquiry or discovery, human reasoning proceeds from certain things understood simply, and these are first principles.

---

56 Thomas Aquinas [17], *Super Post. An.* II lectio 9: "medium demonstrationis sit causa'; 'per medium demonstrationis omnes hae causae manifestantur; quia quaelibet harum causarum potest accipi ut medium demonstrationis."

57 Paul T.Durbin, *Blackfriars ST*, vol. 12 (New York: McGraw-Hill 1968), 82, n. a

> And, again, following the path of judgment, human reasoning returns by analysis to first principles, which it ponders once it has discovered them.[58]

So, according to Aquinas, when we are engaged in what he calls 'discovery,' we proceed from first principles, reasoning *from* them to other things; when we are concerned with what he calls 'judgment,' we reason *to* first principles by means of analysis. On the common account of Aquinas as a Foundationalist, his commentary on the *Posterior Analytics* and his other discussions of epistemology would count as descriptions of discovery, since in those discussions Aquinas is supposed to be explaining how we proceed from first principles to other things known with certainty. But in his introduction to his commentary on the *Posterior Analytics*, Aquinas takes the opposite view. He thinks there are three different reasoning processes examined in Aristotle's logical works. The first process yields *scientia*.

> The part of logic which is principally devoted to the first process is called the judicative part, because judgment goes with the certitude of *scientia* And because we cannot have certain judgment about effects except by analysis into first principles, this part is called "Analytics"....[59]

Sometimes this judgment is based on the matter rather than the form of a syllogism, and "the *Posterior Analytics*, which has to do with the demonstrative syllogism, is devoted to this."[60]

---

58 Thomas Aquinas [3], ST Ia q.79 a.8: "ratiocinatio humana, secundum viam inquisitionis vel inventionis, procedit a quibusdam simpliciter intellectis, quae sunt prima principia; et rursus, in via iudicii, resolvendo redit ad prima principia, ad quae inventa examinat."

59 Thomas Aquinas [17], *Super Post. An. proemium*: "Pars autem Logicae, quae primo deservit processui, pars Iudicativa dicitur, eo quod iudicium est cum certitudine scientiae. Et quia iudicium certum de effectibus haberi non potest nisi resolvendo in prima principia, ideo pars haec Analytica vocatur, idest resolutoria."

60 Ibid., proemium: "ad hoc ordinatur liber Posteriorum analyticorum, qui est de syllogismo demonstrativo."

But there is also a second reasoning process, another part of of logic, which doesn't yield *scientia*, and "this is called 'discovery'.... The *Topics* or dialectic is devoted to this." And so, as it turns out, is the *Rhetoric*.[61]

So on Aquinas's account discovery is a part of dialectic or rhetoric, rather than of demonstration, and what is covered in his commentary on the *Posterior Analytics* is judgment. But, according to Aquinas, judgment is a matter of returning to first principles, rather than beginning from them and deducing other propositions from them. The subject matter Aquinas takes to be covered both in Aristotle's *Posterior Analytics* and in his own commentary on it, then, has as its main emphasis finding causal explanations for the states of affairs described in claims which become the conclusions of demonstrative syllogisms, and tracing those causal explanations back to first principles. And the point of this process is to yield a deeper understanding of the nature of the state of affairs being described. So a demonstrative syllogism produces *scientia* in virtue of the fact that it shows the causes and so provides an explanation of the syllogism's conclusion. This account of Aquinas's views helps to clarify some of his examples, presented above. For example, on this interpretation, it is easier to understand his example involving the lunar eclipse. Both the person who is on the moon watching an eclipse of the moon and the physicist who understands eclipses know that the moon is sometimes eclipsed (or is now eclipsed). But only the physicist has *scientia* of that fact because only the physicist understands in general the causes of eclipses. On this interpretation, then, a person has more *scientia* in virtue of knowing more, and more ultimate, causal explanations of more states of affairs.

---

61 Ibid., proemium: "Secundo autem rationis processui deservit alia pars logicae, quae dicitur Inventiva.... Per hiusmodi enim processum, quandoque quidem, etsi non fiat scientia, fit tamen fides vel opinio propter probabilitatem propositionum, ex quibus proceditur ... et ad hoc ordinatur Topica sive Dialectica.... Quandoque vero, non fit complete fides vel opinio, sed suspicio quaedam.... Et ad hoc ordinatur Rhetorica."

On this interpretation of Aquinas, then, how shall we translate *scientia*? 'Discipline,' 'expertise,' 'body of knowledge' are all possibilities, except that they leave us no handy analogue for the verb *'scire.'* 'Understanding' might do the job, except that it has unfortunately become the conventional translation for *'intellectus.'* Perhaps the best possibility is just to translate it by its cognate, 'science,' with a reminder to the reader that science so understood also includes, for example, mathematics and metaphysics. Understanding *scientia* as science in this broad sense will help us to digest some of Aquinas's examples of demonstration, which are surprising and perplexing on the Foundationalist interpretation.

In illustrating the different kinds of causes that can serve as the middle of a demonstration, Aquinas gives this example as an instance of a demonstration in which the middle is an efficient cause:

> [Aristotle] presents an example of an efficient cause using a certain story about the Greeks. Allied with certain other Greeks, the Athenians once invaded the Sardians, who were subject to the king of the Medes, and therefore the Medes invaded the Athenians. He says, therefore, that one can ask the reason why the war of the Medes with the Athenians occurred, and this reason why is a cause of the Athenians' being attacked by the Medes.... The middle ... in this case has to do with the Athenians who first began the war. And so it is clear that here a cause which is efficient (*primo movit*) is taken as a middle.[62]

I am not at all clear on how this example could be construed on the Foundationalist interpretation of Aquinas. What combination of self-evident propositions and propositions evident to the senses of a person living in Aquinas's time could yield the conclusion that the Medes made war on the Athenians? But on the account I have been

---

62 Ibid., II lectio 9: "ponit exemplum de causa movente, tangens quamdam Graecorum historiam: videlicet quod Athenienses quondam, adiunctis sibi quibusdam aliis Graecis, invaserunt Sardenses, qui erant subiecti regi Medorum; et ideo Medi invaserunt Athenienses. Dicit ergo quod quaeri potest propter quid bellum Medorum factum est cum Atheniensibus; et hoc propter quid est causa quare Athenienses impugnati sunt a Medis.... Hoc autem, scilicet B, quod est medium, pertinet ad Athenienses, qui prius bellum inceperunt. Et sic patet quod hic accipitur quasi medium causa quae primo movit."

developing here it isn't difficult to accommodate this example if we take 'science' broadly enough to include the social sciences as well.

The fact that in this passage Aquinas is obviously discussing an example of Aristotle's should serve to remind us that the question of Aquinas's relation to Aristotle still remains. On Irwin's view of Aristotle's *Posterior Analytics*, Aristotle is a foundationalist, at least at the time of writing that work. I have been at pains to show that Aquinas's commentary on the *Posterior Analytics* cannot be interpreted as presenting his theory of knowledge, that *scientia* in that work is not equivalent to 'knowledge,' and that Aquinas's epistemological position is not correctly characterized as Foundationalism. I am not clear what species of foundationalism Irwin is attributing to Aristotle, but if it is an internalist theory of knowledge or if it bears a family resemblance to Foundationalism, then, on my interpretation of Aquinas, there are two ways of thinking about Aquinas's relation to Aristotle. One is that Aquinas completely misunderstood the nature of Aristotle's treatise and that although he thought he was simply explaining and developing Aristotle's thought, in fact he was radically altering the nature of Aristotelian epistemology. And the other is that we suppose Aquinas was an astute reader of Aristotle and that the evidence gathered here to reject the view of Aquinas as a Foundationalist is some reason to rethink at least one current account of Aristotle. Either of these possibilities is compatible with the interpretation of Aquinas I have defended here, but deciding which one to accept seems to me to belong decidedly to the province of the historians of ancient philosophy. On that score, then, this paper will come to no judgment. When the issue is adjudicated, however, it should be resolved with a clear recognition of Aquinas as holding not Foundationalism but rather an interesting theological externalism with reliabilist elements.[63]

---

63 I am grateful to William Alston, Scott MacDonald, and Alvin Plantinga for many helpful comments and suggestions on an earlier draft of this paper, and I am especially indebted to Norman Kretzmann, whose help at earlier stages of the paper was invaluable.

CANADIAN JOURNAL OF PHILOSOPHY
Supplementary Volume 17

Infallibility, Error, and Ignorance

NORMAN KRETZMANN

I Introduction

Eleonore Stump argues in her article in this volume[1] that Aquinas's theory of knowledge is not classical foundationalism, as it has sometimes seemed to be, but, instead, a version of reliabilism. I'm convinced that her thesis is important and well-supported, and it has led me to begin a re-examination of one aspect of Aquinas's theory of knowledge from the new viewpoint Stump's work provides. I think the results tend to confirm her account while revealing further details of Aquinas's reliabilism.

My topic is not reliabilism itself. Instead, I am focusing on Aquinas's account of the reliability of the fundamental operations of the two human cognitive faculties, sense and intellect. Accounts of cognitive reliability have a place in most theories about the justification of belief, of course, and so they are found in more than one sort of epistemology; but reliabilism might be said to need them most.[2]

Questions of cognitive reliability arise in connection with acquiring data and processing data. Reliability in our cognitive faculties for either acquiring or processing data admits of two broadly distinguished types of guarantees, or explanations: natural and

---

1 'Aquinas on the Foundations of Knowledge,' infra, 125-58

2 Especially because reliabilists tend to take cognitive reliability to be a sufficient condition for justification or even to reduce justification to reliability.

supernatural. For example, our faculties have attained reliability through natural selection; or, a creator makes our faculties reliable. A twentieth-century reliabilist who is also a theist might be expected to combine the evolutionary and theistic accounts, incorporating the natural within the supernatural explanation. Although Aquinas hadn't heard of natural selection, his thirteenth-century reliabilism also has natural and supernatural components, with Aristotelianism playing the role of the natural account incorporated within the supernatural.

The resemblance between the roles of evolution and Aristotelianism is not just structural. Like the theory of evolution, the Aristotelianism incorporated into the theological component of Aquinas's theistic reliabilism offers natural (as well as metaphysical) confirmation and elaboration of what would otherwise be purely theological explanations of the reliability of cognition. Of course, the resemblance isn't precise, either. Unlike evolution, Aquinas's Aristotelianism offers no historical or prehistorical answer to the question *why* our faculties are reliable. Instead, proceeding on the conviction that the very nature of the relationship between reality and our faculties guarantees the fundamental reliability of our acquisition and processing of the data, it tries to say *how* that happens, to say what must be the case regarding our faculties and their objects, given that cognition is reliable.

For Aquinas, the theological component of his theistic reliabilism naturally comes first. It will come first also in my investigation of his position, because it provides a sketch of the whole story. The Aristotelian component fills in the details.[3] Employing Aristotle's epistemology to fill in details of a theological account might seem offhand to threaten a distortion of it. I can't offer an expert assessment of the interpretation of Aristotle underlying this Aristotelian component,

---

3 Aquinas notably prefers the non-theological, Aristotelian sort of account of certain details even when a supernatural alternative is available to him — e.g., in his well-known rejection of the theories of the agent intellect and the possible intellect as separate substances (see, e.g., Thomas Aquinas [3], *Summa theologiae* [ST] Ia.79.4 & 5).

but I don't think it involves any serious distortion of Aristotle. In fact, I think Aquinas's use of Aristotle in this way may provide grounds for a different sort of expectation. Just because Aquinas is the paradigmatic thoughtful Aristotelian, Stump's revision of an initially plausible account of *Aquinas's* epistemology raises interesting questions about standard interpretations of *Aristotle's* epistemology. In her paper Stump understandably leaves those questions to specialists in Greek philosophy. Neither will I say anything explicit here about any possible reinterpretation of Aristotle in the light of Aquinas's constant and varied use of Aristotelian material in his epistemology, even in developing its theological component.[4]

II The Theological Component: Basic Doctrines

The component of cognitive reliability in theistic reliabilism could reasonably be said to be implied by a few basic theological doctrines which Aquinas of course argued for, quite independently of their implications for epistemology: God, the creator, is omniscient, omnipotent, and perfectly good; and part of his purpose in creating is

---

4 In this paper references to Aristotle will have the name of the work spelled out followed by the number of the book, etc.; references to Aquinas's commentaries on Aristotle will have the number of the book followed by an abbreviated form of the name of the work, etc. The Aristotelian texts relevant to my purposes include a few prominent, extended passages (e.g., esp. *De Anima* III 6 [Aristotle (3)] and *Metaphysics* IX 10 [Aristotle (4)]) but also many scattered bits and pieces. And almost all these texts, long and short, were discussed in Aquinas's commentaries on Aristotle as well as cited frequently by him as he developed his own position. This vast array of sources and Aquinas's intricate weaving of his own epistemology through Aristotle's would make it intolerably distracting to try to trace the Aristotelian thread in every Thomistic doctrine. So I will only occasionally point to a relationship between them, and I will often speak only of Aquinas's position when I might appropriately have referred to Aristotle's as well. But it seems clear to me that although Aquinas no doubt thought of himself as developing an Aristotelian account, he was not merely expounding Aristotle, not even in his commentaries.

the manifestation of himself to rational creatures.[5] From those central doctrines alone it seems to follow that skepticism is frivolous — that human beings must have been created with reliable access to created reality and with reliable faculties for the processing of the reliably acquired data.

In fact, skepticism never is a serious issue for Aquinas, probably for just such reasons.[6] But he does not leave us to discover the guarantee of reliability only by drawing this obvious inference for ourselves. He also offers several explicit explanations of the creator's provision of reliable cognitive faculties. "The immediate purpose of the human body," he says, "is the rational soul and its operations, since matter is for the sake of the form, and instruments are for the sake of the agent's operations. I maintain, therefore, that God designed the human body in the pattern best suited to that form and those operations" (ST Ia.91.3c). Sensory cognition, although not part of the rational soul in the narrow sense, is indispensable to intellection, the cognitive operation of the rational soul, and so the senses, too, he says, "have been given to human beings not only in order to get the necessities of life, but also in order to acquire cognition" (ST Ia.91.3, ad 3).[7] Consequently, the *human* animal, unlike all the others, is not called a *sensory* substance, "because sensation is less than

5 See Thomas Aquinas [2], I *Scriptum super Sententias* (*Sent.*) 44.1.2: "... a likeness of God's goodness is the purpose of all things"; see also my article 'Why Would God Create This World? A Particular Problem of Creation' (in Scott MacDonald, ed., *Being and Goodness* [Ithaca: Cornell University Press 1990] 229-49, esp. 242-3).

6 As William Alston observes after summarizing the importance of skepticism in epistemology, "I do not deny that skepticism is worthy of serious and prolonged consideration, but I do deny that it must find a place on every worthwhile epistemological agenda" (*Epistemic Justification* [Ithaca: Cornell University Press 1989], 2).

7 See also ST IIIa.11.2, ad 3: "the senses are given to a human being not only for intellective *scientia* but also for the necessities of animal life"; and ST IaIIae.31.6c, which cites the opening passage of Aristotle's *Metaphysics* (I 1, 980a21-4), where human delight in the senses and especially in sight is explained by reference to their indispensable contribution to knowledge.

[rationality], which is proper to a human being"; still, just because of sensation's contribution to intellection, sensing "is more excellently suited to a human being than to other animals" (ST Ia.108.5c).[8] In fact, he explains even the location of most of the sense organs in the head and the upright posture of the rational animal as designed by God "so that through the senses, and especially through sight, which is more acute [than the other senses] and discloses more distinctions among things, a human being can freely cognize sensible things in all directions, in the heavens and on earth, in order to gather intelligible truth from all of them" (ST Ia. 91.3, ad 3).[9] So human senses are provided not just for ordinary animal purposes but, more importantly, for starting theoretical cognition generally (and theology in particular).[10]

The passages I have just presented show that the importance of the senses as regards human *cognition* lies in their contribution to *rational* cognition, intellection, the activity of the speculative intellect.[11] Intellect is of course the pre-eminent cognitive faculty in Aristotelian-Thomistic epistemology generally, but it also enjoys special pre-eminence in Christian doctrine, a status that enhances the plausibility of theistic reliabilism in a Christian context. For one thing, it is the

---

8 See also Thomas Aquinas [11], II *De anima*, lect. 6, n. 301: "In mortal beings possessed of intellect, however, it is necessary that all the other [faculties] exist before it, as instruments of and preconditions for intellect, which is the ultimate perfection aimed at in the operation of nature."

9 See also ST IIaIIae.164.2, ad 1; Thomas Aquinas [6] (DM) 5.5; Thomas Aquinas [5] (QDA) 8.

10 As for the senses' contribution to theology in particular, there is also familiar scriptural backing: "The heavens declare the glory of God; and the firmament showeth his handiwork" (Psalms 19:1); "For the invisible things of him from the creation of the world are clearly seen, being understood by the things that are made, even his eternal power and Godhead..." (Romans 1:20).

11 In this paper I will have nothing to say about the practical intellect. Aquinas's term '*intellectus*' is usually translated correctly as 'intellect' (the faculty), but he sometimes uses it in contexts where 'intellection' (the faculty's operation) is called for in English, and so I will vary my translation of it.

human *intellect*, not the human body or its senses, in respect of which human beings are made in the image of God,[12] and so it is entirely reasonable that *that* cognitive faculty in particular should manifest special excellence. And since the human intellect depends on the human senses, the creator who leaves his image in the intellect can hardly leave the senses less than superbly suited for cognitive service to intellect. Furthermore, the beatific vision, the transcendent culmination of cognition and the creator's intended perfection of human existence, is an act of the perfected human *intellect*, released from its terrestrial dependence on the senses.[13] Even as a dim foreshadowing of that culmination, the activity of intellect in this life, particularly but certainly not exclusively in theology, may be expected divinely to have provided access to truth.[14]

III The Theological Component: Adamic Cognition

So far, theistic reliabilism's account of cognitive reliability sounds unbelievably rosy. Nothing in these relevant basic doctrines explains even the occurrence of error and ignorance, never mind their prevalence. The basic ingredient in Aquinas's explanation of such cognitive shortcomings can be seen most clearly in his account of the creation

---

12 See, e.g., ST Ia.3.1, ad 2; 93.2c; 93.6c.

13 See, e.g., ST Ia.12, esp. a. 1; IaIIae.3.8c; Suppl. 92.1c (IV *Sent.* 49.2.1); Thomas Aquinas [4] (SCG) III.51, n. 2285. The role of *intellectus* as one of 'the gifts of the Holy Spirit' might seem particularly well-suited to bear out the fundamental claim of theistic reliabilism, but in fact '*intellectus*' in that context refers only to a gift of special understanding regarding matters that in this life are ordinarily accessible only to faith, and so this special theological status has no bearing on theistic reliabilism as a general epistemological theory. (See, e.g., ST IaIIae.8.1 and III *Sent.* 35.2.2.)

14 On relationships between celestial and propositional understanding see my article 'Faith Seeks, Understanding Finds: Augustine's Charter for Christian Philosophy' (in Thomas P. Flint, ed., *Christian Philosophy* [Notre Dame: University of Notre Dame Press 1990] 1-36, esp. 13-16).

of human beings. But the way he begins that account strengthens the impression that human cognitive faculties are eminently reliable.

Aquinas develops his theory of what I'm calling Adamic cognition in at least three places.[15] Taking his cue from Augustine,[16] he argues for this very strong thesis: "in the state of innocence the human intellect *could not* accept *anything* false as true" (ST Ia.94.4c). Although Aquinas turns to Augustine for his description of Adamic cognition, for his argument supporting that description he draws on Aristotle: "just as *true* is intellect's *good*, so *false* is what is *bad* for it, as is said in *Ethics* VI [2, 1139a27-31]" (Ibid.).[17] In pre-fall Eden, in circumstances optimal for all aspects of earthly human existence, that Aristotelian premiss does not preclude ignorance, but it definitely rules out error of any kind: "although in the state of innocence there could have been the *lack* of some good, in no way could there have been any *corruption* of a good" (DV 18.6c). And so in Adam's "intellect there could have been a lack of some knowledge, but no false opinion" (ST Ia.94.4c).[18]

Drawing on another Aristotelian premiss in arguing for his account of Adamic cognition, Aquinas claims that since "intellection is always true in respect of its proper object"[19] (a claim I will be examining later in this paper), "intellect is never deceived on the basis of anything

---

15 In order of composition, II *Sent.* 23.2.3; Thomas Aquinas [8] (DV) 18.6; ST Ia.94.4.

16 Augustine [1] *De libero arbitrio* III.xviii.52

17 That is not quite what Aristotle says there, even in Aquinas's Latin text: "*Speculativae autem mentis, et non factivae neque practicae, bene et male, verum et falsum.*" See also Thomas Aquinas [16], I *Peri Herm.*, lect. 3, n. 7, and Spiazzi's editorial note (8). For some other interpretations and applications of this line, see, e.g., Thomas Aquinas [14], VI *Eth.*, lect. 2, n. 1130; Thomas Aquinas [15] VI *Metaph.* (4, 1027b25-27), lect. 4, n. 1231; ST IaIIae 60.4, ad 2.

18 On the kinds of knowledge Adam had to have and the kinds he could or must have lacked, see esp. the articles closely associated with the ones on which this discussion is based: II *Sent.* 24.2.2; DV 18.4; ST Ia.94.3 ("Did the first human being have *scientia* of all things?"). Briefly, he could not have lacked any knowledge he needed for his own welfare and the raising of children.

19 Aristotle [3], *De Anima* III 6, 430b27-31

stemming from itself (*ex seipso*). ...Thus it is clear that the rightness of the original [human] condition was incompatible with any deception involving intellect" (Ibid.).

But Aquinas realizes that his strong thesis about the infallibility of Adamic cognition in the original condition has to face up to at least three modest, plausible objections,[20] all of which can be recognized in other versions elsewhere in the history of epistemology: (1) Dreams deceive us, and Adam must have had dreams; (2) Like any of us, Adam was ignorant about other people's thoughts and about future contingents, so someone could have misled him about such things; (3) Adam's eyes were, presumably, no better than ours at their best, so, like us, he could have been mistaken about the size of something seen in the distance.

Objection (1), the dream argument, appears to borrow strength from something Aquinas says in arguing *for* his infallibility thesis: "we are not deceived by ... appearances when the natural faculty of judgment [intellect] is not impeded, but *only* when it *is* impeded, as is the case in people who are *asleep*" (Ibid.). Nevertheless, Aquinas has a ready rejoinder to the dream argument, one that applies as well to post-fall human beings. Dreaming, he says, takes place not in the intellect, but in the sensory part of the soul. If there is deception in a dream, it occurs because sleep impedes, or 'binds,' intellect so that the sensory part of the soul can impose on it; for "every deception in intellection occurs accidentally, stemming from something inferior to intellect — imagination [*phantasia*], for example, or something of that sort" (Ibid.). That's why nothing that "happens in sleep is attributed to the *person*, because [a sleeping person] does not have the use of reason, which is the activity *proper* to a human being" (Ibid., ad 4).[21] So even if Adam's intellect was imposed upon in a dream, Adam

---

20 I have chosen only the three that strike me as not only effective but also philosophically familiar. There are four objections in II *Sent.*, including (2) and (3), five in ST, including all three of these, and fifteen in DV, including (1) and (3).

21 Cf. DV 18.6, ad 14.

himself was not then deceived any more than we are in such circumstances. Adam himself is the fully conscious, normal person whose intellect cannot be imposed on unless his will acquiesces or connives in the deception.

As for objection (2), the misinformation argument, if Adam had encountered "someone saying something false about future contingents or the thoughts of [human] hearts, the man in the state of innocence would *not* have believed that it was *so*, but he *would* have believed that it was *possible* — which would not count as thinking anything false" (Ibid., ad 5).[22] And the same sort of rejoinder, broadly speaking, is offered to (3), the optical illusion argument: "if anything had been represented to the first man's sense or *phantasia* otherwise than it is in fact, he would not have been deceived, because through reason he would have discerned the truth" (Ibid., ad 3).[23] These two rejoinders are alike in implying that in these sorts of cases Adam *was* different from us, since we, of course, are regularly deceived in our judgments about distant objects, predictions, and purported revelations of the thoughts of human hearts.

What made Adam our cognitive superior in these respects? Aquinas does not say, in so many words, but his answer seems clearly implied in what he says about Eve's being deceived in her assessment of the serpent's speech and about Adam's being deceived in his judgment that eating the forbidden fruit was a venial rather than a mortal sin. Those crucial mistakes in both of them were consequences of the at least logically prior sin of pride; if they had not erred in that act of will, they would not have erred cognitively either.[24] Basing

---

22 Cf. the earlier II *Sent.* 23.2.3, ad 3, where Aquinas takes quite a different line, claiming that God would have intervened "so that he [Adam] would immediately have had intellective cognition of it if anyone had told him anything false as true."

23 Cf. II Sent.24.2.3, ad 4, a fuller version of this rejoinder, and DV 18.6, ad 15, where the unmisleadable waking intellect is contrasted with intellect in sleep.

24 See II *Sent.* 24.2.3, obj. 1; ad 1; DV 18.6, obj. 5; obj. 11; ad 5; ad 11; ST Ia.94.4, obj. 1; ad 1.

definite judgments on insufficient evidence — especially judgments as important as those — is an immediate consequence of the sin of pride if not itself an instance of it, a case of desires influencing beliefs.[25] And such an explanation, even detached from its theological context, does have some claim to general applicability. Pride goeth before many a cognitive fall. We make at least the vast majority of our cognitive mistakes because we overestimate our grasp of the evidence or our ability to assess it, or because we'd be too embarrassed to say as often as innocent Adam would have said in our circumstances, 'Well now, what you say is *possible*, at any rate.'

IV The Aristotelian Component Generally

Against the background of this survey of the theological component in Aquinas's reliabilism, I turn to its Aristotelian component.

Aquinas's theistic reliabilism depends on Christian doctrine for its starting points and its outline. But its account of the *mechanism* of cognition and of the *details* of sensory and intellective reliability is largely drawn from Aristotle's epistemology, which Aquinas found readily adaptable to his purposes. In fact, even Aquinas's comments on 'All human beings desire to know' and the rest of the opening passage of the *Metaphysics* contain all the elements needed for an argument on natural grounds that would confirm his own theological considerations supporting reliabilism. For example: "the proper activity of a human being considered just as a human being is to think and understand,[26] for it is in this respect that a human being differs

---

25 Or, as Aquinas would say, of will's misdirecting intellect. On this basis someone — W.K. Clifford, for instance — might be moved to conclude that evidentialism is the will of God. See my forthcoming article 'Evidence Against Anti-Evidentialism.'

26 'Understand,' the standard translation for the verb '*intelligere*,' is often too narrow in the context of this discussion; in such cases I will use 'think and understand,' or (far more often) 'have intellective cognition of,' instead. In translating nominalizations of the infinitive I tend to use 'intellection.'

from all others. That is why a human being's desire is naturally inclined to thinking and understanding and, as a consequence, to acquiring organized knowledge.[27] ... [But] a natural desire cannot occur in vain" (I *Metaph*. lect. 1, nn. 3 & 4). Therefore, we might fairly conclude, nature, including human cognitive faculties, must be organized in such a way as to enable human beings to satisfy their natural desire to know. And since the object of a thing's natural desire is that thing's natural good, it is not surprising to find Aquinas often alluding to the Aristotelian observation that truth is intellect's natural good,[28] the very thing to which a perfectly good God would guarantee intellect's access.

How direct is the access? How solid is the guarantee? In Aquinas's Aristotelian reliabilism, the access is utterly direct, to the point of formal identity between the extra-mental object and the actually cognizing faculty — an extremely strong version of direct realism.[29] As for the guarantee, it is expressed not in the sober terms of mere reliability but in the initially astonishing terms of infallibility. For someone who knew no Aristotle it would be natural to suppose that the role of an omnipotent, perfectly good God as the guarantor in

---

27 Since I ordinarily translate '*scientia*' (if at all) as 'organized knowledge,' I here translate '*ad sciendum*' as 'to acquiring organized knowledge.'

28 For the grandest version of this line, see SCG I.1, n. 4: "The ultimate end of any thing is what is intended [for it] by its first author or mover. Now the first author or mover of the universe is intellect, as will be shown below. Therefore, the ultimate end of the universe is intellect's good. But that is truth. Therefore, truth must be the ultimate end of the whole universe...."

29 See, e.g., ST Ia.85.2, ad 1: "What is cognized intellectively [*intellectum*] is in the one who has the intellective cognition [*intelligente*] by means of its likeness. And it is in this sense that we say that what is actually cognized intellectively *is* the intellect actualized [*intellectum in actu est intellectus in actu*], insofar as a likeness of the thing that is cognized intellectively is the form of the intellect, in the way that a likeness of the sensible thing is the form of a sense actualized." I'm grateful to Scott MacDonald for reminding me of Peter Geach's stimulating account of this direct realism in G.E.M. Anscombe and P.T. Geach, *Three Philosophers* (Oxford: Basil Blackwell 1963), 94-7.

Aquinas's reliabilism is all that accounts for its direct realism and its infallibilism, but in fact he derives his detailed developments of those aspects of it from his reading of Aristotle.

The Aristotelian doctrine at the heart of Aquinas's infallibilism derives from Aristotle's claims that it is impossible for either sense or intellect to be mistaken in respect of its proper object. The proper objects of a sense are, of course, those to which it and no other sense has access: colors for sight, sounds for hearing, and so forth.[30] The notion of intellect's proper object is, naturally, more complicated and controversial, but it isn't misleading to begin by thinking of it as the *nature* of a thing.[31] As regards intellect, however, Aristotle can be read as going even further than the already very strong claim of its infallibility in respect of its proper object; for he says in *De anima* III 10 (433a26) that "*All* intellection is right."

I can set the stage for my examination of Aquinas's development of these Aristotelian elements by briefly considering some comments of his on this last sweeping claim. In this passage Aristotle is contrasting the universal rightness of intellection with the occasional wrongness of desire and imagination, and so, Aquinas says, Aristotle is explaining "why we go wrong in our actions and movements." In that context the sweeping claim about intellection "must be understood as having to do with the intellection of ... *first principles* of action," which, like the intellection of general first principles of speculative reason, *never* goes wrong (III *De an.* lect. 15, n. 826). Moreover, *in theory* the super-reliability of the intellection of principles extends throughout the structure of organized knowledge: "in connection with things that come *after* the principles, if we consider [them] rightly, [our intellection] proceeds on the basis of the rightness there is regarding the first principles. If, on the other hand, we deviate from rightness, it proceeds on the basis of an error that occurs acci-

---

30 On a sense's infallibility regarding its proper object see, e.g., Aristotle [3], *De anima* II 6, 418a11-16.

31 On the infallibility of intellect regarding the nature of a thing see, e.g., Aristotle [4], *Metaphysics* IX 10, 1051b25-6.

dentally in the reasoning process" (Ibid.). "The rightness *there is*" is built into the equipment: "*we* deviate from rightness." Our God-given faculty of rational cognition is infallible but not fool-proof. It starts us off unerringly, and it will never steer us wrong. But *we*, who sometimes "go wrong in our actions and movements" when desires influence beliefs, may easily steer *it* wrong.[32] The equipment is flawless but, like any flawless equipment, it can be misused.

V The Mechanism of Reliability: External Senses

In Aristotelian and Thomistic epistemology intellection is of course emphasized over sensation, but since "intellect's operation arises from sensation" (ST Ia.78.4, ad 4),[33] all cognitive reliability depends on reliability in sensation.[34] The nature and limits of that reliability are to be understood in terms of Aquinas's Aristotelian distinction of three types of objects of sensation: proper, common, and incidental.[35] In the case of sight, for instance, *red* is proper (to sight), *round* is common (to sight and touch), and *apple* is incidental (to any one sense and to sensation generally). Claims of infallibility are made only in connection with *proper* sensation. Roughly speaking, if something looks round, it probably is round to the senses; but looking round isn't all there is to being round to the senses. And if it looks like an apple, it probably is one; but looking like an apple is a long way from being an apple to all the senses and to intellect besides. If anything

---

32 See also DM 16.6c: "false opinion in us occurs for the most part as a result of reasoning carried on as it should not be [*ex indebita ratiocinatione*]."

33 See also, e.g., ST Ia.84.6, s.c.: "The Philosopher proves that the source of our cognition is in sensation"; cf. *Metaphysics* I 1, 981a2; Aristotle [12], *Posterior Analytics* II 15, 100a3.

34 Aquinas even suggests at one point that it is the special character of the apprehension a sense has of its proper object that leads us to say even in cases of indubitable *intellectual* apprehension that we '*sense*' something (ST Ia.54.5c).

35 See, e.g., ST Ia.17.2c; 85.6c.

looks *red*, however, it *is* red to the senses; looking red *is* all there is to being red as an object of sensation. A wall, of course, is not a proper object of sight, and so its looking red is not all there is to *its* being red. Still, if my vision is normal, then when I'm shown a white wall bathed in red light, *what* I see (and don't also touch, or infer the corporeal existence of) *is* red. If I judge, solely on that basis, that *the wall* is red, *I*, of course, am *processing* the infallible data, and the error is mine, not the sense's.

This crude account can be refined by looking at Aquinas's explanations of the infallibility of proper sensation. I'm confident that his understanding of infallibility is founded ultimately on the theological considerations I reviewed earlier. If I'm right, then the Aristotelian explanations he explicitly offers in this connection may be viewed as developing those considerations. They stem from his recognition of any faculty of sense as a potentiality designed to be actualized or to receive its accidental form as a result of coming into contact with an appropriate physical property that acts on a passive corporeal organ. To the extent to which sense is merely potential and merely passive, it cannot introduce error into this initial transaction between reality and human cognitive faculties, the transaction that actualizes those faculties.

In various places Aquinas offers at least two versions of an argument along these lines. One version stresses passivity: "A sense organ is affected by a sensible thing, because to sense is to undergo something. For that reason the sensible thing, which is the agent [in sensation], makes the organ be actually as the sensible thing is, since the organ is in a state of potentiality to this [result]" (II *De an.* lect. 23, n. 547).[36] The other version stresses potentiality: "Any power or

---

36 Cf. IV *Metaph.* lect. 12, n. 672: "Sensory cognition takes place through an alteration of sense in response to sensible things in such a way that a sense's sensing something results from the sensible thing's impression on the sense." Also III *De an.* lect. 1, n. 577: "Any things that are sensed in virtue of the fact that they alter a sense are sensed *per se* and not incidentally; for to sense *per se* is to undergo something from a sensible thing." (Both proper and common sensing are sensing *per se*.)

potentiality stands in an ordered relationship to an object that is proper to it, just in virtue of being that very power or potentiality. But things of that sort are always related [to each other] in the same way. For that reason, as long as a [sensory] power or potentiality remains, its judgment regarding its proper object is not defective" (ST Ia.85.6c).

In the first place, then, this externalist account of proper sensation in terms of passivity and potentiality warrants a claim of veridicality or sub-propositional accuracy. Veridicality or accuracy generally need not and in this case does not involve precision as to all details. Aquinas seems not to have a term as narrow as our word 'veridical,' and he is understandably uncomfortable with the use of 'true' [*verum*] in this context. On at least one occasion, when he is arguing for intellect as the only proper locus for truth, he is confronted with the objection that "the Philosopher says in *De anima* III (6, 430b27-9) that ... the senses are always true of their proper objects." Aquinas's reply reveals another connection between the Aristotelian and the theological components of his reliabilism: "Since every thing is 'true' insofar as it has the form proper to its nature ... there can indeed be truth in sense ... as in a true thing [of a certain sort]" (ST Ia.16.2c). And, "since all natural things are related to the divine intellect as artificial things are related to their art, the result is that each thing is called true insofar as it has its proper form, in which it reflects the divine art.... That is why sense is called true when it is in conformity through its form with a thing existing outside the soul, and it is in this way that we mean that the sensation of a proper object is true" (I *Peri herm.* lect. 3, n. 30).[37]

So, at a level below judgment of any kind, a sensation of a sense's proper object is always 'true,' necessarily free from error, infallible,[38]

---

37 See also, e.g., ST Ia.16.1c; 17.1c; DV 1.3c.

38 Among the very many passages in which this Aristotelian point is made, those in Aquinas's commentary on *De anima* are closest to the source: II *De an.* lect. 13, n. 384; III *De an.* lect. 4, n. 630; lect. 5, n. 645; lect. 6, n. 661.

though naturally lacking any number of the original's details and, in that sense, 'ignorant.'

But a semi-automatic, sub-deliberative kind of judgment occurs immediately above this purely acquisitive level in the cognitive process, a judgment that Aquinas assigns to sense itself, an ordinarily unexpressed judgment which, if it were expressed generally would take the form of a crude realism: *Extramental reality here and now is as it appears to be.* We've already seen a reference to this semi-automatic sense judgment at the end of the potentiality argument: 'as long as a [sensory] power or potentiality remains, *its judgment* regarding its proper object is not defective.' If I'm right about this sense judgment, then in my example of being confronted with the white wall bathed in red light, the appropriate sense judgment would go beyond 'I am being appeared to redly' but not beyond something like *Red is a feature of extramental reality here and now.*

But even sense judgment of this kind can be mistaken *per accidens*.[39] In one of Aquinas's favorite examples, a diseased sense of taste brought into contact with something sweet judges that it is tasting something bitter — that *bitter* is a feature of extra-mental reality here and now.[40] This disease affecting the tongue constitutes a violation of the condition 'as long as the [sensory] power or potentiality remains' — i.e., remains normal. "Even though a sense is altered by sensible things, the sense's judgment need not be true to the conditions of the sensible thing; for the action of the agent [i.e., the sensible thing] need not be received in the patient in accord with the state of the agent, but rather in accord with the state of the patient and recipient. That is why a sense is sometimes not disposed to receive a sensible thing's form as it is in the sensible thing itself, and that is why sense sometimes

---

39 See, e.g., ST Ia.17.2c: "a sense cannot have false cognition about sensible things that are proper to it, except *per accidens* and relatively rarely"; 85.6c: "a sense is not deceived about its proper object ... except perhaps *per accidens*, because of a contingent impediment in its organ."

40 See, e.g., III *De an.* lect. 6, n. 661; ST Ia.17.2c; 85.6c.

judges otherwise than the truth of the thing is constituted" (IV *Metaph*. lect. 12, n. 673).[41]

So Aquinas of course acknowledges the real possibility, not so rarely realized, of non-veridical sensation. But it is very important to notice that at this level the only defect is in the corporeal organ, and the only error is in the *sense's* sub-deliberative, sub-rational judgment. As for the *person* who *has* the defective sense of taste, *she* need not be and *should* not be deceived or mistaken at all. "A sense's being affected just is its sensing. Thus in virtue of the fact that the senses report as they are affected, it follows that we are not deceived in the judgment in which we judge that we are sensing *something*. But because a sense is occasionally affected otherwise than the thing is, it follows that *it* will sometimes report a thing to us otherwise than the thing is. And on that basis *we* are [sometimes] mistaken about a thing *through* the sensing, but *not* [ever] about the sensing itself" (ST Ia.17.2, ad 1). If the cognizer's intellective judgments set aside her sense *judgments* and are concerned with no more than her sense *reports*, they are incorrigible in the manner of 'I am being appeared to bitterly.' Even when the reports are nonveridical, transmitted through a defective organ, her intellective judgments of this sort cannot be mistaken. And since her intellect is itself unimpaired by the defect in her sense of taste, she *should* not make mistaken intellective judgments about the real, extramental presence of *bitter* on the basis of her sense's report even if the relevant sense judgment is mistaken.[42]

One reason why intellection is to be relied on even when some physical defect is causing non-veridical sense reports is that, according to Aristotle and Aquinas, intellect uses no organ of its own and so is immune to that sort of cognitional disability.[43]

---

41 Cf. IV *Metaph*. lect. 14, nn. 692-3, where error in a sense's judgment about its proper object is attributed not to the sense itself but to a defective *phantasia*.

42 See, e.g., the treatment of the sense-of-taste example in ST Ia.85.2c.

43 See, e.g., ST Ia.12.4c; and esp. 85.6c: intellect cannot be deceived in regard to its proper object 'because of an organ, since intellect is not a power that uses an organ'; also III *De an*. lect. 7, n. 687.

Far more importantly, intellect naturally has a capacity for reflexive judgment that sense cannot attain to.[44] "Now it must be considered that even though a sensation of [a sense's] proper object is true, sense can have no cognition of its being true. For it can have no cognition of the relationship that is its conformity to the thing; instead, it only apprehends the thing. Intellect, on the other hand, can have cognition of this sort of relationship of conformity, and so intellect alone can have cognition of *the truth*.... Now to have cognition of that relationship of conformity is nothing other than to judge that it is or is not so in reality" (I *Peri herm.* lect. 3, n. 31).[45] The person of unimpeded intellect whose sense of taste is diseased is often in a position to realize that that is the case — e.g., when she notices that she has a fever, that what tastes bitter to her is sugar, that what tastes bitter to her tastes sweet to others, and so on. If she fails to take cognizance of those circumstances, or if she unreflectively accepts the report of her impaired sense in such circumstances, she is committing the cognitive version of the sin of pride — a sin that, like all others, takes place in the rational, not the sensory, part of the soul.

So what may at first have looked like Aquinas's infallibilism regarding sensation turns out to have been sensibly watered down to reliabilism regarding the sense judgments of normal senses (presumably in normal circumstances), and so the claims made for the senses

---

44 As Scott MacDonald has suggested to me, Aquinas's acknowledgement of the epistemic importance of intellect's capacity for reflexive judgment introduces an internalist component into his theory of cognition, however much it may seem otherwise to be a kind of externalism.

45 See also, e.g., DV 1.9c, where a limited sort of reflexive cognition is assigned to sense: "for although a sense cognizes itself sensing, it does not cognize its own nature; as a consequence, it also does not cognize the nature of its act or the degree of its correspondence to the thing, and so neither does it cognize its truth"; ST Ia.16.2c: "Thus to have cognition of the conformity is to know the truth. But sense in no way has cognition of it. For although sight has the likeness of the visible thing, it has no cognition of the relationship there is between the thing seen and the sense's apprehension of it." Cf. ST Ia.78.4, ad 2, where at least one aspect of this otherwise intellective reflexive cognition is assigned to the common sense.

in Aquinas's reliabilism are, after all, not unbelievable. But part of what makes his account of sensation less worrisome than it might at first seem to be is intellect's crucial role in it.[46] In Aquinas's philosophy of mind the deliverances of the senses are the necessary precondition for any intellective activity, but we have seen by now that certain activities of intellect are indispensable to our reliance on sensation.[47] It is time to move toward an examination of the reliability of intellection, which, of course, depends on the reliability of the transmission of data from sense to intellect.

VI The Mechanism of Reliability: Internal Senses

In considering that transmission of data, I have to restrict myself to the briefest sketch of the interrelated elements and their relationships. Sensible species, the impressions things make on the *external* senses, are copied and stored by *internal* senses, especially *phantasia*,[48] and transmitted by *phantasia* to intellect as phantasms.[49] The agent intellect by abstracting from the phantasms' particularities produces intelligible species,[50] which form the contents of the possible intellect, and

---

46 Although intellect's role is crucial (in ways that will become clearer in what follows), some of the possibly erroneous judgments near the beginning of the processing of the sensible species (the data) can be attributed to internal senses, faculties between the external senses and the intellect in the processing of data (see, e.g., ST Ia.78.4; QDA 13). See also n. 41 above.

47 "Although intellect's operation arises from sensation, in connection with a thing apprehended by sense intellect has cognition of many things that sense cannot perceive" (ST Ia.78.4, ad 4).

48 See, e.g., ST Ia.84.6c; 84.7, passim; 85.1, s.c.; ad 3; 85.2, ad 3; SCG II.80 & 81, n.1618.

49 See, e.g., ST Ia.84.6c; ad 2; 84.7c; ad 2; 85.1, passim. The Aristotelian source of this account of *phantasia* is in *De anima* III 3, 427a16-429a9; see III *De an.* lect. 5 & 6. On this aspect of Aristotle's philosophy of mind see esp. Michael V. Wedin, *Mind and Imagination in Aristotle* (New Haven: Yale University Press 1988).

50 See, e.g., ST Ia.85.1.

which are not themselves the objects of intellective cognition but the means of having intellective cognition of real, extramental things.[51]

A chain of cognitive processes is only as reliable as its least reliable link, and the phantasm certainly seems unreliable. It is primarily the product of *phantasia*, as its name suggests, but *phantasia* also plays the role of imagination (as *we* conceive of imagination),[52] and imagination is characteristically non-veridical. Aristotle attributes sub-intellective falsity to *phantasia*, or imagination, rather than to the external senses.[53] Aquinas explains that "Falsity is attributed to *phantasia* because it represents the likeness even of a thing that is absent" (ST Ia.17.2, ad 2).[54] And that's not all. Dream-images, too, are phantasms, but many phantasms that appear in dreams, Aquinas observes, are "distorted and disordered" (ST Ia.84.8, ad 3). To top off the bad news with something we've already heard, "every deception in intellection occurs accidentally, stemming from something inferior to intellect — *phantasia*, for example, or something of that sort" (ST Ia.94.4c).[55] If the

---

51 See, e.g., ST Ia.85.2.

52 Aquinas sometimes uses the Latin word *'imaginatio'* for this faculty, but he seems to prefer Aristotle's Greek word *'phantasia.'*

53 *Metaphysics* IV 5, 1010b1-3; see also, e.g., ST Ia.17.2, obj. 2.

54 Cf. III *De an.* lect. 5, n. 644: "The Philosopher says that the animals that have *phantasia* are those to which something appears in a phantasm even when it is not actually sensed"; also lect. 6, n. 665: "But when the movement of *phantasia* takes place in the absence of sensation, it can be deceived even about proper sensibles, for it sometimes imagines absent things as white even though they are black. Other movements of *phantasia*, however, those that are caused by the sensing of incidental sensibles and by the sensing of common sensibles, can be false whether the sensible is present or not. But they are more false in the absence of the sensible than when it is [*est/sunt*] at a distance."

55 Cf. 166-7, above. See also ST Ia.85.2, ad 3: "Two operations are found in the sensory part of the soul. One occurs only by way of a change effected in it, and the operation of sense in this respect is completed by means of having a change effected in it by a sensible thing. The other activity is *formation*, which occurs when the imaginative power forms for itself an image [*idolum*] of a thing that is absent, or even of a thing that has never been seen...." Although the passage is

deliverances of sense are the indispensable starting points for intellection, and if the deliverances of sense to intellect are phantasms,
how can the reliability of the cognitive process be maintained past
this juncture?[56]

I think we've already seen Aquinas's general answer to this question in his rejoinder to the dream argument against Adamic infallibility. No matter what non-veridical, distorted, disordered phantasms
our imaginations may present us with, "we are *not* deceived by
appearances of that sort when the natural faculty of judgment [i.e.,
intellect] is *not impeded*" (Ibid.). If your imagination is healthy, any
non-veridical phantasms it presents to your unimpeded intellect will
be seen for what they are; your own imagined purple cow will not
deceive you.[57] But since imagination, like every other sense, external
or internal, uses a corporeal organ, it can suffer a physical accident.
Intellect must learn to watch for signs of that sort of impairment in
order to compensate for the damaged equipment of an internal sense
as it does for the damaged equipment of an external sense — e.g., in
the case of the defective sense of taste. "If one objects that sometimes
error occurs even regarding the proper sensibles, [Aristotle] replies
that it stems not from the sense, but from the *phantasia*. Sometimes,
because of some defect in the *phantasia*, what is picked up by a sense
arrives in the *phantasia* otherwise than it is perceived by the sense —
as is clear in the case of frenetics (*phreneticis*), in whom the organ of
phantasia [i.e., a certain region of the brain] has been injured" (IV

---

ambiguous, I'm inclined to think that veridical phantasms are products of the
first of these two activities, and that all potentially deceptive, non-veridical
phantasms are products of *formation*. Cf. Ia.77.4c (near the end).

56 Whatever other sources of unreliability there might be at this juncture, the mere
abstraction of intelligible species from phantasms by intellect is, as might be
expected in Aquinas's reliabilism, no more capable of introducing error than is
a sense's reception of its proper objects: "Even though intellection is not an
activity carried out by means of any corporeal organ, its objects are phantasms,
which are related to it as colors to sight" (SCG II.80 & 81, n. 1618).

57 On healthy imaginations, orderly phantasms, and the possibility of an intellect
only slightly impeded even in sleep, see esp. ST Ia.84.8, ad 2.

Norman Kretzmann

Metaph. lect. 14, n. 693). It may not be impossible even for a frenetic's intellect to override the deliverances of the damaged corporeal equipment. But when there is no injury to the organ of *phantasia*, the common sort of deception associated with mirages and hallucinations is altogether a matter of pilot error — i.e., of a mistake made in the rational part of the soul. For, as we've seen, there are (there must be) phantasms of things that are not actually present: "that is why when someone turns [intellectively] to the *likeness* of the thing *as* to the thing *itself*, the falsity stems from that sort of [intellective] apprehension" (ST Ia.17.2, ad 2) and not from the phantasm whose original is just then absent from the extramental scene.

And so, at least for present purposes, it may be enough to say that the phantasm and its role in the cognitive process provide no threats to reliability different from those already encountered at the level of the external senses, and that the remedy remains the same. The general design of the external and internal sensory equipment is essentially flawless. Day-to-day reliability in particular instances is in theory guaranteed by a vigilant, reliable intellect's capacity to recognize and compensate for innate or acquired defects in the particular sensory equipment it is dependent on.[58] In cognition as in other action, error occurs only when the cognizer's desires influence intellect to make judgments that go beyond the evidence or ignore the

---

58 In interpreting Aristotle's observations on imagination in animals generally, Aquinas comes close to saying this in so many words, although the focus is on error in action rather than in cognition: "many animals behave on the basis of their *phantasiae*, but this happens because of an absence (*defectum*) of intellect; for because intellect is superior [to *phantasia*], when intellect is present, its judgment governs action. And so when intellect is *not* in control, animals act on the basis of *phantasia* — some (the beasts) because they have no intellect at all, others (human beings) because they have a darkened [*velatum*] intellect. This happens in three ways. Sometimes because of some passion of anger, desire, fear, or the like; sometimes because of some weakness, as happens in frenetics and madmen; and sometimes in a dream, as happens to people in sleep. For it is from these causes that it happens that intellect does not prevail over *phantasia*, so that a person follows an imaginary [*phantasticam*] apprehension as if it were true" (III *De an.* lect. 6, nn. 669-70).

symptoms of non-veridicality in the deliverances of sense: "in things that depend on God [for their nature and existence] no falsity can be found on the basis of their relationship to the divine intellect ... except, perhaps, in voluntary agents alone, who have it in their power to seduce themselves away from the divine intellect's plan" (ST Ia.17.1c). Aquinas goes on to remark that this is why Scripture sometimes calls sin 'falsity' and 'lying.' The converse inference is strongly suggested by everything he has to say about cognitive error: it is, or stems from, a kind of sin.[59]

VII The Mechanism of Reliability: Intellect

In considering the mechanism of reliability in intellection, I will suppose that we are considering only cases in which the phantasms at the bottom of the intellection are veridical. These phantasms are likenesses of particular material things, the sort of things it is natural for us to have cognition of, Aquinas says, "in virtue of the fact that our soul, through which we have cognition, is the form of some matter. But the soul has two cognitive powers. One is the act of a corporeal organ, and it is natural for *it* to have cognition of things as they exist in individuating matter, which is why sense has cognition only of individuals. But the soul's other cognitive power is intellect, which is not the act of any corporeal organ. And so through intellect it is natural for us to have cognition of *natures*. Natures, of course, do

---

59 I'm grateful to Sydney Shoemaker for reminding me that this interpretation of Aquinas's account of error bears a strong resemblance to the line Descartes takes in his *Fourth Meditation*. There Descartes brings out explicitly the central idea of the account I find adumbrated in Aquinas. For example, "So what then is the source of my mistakes? It must be simply this: the scope of the will is wider than that of the intellect; but instead of restricting it within the same limits, I extend its use to matters which I do not understand. Since the will is indifferent in such cases, it easily turns aside from what is true and good, and this is the source of my error and sin" (trans. from Descartes [1], vol. 2, 40-1).

not have *existence* except in individuating matter. It is natural for us to have *cognition* of them, however, *not* as they are in individuating matter but as they are *abstracted* from it by intellect's consideration. Thus in intellection we can have cognition of such things in universality, which is beyond the faculty of sense" (ST Ia.12.4c). So our intellect has cognition of things only after the active intellect has carried out an abstraction whose raw material is phantasms and whose product is intelligible species.[60]

Aquinas sees this abstraction of the universal from its particular as required by an Aristotelian principle he accepts: "Things have to do with intellect to the extent to which they can be separated from matter" (*De anima* III 4, 429b21).[61] But the real complex substances outside the mind are themselves concrete individuals, and Aquinas admits that "abstracting the form from the individuating matter, which the phantasms represent, is to have cognition of that which is in individuating matter, but not *as* it is in such matter" (ST Ia.85.1c). So abstraction, the very first move in intellection, seems already to have forfeited the veridicality transmitted in the phantasms.[62] And since the divinely designed mechanism and process of cognition absolutely require abstraction for the transmission of data from sense

---

60 See, e.g., ST Ia.13.9c; 57.1, ad 3; 57.2, ad 1; and esp. 85.1, passim.

61 See, e.g., ST Ia. 85.1, s.c.; Thomas Aquinas [12], *Expositio super librum Boethii De trinitate* qq. 5 and 6; and esp. III *De an.* lect. 8, n. 716: "Thus things that are separated from matter in their existence [i.e., separated spiritual substances] can be perceived by intellect alone, while those that are not separated from sensible matter in their existence but rather conceptually [i.e., mathematical entities] are cognized by intellect without sensible matter but not without intelligible matter. Natural entities, however, are intellectively cognized on the basis of abstraction from individuating matter but not from sensible matter entirely. For a human being is intellectively cognized as composed of flesh and bones, but on the basis of abstraction from this flesh and these bones. And that is why it is sense or imagination (*imaginatio*), not intellect, that has direct cognition of individuals." In this article I consider only natural entities as objects of intellection, not also mathematical entities or spiritual substances.

62 See ST Ia.85.1, obj. 1.

to intellect, if abstraction itself introduces non-veridicality, even only sometimes, cognitive error is not always attributable to the person who uses the equipment, as I've been maintaining it is in Aquinas's reliabilism. So Aquinas must defend the infallibility of this sort of abstraction, and he does so: "if we consider a color and its characteristics without at all considering the apple that has the color, or even [if we] express verbally what we have intellective cognition of in that way, there will be no falsity of opinion or of speech. For the apple has no part in the nature [*ratio*] of the color, and so nothing prevents our having intellective cognition of the color without any such cognition of the apple. ... For there is no falsity in the fact that the intellect's way of having intellective cognition [of a thing] is different from the thing's way of existing" (ST Ia.85.1, ad 1)!63 not, at any rate, if the difference consists just in the fact that in abstraction *only an unaltered part* of the phantasm's content becomes the intelligible species.

On the basis of this general account of abstraction and its preservation of veridicality, Aquinas moves to the direct consideration of the kind of case at the center of his theory of intellection. Just as the apple's color can be considered independently of any consideration of the apple without introducing falsity, so "those things that pertain to the specific nature [*ratio speciei*] of any material thing — a stone, a man, a horse — can be considered without the individuating principles that have no part in the specific nature. And that is what abstracting the universal from a particular, or the intelligible species from phantasms, amounts to — viz., considering the specific nature [*natura speciei*] without considering the individuating principles that are represented by phantasms" (Ibid.). And, as we've seen, the purely mental, abstract entities that are the intelligible species are not themselves the proper objects of intellect but only intellect's means of

---

63 See also, e.g., ST Ia.13.12c; 50.2c; Thomas Aquinas [13], *In Dionysii De divinis nominibus* 7, lect. 3, n. 724: "all cognition is in accord with the mode of that by which something is cognized, just as every activity is in accord with the mode of the form by means of which someone carries out the activity."

Norman Kretzmann

access to those extramental specific natures that exist only in material individuals.[64] Those natures are intellect's proper objects.[65]

Aquinas uses many different designations for the proper object of intellect,[66] perhaps 'quod quid est' (his version of Aristotle's 'to ti esti') more often than any other.[67] Offhand, these designations strike me as not significantly different in ways that affect this discussion. For the sake of uniformity, I will adopt one of them — 'the quiddity of a thing' — as my standard designation for intellect's proper object.[68]

---

64 See, e.g., ST Ia.85.2c; ad 2.

65 Aquinas thinks this feature of intellect is apparent even etymologically: "The name 'intellect' derives from the fact that it has cognition of the *intimate* characteristics of a thing; for 'intelligere' [to have intellective cognition] is by way of saying 'intus legere' [to read penetratingly]. Sense and imagination [*imaginatio*] have cognition of external accidents only; intellect alone succeeds in reaching a thing's essence" (DV 1.12c).

66 E.g., 'ens': ST Ia.5.2c; 11.2, ad 4; 12.1, obj. 3; 16.4, ad 2; IaIIae.55.4, ad 1; SCG II.83, n. 1678; 'ens intelligibile': SCG II.98, n. 1835; 'ens universale': ST Ia.105.4c; SCG III.25, n. 2066; 'ens vel verum commune': ST Ia.55.1.c; 79.7c; 87.3, ad 1; IaIIae.9.1c; 10.1, ad 3; 'verum': ST Ia.20.1c; 54.2c; IaIIae.3.7c; 10.1c; IIaIIae.25.2c; 'substantia': ST IIIa.75.5, ad 2; 'intima rei': DV 1.12c; 'interiora rei': SCG IV.11, n. 3475; 'essentia rei': ST Ia.57.1, ad2; IaIIae.31.5c; DV 1.12c; 'quidditas rei': ST Ia.17.3, ad 1; 18.2c; 85.5c; 85.6c; 86.2c; 88.3c; 'quidditas sive natura in materia corporali existens': ST Ia.84.7c; 84.8c; ad 1; 85.5, ad 3; 85.8c; 87.2, ad 2; 87.3c; ad 1; 94.2c.

67 E.g., ST Ia.16.2, obj.1; 17.3, ad 1; 57.1, ad 2; 58.4c; ad 1; ad 3; 58.5c; ad obj.; 67.3c; 89.5c; IaIIae 3.8c; 10.1, ad 3; 31.5c; IIaIIae.8.1c; IIIa.10.3, ad 2; 76.7c; SCG I.58, n. 489; 59, n. 496; 61, n. 508; 66, n. 545; III.41, n. 2182; 46, n. 2236.

68 In III *De An.* lect. 8, nn. 705, 706, 712, 713, Aquinas offers some helpful introductory remarks on quiddities in this connection: "the quiddities of things are other than the things only *per accidens*. For example, the quiddity of a white man is not the same as the white man, because the white man's quiddity contains in itself only what pertains to the species *human being*, but what I call a white man has within itself more than what belongs to the human species.... [I]n all things that have a form in matter the thing and its *quod quid est* are not entirely the same: Socrates is not his humanity.... [Intellect] has cognition of both [the universal and the individual], but in different ways. For it has cognition of the nature of

Understandably, Aquinas counts intellect's cognition of its proper object as the *first* operation of intellect[69] even though, as we've seen, the active intellect's abstraction of intelligible species is a necessary precondition of the cognition of the quiddities of things.[70] For my present purposes what is important (and, at least initially, impossible to credit) is Aquinas's claim, in which he thinks he is following Aristotle, that intellect in its cognition of the quiddities of things no less than in its abstraction of intelligible species is infallible.

The Aristotelian antecedent of this claim is a passage in *De anima* III 6 (430b26-31),[71] which, as Aquinas interprets it, presents the thesis that just as a sensation of a sense's proper object is always veridical, so is an intellective cognition of intellect's proper object, which he identifies as the quiddity of a thing. Aquinas more than once paraphrases the passage along these lines: "Intellection regarding the quiddity of a thing is always true, as is a sensation regarding its proper object."[72]

---

the species, or of the *quod quid est*, by directly extending itself into it; it has cognition of the individual, however, by a kind of reflection, insofar as it turns back to the phantasms from which the intelligible species are abstracted."

69 See, e.g., I *Sent.* 19.5.7, ad 7.

70 Infallible abstraction plays an essential part in the cognition of quiddities: "intellect apprehends the quiddities of things differently from the way they exist in sensible things; for it does not apprehend them with the individuating conditions that are adjoined to them in sensible things. And intellect can manage this without any falsity, since nothing prevents one of two conjoined things being understood without the other's being understood" (III *De an.* lect. 8, n. 717). See also III *De an.* lect. 10, n. 731.

71 "Every assertion says something of something, as too does denial, and is true or false. But not every thought is such; that of what a thing is in respect of 'what it is for it to be what it was' is true, and does not say something of something. But just as the seeing of a special object is true, while the seeing whether the white thing is a man or not is not always true, so it is with those things which are without matter" (Hamlyn's translation). The Aristotelian technical term in inverted commas is '*ti esti kata to ti en einai,*' which Aquinas encountered as '*quid est secundum hoc quod aliquid erat esse.*'

72 See, e.g., ST Ia.58.5c; 85.6c; I *Peri herm.* lect. 2, n. 20; lect. 3, n. 31.

Norman Kretzmann

I imagine almost everyone will find this claim unbelievable on the face of it without any help from me, but I want to be sure that the widespread incredulity is deepened by two particular considerations. In the first place, since Aquinas carefully explains that intellect's proper objects are *outside* the mind, the infallibility he is claiming for our intellection of them does not reduce to mere, sterile incorrigibility. In the second place, and more obviously, it is the *quiddities* of things, their *essential natures*, about which he is claiming universal infallible intellection. This feature of his claim looks, if possible, even less plausible when we notice that on his view the *science* of nature *also* has the quiddities of things as its objects.[73] Quiddities, the proper objects of intellect's first operation *and* the objects of the culminating cognition of nature might, then, fairly be called the alpha and omega objects of intellective cognition.[74] But if this pre-theoretic, *alpha* cognition of them, intellect's *first* operation, is infallible, what could be the point of struggling toward the *omega* cognition, the distant goal of *scientia* regarding natural things?

Having posed this problem, I want to offer two mitigating considerations before developing Aquinas's solution to it. The first consideration draws on another Aristotelian passage Aquinas frequently appeals to in this connection. In *Metaphysics* VI 4 (1027b25-9) Aristotle says, as Aquinas interprets him, that the infallible alpha intellection

---

73 See, e.g., III *De an.* lect. 8, n. 718: "what intellect has cognition of is the quiddity that is in things.... For it is obvious that the *scientiae* are about the things intellect has cognition of..."; *In Ioan.* 1, lect. 1, n. 26: "When I want to grasp (*concipere*) the nature of a stone, I have to arrive at it by reasoning. And that is how it is in connection with all the other things we have intellective cognition of, with the possible exception of first principles, which are known (*sciuntur*) without discursive reason when they are known (*nota*) simply"; cf. III *Sent.* 23.1.2.

74 Cf. Bernard J. Lonergan, *Verbum: Word and Idea in Aquinas*, David B. Burrell, ed. (Notre Dame: University of Notre Dame Press 1967): "the *quod quid est* is at the very center of Aristotelian and Thomist thought. For *quod quid est* is the first and immediate middle term of scientific syllogistic demonstration; simultaneously, it is the goal and term of all positive inquiry, which begins from wonder about data and proceeds to the search for causes.... The *quod quid est* is the key idea not only in all logic and methodology, but also in all metaphysics" (24).

186

of the quiddities of things cannot be false just because it cannot be true, either: it occurs below the level of intellection at which (paradigmatic propositional) truth and falsity apply properly.[75] So the infallibility claim is by no means a claim that the first operation of intellect delivers to us something like a set of true propositions regarding the quiddity that is its object. Whatever it delivers *infallibly* leaves us in a state close to total *ignorance* about that quiddity. Still, it does look as if intellect is supposed to cognize quiddities the way sight sees colors, and that's implausible enough.

My second mitigating consideration addresses this residual implausibility. If I had nothing else to draw on, I'd express it as an appeal to common sense, or to the principle of charity: Aquinas *couldn't* have been claiming anything as wild as this claim has been sounding.[76] Aside from the details of his solution to the problem I've posed, there are plenty of scattered observations to show that he didn't — e.g., "the essential principles of things are unknown to us" (I *De An.* lect. 1, n. 15); "our cognition is so feeble that no philosopher has ever been able to investigate completely the nature of a fly" (*In symbolum Apostolorum*, preface).[77] Aquinas appears to have had a just estimate of the state of thirteenth-century natural science, and, if we are really to focus on what he would have considered 'the *essential* principles of things,' his appraisal might suit twentieth-century science as well.

So, then, what *does* he mean by his claim that "the proper object of intellect is the quiddity of a thing, and that is why intellect is infallible (*non fallitur*) regarding the quiddity of a thing, speaking of it just as such [*per se loquendo*]" (ST Ia.85.6c)?

---

75   See, e.g., VI *Metaph.* lect. 4, nn. 1230-40; ST Ia.16.2, s.c.; I *Peri herm.* lect. 3, n. 31.

76   I found Paul T. Durbin's discussion helpful (in Appendix 2 to his edition and translation of ST Ia.84-9, vol. XII in the Blackfriars edition [1968], 170-2), and in these paragraphs I make use of some of the passages he provides.

77   See also, e.g., DV 4.1, ad 8; 6.1, ad 8; 10.1c; ad 6; *De spiritualibus creaturis* 11, ad 3; SCG I.3, n. 18; ST IIaIIae 8.1c; Thomas Aquinas [17], I *Post. an.*, lect. 4, n. 43; II *Post. an.*, lect. 13, n. 533. I'm grateful to Scott MacDonald for some of these references.

We can make progress toward answering that question by noting what seems to be an important ambiguity in Aquinas's characterizations of the first operation of intellect. Sometimes he describes it simply in terms of *the proper object generally,*[78] and then it may be thought of simply as any cognition of the quiddities of things, deserving the designation 'first' in virtue of the primacy of its object. On this description of it the first operation covers the whole range of the cognition of quiddities, from alpha to omega. But Aquinas also describes the first operation, perhaps more often, in terms of only the initial stage of the cognition of quiddities, *the acquisition of the concepts of quiddities.* On this description of it the first operation is confined to the pre-theoretic alpha cognition. And this narrow description of the first operation provides a clear contrast with the standard description of the *second* operation as the making of judgments, affirming by propositionally compounding concepts acquired in the first operation with each other, denying by dividing them from each other. At every stage past the initial stage the cognition of quiddities must involve the second operation, and reasoning as well:[79] "the human intellect does not immediately, in its first apprehension, acquire a complete cognition of the thing. Instead, it first apprehends *something* about it — viz., its quiddity, which is the first and proper object of intellect; and *then* it acquires intellective cognition of the properties, accidents, and dispositions associated with the thing's essence. In doing so it has to compound one apprehended aspect with, or divide one from, another and proceed from one composition or division to another, which is reasoning" (ST Ia.85.5c). No one could, and Aquinas does not, claim infallibility for cognition that involves judging and

---

78 See, e.g., I *Sent.* 38.1.3c, where the first and second operations are explained as required in order to attend either to a thing's quiddity or its *esse*, respectively.

79 As abstraction precedes the first operation, so reasoning, the use of the second operation's propositions in inferences, follows the second. In at least one place Aquinas expressly identifies it as the third operation — not of *intellect* but, more broadly, of *reason* (I *Post. an.* lect. 1, n. 4).

reasoning.[80] His claim of infallibility for the first operation turns out to be restricted to the alpha cognition.

But that restriction alone doesn't make the claim easy to accept. The revised claim that only our initial acquisition of our concepts of the quiddities of things is infallible is not exactly disarming. How does Aquinas intend it to be understood? Along these lines, I think.

In acquiring the concept *water*, as we all do at a very early age — abstracting it from phantasms, let's suppose — we acquire a full, unopened package. Everything that analysis and experimentation can reveal about water is confusedly contained within that primitive concept,[81] which wouldn't be a concept of water at all if it weren't veridical, no matter how internally confused and imprecise it may be. Or, putting the point less tendentiously, everything that is or could be eventually discovered about water must fit back into that package, saving the phenomena. [82] Our pre-theoretic, alpha cognition of water *is* the cognition of a quiddity, especially if we emphasize the non-technical sense of 'quiddity,' since it surely is the concept of a *whatness*. Even if a single childish concept were abstracted confusedly from phantasms of water, milk, and juice, it would be, even so, the cognition of some quiddity, one that has and needs no established name of its own, one that will in the natural course of the child's development get sorted into three or more quiddities. Nevertheless, that hybrid, stuff-in-my-cup quiddity would be a proper object of intellection, and

---

80 See, e.g., ST Ia.85.6c: "Intellect is fallible [*potest falli*] regarding the aspects associated with a thing's essence or quiddity when it relates one of them to another in compounding or dividing, or even in reasoning."

81 See, e.g., ST Ia.14.6c: "Since our intellect [unlike God's] moves from potentiality to actuality, it attains a universal, confused cognition of things before attaining to a proper cognition of them, proceeding from the imperfect to the perfect, as is clear in *Physics* I [1, 184a18-25]"; 85.3c; ad 3: "we have a confused kind of cognition of *human being* before we know how to distinguish everything belonging to the nature of a human being"; 85.4, ad 3; 75.5c.

82 SCG III.56, n. 2328: "The proper object of intellect is *quod quid est*, the substance of a thing.... Therefore, whatever is in a thing that cannot be cognized through the cognition of its substance must be unknown (*ignotum*) to intellect."

the child's alpha cognition of it would be infallible. Where, after all, is there any room for error?

Of course, error will have crept in if the first word the child associates with this hybrid quiddity is 'water.' But even naming the object of one's alpha cognition is obviously more than just *having* the cognition. Associating a name with the object already involves the *second* operation of intellect, compounding one's concept of the sound 'water' with one's concept of that quiddity, and we've already seen that Aquinas emphatically recognizes the fallibility of judgment.[83]

If we temporarily set aside error, it should already be clear that recognizing the alpha cognition as infallible in this way entails leaving lots of room in it for *ignorance*. The alpha cognition is inchoate — unanalyzed, confused, imprecise, characterized by ignorance more than by cognition. All the same, it is the cognition with which organized knowledge begins its quest for the omega cognition of that same quiddity. Moving toward an omega cognition of water, learning or constructing a *scientia* that has water among its objects, is the fallible process of reducing the ignorance in the infallible alpha cognition.

The fallibility sets in so close to the alpha cognition that Aquinas sometimes picks out errors of a sort he thinks must be counted as incidental to this *first* operation of intellect (which shows that on such occasions he is thinking of the first operation as the cognition of quiddities generally). As far as I know, he doesn't recognize the mere associating of a name with a quiddity as a locus of fallibility at this lowest level, but his own two standard examples are almost as simple: "even in the operation of intellect by which it has cognition of quiddities there can be falsity *per accidens* insofar as intellect's compound-

---

83 See also, e.g., III *De an.* lect. 11, n. 761, which illustrates, among other things, Aquinas's interpretation of *'intelligentia indivisibilium'* as another description of what I am calling the alpha cognition. On this interpretation what is 'indivisible' is not, e.g., a point or an instant, but the as yet undivided (i.e., unanalyzed) concept of the quiddity. See also, e.g., ST Ia.85.8c; I *Peri herm.* lect. 3, n. 25; I *Sent.* 19.5.1, ad 7; 38.1.3c. On the association of names with natures see, e.g., DV 4.1, ad 8; ST Ia.13.8.

ing is mixed into it.[84] This can happen in two ways: first, in intellect's attributing the definition of one [quiddity] to another" — mistakenly compounding definition and definiendum; "second, in its compounding together [as] parts of a definition [quiddities] that cannot be associated with each other ... e.g., if it forms such a definition as *four-legged rational animal*" (ST Ia.17.3c).[85] Errors of this sort, no matter how near the alpha cognition they occur, really occur on the way to the omega cognition, the only sort of cognition that has a thing's quiddity or essence *clearly* in its sights: "sometimes one does not attain to the innermost aspects [of a thing] except by way of things associated with it, as if through doors of some sort. And this is the mode of apprehending for human beings, who proceed from effects and properties to a cognition of a thing's essence. And because there must be some discursiveness in this [mode of apprehending], a human being's apprehension is called *'reason'* even though it terminates in intellection in case this sort of investigation leads all the way to the thing's essence" (III *Sent.* 35.2.2ac).[86]

---

84 Cf. III *De an.* lect. 11, n. 751: "we have to bear in mind that the composition of a proposition is a production of reason and intellect, not a production of nature."

85 See also, e.g., ST Ia.58.5c; 85.6c; I *Sent.* 19.5.1, ad 7; SCG I.59, n. 496; DV1.12c; III *De an.* lect. 11, n. 763; IX *Metaph.* lect. 10, n. 1908.

86 See also, e.g., ST Ia.58.5c: "Sometimes we arrive at intellective cognition of a quiddity by compounding and dividing, just as we find out a definition by means of dividing [i.e., analyzing] or demonstrating"; I *De an.* lect. 1, n. 10: "a definition lays out [*notificat*] the essence of a thing, which cannot be known [*sciri*] unless the principles are known [*sciantur*]"; SCG III.58, n. 2836: "In the operation of intellect by which it apprehends a *quod quid est*, falsity does not occur except *per accidens*, insofar as something of intellect's operation of compounding and dividing is mixed into this operation. That happens to the extent to which our intellect attains to cognizing the quiddity of any thing not at once but in an orderly inquiry...."; Thomas Aquinas [18], *Super Ioannem* 1, lect. 1, n. 26: "when I want to conceive of the nature [*rationem*] of a stone, I must arrive at it by reasoning — as is the case regarding all other things of which we have intellective cognition.... So as long as intellect is driven now this way, now that, in the process of such reasoning, the formation [of the conception of the thing's nature] is not yet complete. It is only when intellect has completely conceived of the very

Progress toward the omega cognition of a thing's quiddity isn't all there is to human intellectual life, but it might fairly be identified as all there is to theoretical inquiry, leading to *scientia*. And Aquinas makes it clear that there is no guarantee of success for our attempt to understand nature: "we are ignorant of very many properties of sensible things and, as for the properties we perceive by the senses, in many cases we cannot completely discover their natures" (SCG I.3, n. 18). But, as we've seen, ignorance, even unremitting ignorance, doesn't tell against theistic reliabilism. No doubt post-fall human beings need to know more than innocent Adam did, but perhaps they really don't need to know all there is to know about nature. Nevertheless, Aquinas maintains an optimistic, Aristotelian assessment of the possibility: "a human being *can* by means of intellect acquire cognition of the natures of *all* bodies" (ST Ia.75.3c); "if the human intellect comprehends the substance of any thing — a rock, say, or a triangle — *none* of the intelligible aspects of that thing exceeds the capacity of human reason" (SCG I.3, n. 16).[87] There is, then, no argument to show that the cognitive equipment comes with divinely imposed limitations: ignorance isn't foreordained.

Even more clearly, neither is error. The way from alpha to omega is made up of many judgments and much reasoning — deciding that certain concepts belong together and that others are to be kept apart, deciding that certain propositions entail others. Without compounding and dividing, without reasoning, there can be no theoretical inquiry, no full-fledged truth or falsity for human intellects or, for that matter, full-fledged human intellects at all. But every act of compounding or dividing concepts — even those that are logically incom-

---

nature of the thing that, for the first time, it completely possesses the thing's nature and then, too, the definition [*rationem*] of the word [associated with the thing]." I am grateful to Jan Aertsen for having called my attention to this last passage.

87 *De anima* III 4, 429a18. See also, e.g., III *De an*. lect. 7, n. 680: "our intellect is naturally suited to have intellective cognition of all sensible and corporeal things"; n. 681: intellect "can have cognition not only of one kind of sensible things ... but rather universally, of sensible nature entirely."

patible or inseparable — and every act of inferring a proposition essentially involves a human decision. And our decisions are free choices of will, no matter how well supported by evidence they may be, especially when the subject matter is characterized by contingency.[88]

All these remarks about cognitive error in the by now predictable vein of *nostra culpa* might well lead someone to think that the initial infallibilities in this epistemology are snares and delusions rather than promises. Is the infallibility of the sensation of proper objects and of the intellection of quiddities any less sterile, after all, than the incorrigibility of judgments regarding nothing but the contents of sense reports? Certainly the equipment's reliability would be a sorry joke if that were the extent of it.

Aquinas's account of reliability goes much farther, of course. Naturally, the operations of judging and reasoning are *fallible*, but they are not fallacious. They are in fact, as might be expected, designed to lead to truth, intellect's good, if they are engaged in prudently. From a cognition of quiddities that is only a little (if at all) advanced beyond the alpha cognition, cognition of first principles combining the corresponding concepts sometimes follows immediately.[89] As for reasoning, and as for judging at levels riskier than that at which first principles are discovered, in those operations, Aquinas says, "there *is* falsity in intellection — but *never* if the analysis [of conclusions] into first principles is carried out *correctly*" (DV 1.12c).

That is not the empty promise it may appear to be. Its purely externalist character makes it difficult or impossible to tell immediately when it's been fulfilled, but the long run shows us that it sometimes is. We, unlike even the apes and dolphins, have been given equipment that can get us to theoretically unlimited theoretical truths about complex substances. As the history of science shows,

---

88 See, e.g., ST Ia.82.2c; IaIIae.10.2, ad 2; 57.5, ad 3.

89 See, e.g., ST Ia.18.3c; 62.8, ad 2; 82.1c; 82.2c; 85.6c.

it's not easy, and it takes a long time, but, with luck, we don't have to stop yet.[90]

---

90 SCG III.48, n. 2258: "As long as something is being moved toward perfection, it is not yet at its ultimate goal. But when it comes to having cognition of the truth, all human beings are always in a state of being moved and tending toward perfection; for those who follow after make further discoveries of other things than those that were discovered by their predecessors (as is said in *Metaphysics* II [1, 993a31])."

I am grateful to Jan A. Aertsen, William P. Alston, Gail Fine, Scott MacDonald, Steve Maitzen, Robert Pasnau, and Eleonore Stump for comments on earlier drafts. I owe special thanks to Eleonore Stump, for having first interested me in these topics, and to Jan Aertsen, who sent me learned, detailed comments on my interpretation of Aquinas's 'first operation' of intellect, about which he has some misgivings.

CANADIAN JOURNAL OF PHILOSOPHY
Supplementary Volume 17

Aristotle and the Sacrament of the Altar: A Crisis in Medieval Aristotelianism

MARILYN McCORD ADAMS

I Transubstantiation as 'Aristotelian'?

In the Anglican theological circles in which I move, the doctrine of transubstantiation is apt to be declared guilty by association with its Aristotelian underpinnings, most notably its 'out-moded' substance-accident ontology. These negative assessments, based as they usually are on cursory acquaintance with the theory's most enthusiastic medieval exponent, Thomas Aquinas, abstract from historical complications. For eleventh-century theologians had already debated the manner of Christ's presence in the Eucharist: whether it was merely symbolic (as Berengar of Tours was accused of holding) and/or spiritual (as some passages of St. Augustine would suggest); or whether the Body and Blood of Christ were really present in the Eucharist under the forms of bread and wine? Once the Church pronounced in favor of 'the real presence,' several competing theories were advanced to explain it: (i) 'impanation,' according to which the Body of Christ assumed the substance of the bread, the way the Divine Word assumes Christ's human nature; (ii) 'annihilation,' according to which the substance of the bread is annihilated; (iii) 'consubstantiation,' which stipulates that the substance of the bread remains and the Body of Christ coexists with it; and (iv) 'transubstantiation,' which says the bread is neither annihilated nor remains, but is converted into the Body of Christ. While many favored transubstantiation, consubstantiation was regarded as a viable option, both defensible and permissible, right up through Albert the Great. Aquinas was the first to insist on transubstantiation as the only legitimate option.[1]

Likewise, the condemnation of transubstantiation as 'Aristotelian' is as philosophically superficial as it is ironic. For while any theory of real presence posed problems, the elevation of transubstantiation to the status of theological norm precipitated a crisis for thirteenth- and fourteenth-century Aristotelians. Among the three judges of theoretical adequacy — reason, experience, and authority — it was the first that had to bow. The scramble to win a theoretical balance at once Christian and Aristotelian was creative, full both of false starts and of startling surprises.

II Thomas Aquinas, Champion of Transubstantiation

Advancing beyond earlier majority favoritism for transubstantiation, Aquinas boldly declared its major competitor out of court on three grounds. (i) First, he appealed to Aristotelian physics to argue that it is impossible for the substance of the bread to remain. For the Body of Christ cannot come to be present where it was earlier absent apart from some change. But Aristotle recognizes only four kinds of natural change: qualitative change (or alteration), quantitative, substantial (generation and corruption), and locomotion. To these, Christian theology adds the supernatural, creation and annihilation, peculiar to Divine power alone. According to doctrinal consensus, the Body of Christ pre-exists the consecration (and so does not come or cease to be by generation or corruption, creation or annihilation, respectively). Moreover, it is and remains in heaven, and undergoes no qualitative or quantitative change thereby. Finally, it is impossible for it to become present on the altar(s) by natural locomotion, and that thrice-over. First, natural locomotion involves both the body's loss of its former location and the acquiring of a new one, while the Body of

---

1 Cf. the excellent article by James F. McCue, 'The Doctrine of Transubstantiation from Berengar through Trent: The Point at Issue,' *Harvard Theological Review* **61** (1968), 385-430.

Christ remains in heaven. Second, natural locomotion from point *a* to point *b* takes a body successively through a continuous path in between, but the Body of Christ does not thus 'travel' through the places between heaven and earthly altars. Finally, the Body of Christ may become present on many altars simultaneously, but it is impossible for one and the same locomotion to have many *termini ad quem*. Since it is obvious to the senses that the accidents of the bread remain, Aquinas concluded that the only remaining change would be one in which the substance of the bread is converted into the Body of Christ; and what is converted, cannot remain.[2]

(ii) Second, the hypothesis that the substance of the bread remains is heretical because contrary to the authority of Scripture. For Christ says, "Hoc *est corpus meum*" — using the neuter gender to agree with *'corpus'* — whereas if the bread remained, He should have said, 'Hic [i.e., *hic panis*] *est corpus meum*." And "what the Truth has spoken, that for truth [we must] hold" (Ibid.).

(iii) Third, the assumption that the bread remains is incongruous with Church law and practice. For it is legal to consume one host after having consumed another, but illegal to receive it after having consumed corporeal food. Yet, if the substance of bread remained, consumption of one host would provide physical nourishment, so that one could not receive another without violating the canons on fasting. Again, the practice of venerating the sacrament would be rendered idolatrous, if the substance of the bread remained along with the Body of Christ under the species (Ibid.).

1. The Nature of the Change

Granted that the substance of the bread does not remain, how does it depart? Here theory and experience are enough to exclude the idea that bread is resolved into its matter. Not into the elements, for the senses would detect that. Not into prime matter either, since according to (Aquinas's) hylomorphism, prime matter is pure potentiality

---

2 Thomas Aquinas [3], *Summa Theologica* III, q.75, a.2 c

and thus cannot exist alone. Besides, when would such matter be present? For Eucharistic doctrine holds that the bread and wine are present right up to the last instant of consecration, and at the last instant the Body of Christ is already there (Ibid., q.75, a.3, c). But Aquinas could not say that the substance of bread is annihilated either: for the *terminus ad quem* of annihilation is *'purum nihil,'* whereas the term of Eucharistic conversion is the Body of Christ. Lest one dismiss this as a piece of ad hoc semantics, Aquinas appealed to an analogy with natural change: it doesn't follow from the fact that forms cease to exist in alteration and corruption, that they are annihilated properly speaking (Ibid., q.75, a.3, c; ad 1um).

Summing up, Aquinas declared that sacramental conversion is a third sort of supernatural change. As finite, the active power of natural agents presupposes the passive power of matter for a change of form and/or location (Ibid., q.75, a.4, c. & ad 3um; q.78, a.8, ad 4um). God's infinite power extends to the whole being of any creature, and so beyond transformation and locomotion, to the conversion of one whole substance into another (Ibid., q.75, a.4, c). Moreover, the change is instantaneous: the last instant of the priest's speech is the first instant at which the Body of Christ is present (Ibid., q.75, a.7, c.; ad 1um). Thus, like natural change, sacramental conversion involves succession; one term passes into another, but neither term is non-being. Like creation, it involves no subject common to both terms (Ibid., q.75, q.75, a.5, ad 4um; a.8, c). Yet, as in natural change, something persists through supernatural conversion: viz., the accidents (Ibid., q.75, a.8, c). Turning to semantics, Aquinas concluded from these analogies that, strictly speaking, *"panis est/erat/erit/potest esse/fit corpus Christi"* cannot be true any more than *"aer/non ens est/erat/erit/potest esse/fit ignis/ens"* can, while *"ex pane fit corpus Christi"* is true, just as much as *"ex non ente fit ens"* and *"ex aere fit ignis"* and *"ex albo fit nigrum"* are (Ibid.).

2. The Manner of Presence

If the Body of Christ is really present in the Eucharist via transubstantiation, questions about the manner of its presence remain. First, since the extended accidents are apparent to the senses, how can the Body of Christ exist simultaneously in the same place (Ibid., q.76, a.4, ad 2um)? Second, since ecclesiastical formulae specify only that the Body and Blood be present, does this mean that Christ is divided, so that His soul and other accidents are not there (Ibid., q.76, a.1, c)?

Aquinas hoped to cut the knot of these puzzles with a distinction between what is present by the power of the sacrament (*ex vi sacramenti*) — viz., precisely what is signified by the form of words in the consecration — and what is present by natural concomitance (*ex naturali ... concomitantia*) — whatever is really conjoined to what is present the first way, 'sacramentally.' Thus, the whole substance of the Body and Blood of Christ are sacramentally present, whereas Christ's Divinity and soul (except during the Triduum, when it is separate from the Body) (Ibid., q.76, a.1, ad 1um). His quantitative dimensions (Ibid., q.76, a.1, ad 1um and ad 3um; a.4, c., ad 1um, and ad 2um) and other accidents are present only the second way, by virtue of their real inherence in the substance. And so the whole Christ is contained under the species, but in different ways (Ibid., q.76, a.2, ad 1um and ad 3um). Because quantity is present only by natural concomitance, it follows that the substance is sacramentally present only in the mode of substance and not in its quantitative mode. Consequently, just as the whole substance nature of air exists under each part of air, so the whole substance nature of Christ's Body exists under each part of the species, and does so whether the host is whole or broken (Ibid., q.76, a.3, c). Likewise, because substance nature is prior to quantity, and dimensive quantity is responsible for extension, the Body of Christ is not sacramentally present insofar as its parts are at a distance from one another (Ibid., q.76, a.3, ad 2um & ad 3um). Nor is it in place, because its parts are not related to the parts of place where the species are located (Ibid., q.75, a.5, c. & ad 3um). A fortiori, the Body of Christ, which is sacramentally present on many altars, is not in place definitively (in such a way as to be confined to one place as opposed to another) (Ibid., q.76, a.5, ad 1um) or circumscriptively (in such a way as to be contained by the surface that contains the species) (Ibid., q.76, a.5, ad 1um).

Marilyn McCord Adams

3. *Accidents without Inesse?*

Any doctrine of real presence will have to face the metaphysical issue of how and whether one body can exist under another (just discussed in section II.2 above). But Aquinas's insistence on transubstantiation (see section II.1 above) gave rise to a further metaphysical difficulty: viz., that of whether and how the accidents of bread can remain without the substance? That the accidents both ante- and post-date the priest's utterance of the consecration formulae is evident to the senses (Ibid., q.75, a.5, c). But what could be more fundamental to Aristotle's metaphysics than his distinction between substances, whose nature and definition it is to exist per se, and accidents, which by their very nature and definition inhere?[3] Moreover, if accidents are individuated by their subjects (as Aquinas construed Aristotle to say), how can they remain individuated when their subject ceases to be? Aquinas himself intensified these problems by dismissing several obvious evasions: (i) Theologically, the arguments from Scripture and congruity used to banish the substance of the bread, would tell against the substantial form's remaining behind to be subject of the accidents (Ibid., q.7, a.1, c). (ii) In general, it will not help to look for a substitute subject, for the metaphysical reason that accidents are individuated by their subjects and so cannot remain numerically the same in different subjects (Ibid., q.77, a.1, c). The surrounding air and the Body of Christ are eliminated by the further metaphysical consideration, that they are not the right sorts of bodies to take on bread-accidents. Anyway, the senses would alert us to such changes in the air, while theology informs us that Christ's post-resurrection glorified body is impassible and so not susceptible of any qualitative change (Ibid., q.77, a.1, c).

---

3 Ibid., q.77, a.1, obj.2: "Praeterea, fieri non potest etiam miraculose, quod definitio rei ab ea separetur; vel quod uni rei conveniat definitio alterius, puta quod homo, manens homo, sit animal irrationale. Ad hoc enim sequeretur contradictoria esse simul: hoc enim quod significat nomen rei est definitio, ut dicitur in IV *Metaphs.* Sed ad definitionem accidentis pertinet quod sit in subiecto: ad definitionem vero substantiae, quod per se subsistant non in subiecto. Non potest ergo miraculose fieri quod in hoc sacramento sint accidentia sine subiecto."

Of the general definitional question, Aquinas made surprisingly short work. At one level of abstraction, his real distinction between *essence* and *esse* implies a rejection of *"ens per se sine subiecto"* and *"ens in subiecto"* as definitions of substance and accident, respectively. It is more accurate to say that "it pertains to the quiddity or essence of substance to have existence not in a subject," while "it pertains to the quiddity or essence of accident to have existence in a subject" (Ibid., q.77, a.1, ad 2um). Because all categorial beings are creatures, their actual *esse* depends on the efficient causality of something else. In particular, according to the common law of nature, substance is an efficient cause that produces and conserves the esse of accidents so long as they exist in it, with the result that accidents are naturally destroyed when their substance is destroyed. Nevertheless, since effects depend more on the first cause (= God) than on any secondary cause, God can, by His infinite power exercized according to a special privilege of grace, supply the efficient causality of the latter and conserve accidents in existence even when their substance is destroyed (Ibid., q.77, a.1, c. & ad 1um).

Such general observations about Divine omnipotence and causal chains do not seem to address the worry regarding the metaphysical possibility of subject-less accident-individuation. For Divine omnipotence pertains to efficient causality; but it is in their capacity as material causes that subjects individuate accidents. Aquinas did not propose, however, that God do the impossible and become the material cause of such accidents. Rather his contention is that once a form — whether substantial as in the case of the human soul, or accidental as in the Eucharist — acquires individuated *esse* via existence in an individual subject, God can conserve the individuated *esse* that the subject in its material causality has already supplied.[4] And in fact, Aquinas's solution to the individuation problem had another, less

---

4 Ibid., q.77, a.1, ad 3um: "huiusmodi accidentia acquisierunt esse individuum in substantia panis et vini: qua conversa in corpus et sanguinem Christi, remanent virtute divina accidentia in illo esse individuato quod prius habebant. Unde sunt singularia et sensibilia."

abstract layer. According to him, the principle of individuation for composite substances is matter signed by quantity: indivisible in itself, matter contributes the aspect of a subject, while quantity is an accident whose parts would be distinct of themselves if only they could exist of themselves.[5] Moreover, on his understanding of the metaphysical structure of composite substances, substance is the subject of quantity, while quantity the subject of the qualities. Thus, if God conserves quantity in *esse* after its substance has ceased to be, the parts of quantity will be individuated per se, while the parts of quality will be individuated by quantity, just as before.[6] Nor would it be right to apply Aristotle's observation that matterless quantity is mathematical; for merely mathematical quantities are not the subject of sensible qualities (Ibid., q.77, a.2, ad 4um).

4. Sensible Species, Causal Powers

Experience suggests that the consecrated host causes and undergoes changes of all the same sorts as the substance of bread would, were it present. Yet, transubstantiation makes these phenomena difficult to account for.

So far as active causal powers are concerned, Aquinas seems to have agreed with his objector, that in the natural case, the subject and its accident form a causal chain, in which the former is the principal and the latter the instrumental cause of the effect. But, as Aquinas was so fond of pointing out in his proofs for the existence of God, when the prior cause is removed, the posterior cannot act. So if the substance of bread ceases to be present, the accidents can no longer serve as instrumental causes, acting on other things (Ibid., q.77, a.3, obj. 2 & ad 3um).

Aquinas's response moves, once again, at the highest level of metaphysical abstraction: things are related to *agere* the way they are related to *esse*. Since God conserves in the species the same *esse* they

---

5 Thomas Aquinas [2], *IV Sent.*, d.12, a.1, q.3; Thomas Aquinas [1], VII. 655

6 Thomas Aquinas [3], *Summa Theologica* III, q.77, a.2, c., ad 1um, & ad 2um

had before, He thereby preserves in them the same active causal powers (Ibid., q.77, a.3, c. & ad 1um & ad 2um).

Efficient causal power is one thing. But what of those changes that naturally call on the *material* causality of the things that undergo them? How could the sacramental species be corrupted, when, strictly speaking, corruption involves separating form from matter, whereas the matter of the bread does not remain? Yet the putrefaction or incineration of the host seems evident to the senses (Ibid., q.77, a.4, obj. 1 & pro). Again, since "the corruption of one is the generation of another," something must be generated from the species (e.g., worms, ashes). But how can this be when the species have no matter out of which new things can be made?

Aquinas handled the former case more easily, by a simple refocusing of the definition: corruption involves the taking away of the *esse* of a thing insofar as it is the *esse* of form in matter. Since God conserves in the species the same *esse* they had before, the taking away of this *esse* will still count as corruption (Ibid., q.77, a.4, ad 1um & ad 2um). Moreover, since the *esse* is the same, natural causes that had the power to take it away before the consecration, will still have that power afterwards, so that the corruption of the species will not be miraculous but natural (Ibid., q.77, a.4, obj.3 & ad 3um).

Accounting for the complement generation is more difficult, because the matter of the new product has to come from somewhere. Aquinas dismissed the suggestion that the worms and ashes are really generated from the air as empirically and theoretically ridiculous: (i) generation is preceded by alteration, but no such changes are observable in the air; (ii) air isn't the kind of substance from which worms and ashes are naturally generated; (iii) sometimes the quantities are greater than could be generated from the surrounding air; and (iv) such changes occur even when the host is surrounded by metal (Ibid., q.77, a.5, c). Likewise contrary to physical theory is the notion shared by Innocent III, Alexander of Hales, and Bonaventure: viz., that in the process of corruption, the substance of bread returns to supply the matter. For when would it return? Not so long as the species remain, because the Body of Christ is present so long as they are, and (Aquinas had insisted) the substance of the bread cannot be there when it is. Not at the last instant of the process either, because that is the instant of generation, and then the substance of bread would have to coexist with the new substance — which is likewise contrary to both theory and experience (Ibid.).

Aquinas's own solution returns to his metaphysical axiom that *agere* follows *esse*. When God conserves the dimensive quantity of the bread without its matter, He thereby miraculously confers on it a mode of existence that is proper to substance, and therewith all of the power (*vis*) of matter (Ibid., q.77, c. & ad 1um) and of substance (Ibid., q.77, a.5, c. & ad 3um). Thus, dimensive quantity can serve as material cause when the species of the bread are corrupted into worms or ashes, and when they nourish the bodies of those who consume them (Ibid., q.77, a.6, c). Moreover, no new miracle will be involved here, any more than in the case of the blind man who naturally exercizes his miraculously acquired power to see (Ibid., q.77, a.5, c).

That the host undergoes quantitative changes after the consecration is evident to the senses in the fraction. Here Aquinas's eye was more on the eleventh century debate — on assuring us that since the Body of Christ is really present in its substantial and not its quantitative mode, it is not literally broken, divided, or chewed; but since frangibility, density etc. remain in the species, they can be broken, ground by the teeth, etc. — than on the problems Aristotelian physics and metaphysics combined with Eucharistic theology would raise (Ibid., q.77, a.7, c., ad 1um, ad 2um, & ad 3um).

5. Summary

Aquinas's development of the doctrine of transubstantiation is marked by boldness, invention, and economy: boldness in his assertion that transubstantiation is the true and hence only workable theory of real presence; invention with his account of conversion as a species of supernatural change; economy as he tried to handle most of the problems with a single distinction and one of his most central and high-level metaphysical doctrines. All the same, serious problems remain. (i) Aquinas intended, with his notion of conversion, to go beyond bald assertion — that the Body of Christ is miraculously present under the species — to explain its presence in terms of a change in something else. Yet, it remains difficult to believe that we are dealing with a genuine species of change and not simply an ad hoc redescription of the occasions under which the Body of Christ will or will not be miraculously present by Divine fiat. (ii) Likewise, if sacramental presence has been partially elucidated, not enough is said about how soul, quantity, and accidents that are present under the species only by natural concomitance, avoid being sacramentally present too. Aquinas's theory of relations has not been brought into play: e.g., to posit a non-mutual relation of presence, with a real relation in the species to substance but none to the accidents of the Body of Christ and a relation of reason of substance but none of the accidents of Christ's Body to the species. Even so, given Aquinas's 'unitarianism' about substantial forms, it is difficult to see how the substance of Christ's Body can be sacramentally present and His soul not, when intellectual soul is His only substantial form. (iii) Again, even if we bracket (as his successors did not) worries about Aquinas's distinctive doctrine of essence and *esse*, we may wonder about his contention that God by conserving in quantity the esse which it first borrowed from substance, preserves not only the being, the individuation, and the efficient causal powers of the accidents, but also endows quantity with the material causality of the substance. For even if quantity does persist through such changes as putrefaction and incineration, where does the matter for worms and ashes come from — a difficulty exacerbated by Aquinas's insistence that such corruption and generation are natural changes that involve no further miracles! To these queries, among others, his successors were to return.

III Giles of Rome and His *Theoremata de Corpore Christi*

In the judgment of Giles of Rome, the theology of the Eucharist posed more difficulties than that of all the other sacraments. Writing his lengthy treatise *Theoremata de Corpore Christi* (38 incunabula folios in the Rome 1554 edition) from the posture of faith seeking understanding, Giles did not shoulder the foolhardy burden of proving the truth of a doctrine containing so much that is 'beyond reason,' but adopted the more limited goal of dispelling the appearance of impossibility through fine-grained explanations. His confidence of success rested on the intriguing if dubious inference, that since Eucharistic doctrine is true (as authority assures us), and the limitations of human reason are universal, infecting those who would attack as much as those who defend it, human reason should be able to undo all purported refutations.[7] At the same time, his sense that full comprehension of the Eucharist is impossible, served to loosen the boundaries of his metaphysical picture and allowed him to entertain as 'perhaps' possible ontological options his predecessors would have dismissed.

Giles took much from Aquinas: (i) the real distinction between *essence* and *esse* in creatures; (ii) unitarianism with regard to substantial forms; (iii) the endorsement of transubstantiation as the change which brings the Body of Christ to the altar(s); (iv) the distinction between 'sacramental' presence and presence 'by natural concomitance.' Nevertheless, Giles's more detailed treatment draws on his extensive speculations in both metaphysics and physics, and contains a number of novel twists.

---

7 Giles of Rome [1], *Theoremata de Corpore Christi*, f.1ra: "Quia inter caetera ecclesiae sacramenta Eucharistiae sacramentum plus difficultatis continere videtur, et quae omnino sensui repugnare et contradicere rationi in praedicto sacramento includi videntur, ne incredulis praestetur occasio contradicere catholicis sacramentis, dicendo quod fides nostra contineant repugnantia rationi, quam fas est: dominio concedente, quae in eo secundum superficiem visa contradictionem implicare cernuntur, declarabimus: ostendentes quod nihil impossibilitatis sacramentum praehabitum continet. Non est enim quod fidem probare non possimus, ex repugnantia veritatis: sed quia quae continet supra rationem sunt, et ad ea probanda ratio non attingit: et si propter sui excellentiam rationes deficiunt comprobantes, multo magis deficiunt improbantes. Quicquid ergo contra fidem potest per hominem ratione concludi, potest ab homine ratione dissolvi. Hanc ergo firmam tenentes fiduciam, aggrediemur quod diximus tractatum praesentem, prout rei congruentia postulat, per Theoremata distinguentes." I am grateful to Francesco del Punta for making a photocopy of this work available.

1. The 'How' of Transubstantiation

At the outset, Giles tackled the problem of making transubstantiation credible as a genuine species of change, by explaining how the Body of Christ comes to be from/out of (*ex*) the bread. (a) Giles began with Aquinas's premiss that the possibility of transubstantiation depends on the independence of Divine productive power from matter. In the production of form, natural agents presuppose the cooperation of the passive power of the matter to receive form, so that they are said to educe form from the potentiality of the matter. Moreover, natural forms are able to affect matter only insofar as it is individuated (and hence quantified), and so only insofar as it is in potency to this individual form of a given species rather than to that.[8] By contrast, Giles claimed, Divine power reaches back beyond individuation to matter as it is in itself (and hence insofar as it is no more this than that). He inferred that unlike natural agents, God can introduce (*inducere*) any individual form into any matter whatever.[9] (b) According to Giles's diagnosis, part of what makes it difficult to understand transubstantiation as a genuine species of change, is the axiom that change must be to something new, whereas the stipulated term of transubstantiation — viz., the Body of Christ — exists already. Giles denied the axiom universal scope: it applies where natural motion is concerned; here Aristotle's arguments that change cannot reproduce numerically the same thing hold good. But Divine power — whose

---

8 Ibid., *Propositio* II, f. 2ra: "naturale agens attingit materiam solum immediate ut est quanta, non ut est quid. Ideo eandem formam numero educere non potest de una materia quam educebat ex alia, quia ab aliquibus ut sunt diversa, solum diversa produci possunt. Et quia propter diversas partes quantitativas, est diversitas in materia. Educere aliquid de materiis ut sub quantitate existunt, est educere ex eis, ut diversitatem habent ad invincem. Propter quod dicebatur, naturale agens non potest educere eandem formam numero ex una materia quam educit ex alia, nec potest unam materiam in aliam convertere."

9 Ibid., *Theorema primum*, f. 1va: "Deus autem qui immediate attingit materiam ut est quid, cum materia sic accepta ab alia materia non differat, quamcumque formam numero potest inducere in materiam unam, potest etiam inducere aliam."

Marilyn McCord Adams

action does not presuppose the collaborative passive power of the subject — is not restricted to production via motion, and so can restore numerically the same thing and hence produce it again.[10] (c) Giles's third premiss is that the individuation of matter is through form. Drawing these together, he suggested, God converts the matter of the bread into the Body of Christ, by acting on the matter as such (and so prior to its individuation) to introduce (inducere) the substantial form of the Body of Christ into it, whereupon the latter individuates the former, and turns that matter into numerically the same as that found in the Body of Christ in heaven.[11]

2. The Placement Problem

Next, Giles turns his analytical attention to the problem of how the Body of Christ is on the altar(s) and how related to place. (a) His account of the layer-like structure of bodies emphasizes the distinction (not unnoted by Aquinas) between indeterminate and dimensive quantity. According to Giles, matter of itself is indivisible; indeterminate quantity divides it into parts, which dimensive quantity may then extend. Layer-wise, matter is the subject of indeterminate quantity, indeterminate quantity the subject of dimensive quantity, and dimensive quantity of the qualities.[12] (b) Giles also brought the 'secundum rem/secundum

---

10 Ibid., *Theorema primum*, f.1rb: "... Quod ergo de natura sua non habet agere nisi per transmutationem et motum immediate materiam ut est quid, prout motui subiecta esse non potest, nullatenus attinget. Deus autem, qui omnes essentias conservat in esse, qui est quodammodo rei intimior quam ipsa sibi, non praesupponens in actione sua transmutationem et motum, etiam prout producit in esse ex aliqua ·materia, eam non solum ut est quanta, sed etiam ut est quid immediate attingit...."

11 Ibid., *Theorema primum*, f.1: "... deum posse unam materiam convertere in aliam materiam cum possit facere materiam aliquam informari eadem forma numero qua alia informatur..."

12 Ibid., *Propositio* XLIV, f. 31va: "quantitas illa, per quam materia est tanta, possunt dici dimensiones indeterminatae; sed dimensiones determinatae dici possunt

modum' distinction to bear. It would be a metaphysical impossibility for a thing (*res*) which by its very nature belongs to one Aristotelian category to come to belong by its very nature to another really distinct from it.[13] Nevertheless, Giles insisted, there is no problem in a thing having the mode that pertains to another category, through being conjoined to or otherwise related to something else. Thus, the tag from *Liber de Causis* that what is received into something is received according to the mode of the receiver, not that of what is received.[14] Likewise, although a substance can never be an accident (say, a quantity or a quality), it can have the mode of accidents when modified thereby, and thus be substance *secundum rem* but quantified or qualified *secundum modum*.[15] (c) Yet, even though substance (and its metaphysical constitu-

quantitas per quam materia occupat tantum locum ... oportet dimensiones indeterminatas subiici dimensionibus determinatis."

13 Ibid., *Propositio* XXVII, f. 16vb: "... Cum ergo unum sit indistinctum a se, et distinctum ab alio, forma dando rei, quod sit hoc, dat ei quod non sit aliud. Nulla ergo res, quae per aliquam naturam est in aliquo praedicamento, potest esse in alio praedicamento differente realiter ab illo. Bene ergo dictum est quod diversorum generum, et non subalternatim positorum, diversae sunt species et differentiae. Non ergo res unius praedicamenti per se loquendo potest esse in alio praedicamento realiter differente ab illo; tamen si duo aliqua praedicamenta realiter non different, non esset inconveniens idem secundum rem esse in duobis diversis praedicamentis. Et inde est quod quia actio et passio...."

14 Ibid., f.16vb: "...non tamen est inconveniens rem unius praedicamenti habere modum alterius praedicamenti, et universaliter unam rem habere modum alterius praaedicamenti, et universaliter unam rem habere modum alterius; quia licet reale esse competat rei per suam essentiam et naturam, modus tamen potest rei competere ex eo quod alteri coniungitur, vel secundum quod ad aliud comparatur, et prout alii et alii connectitur, alium et alium modum induit; quod declarari potest tam in his, quae naturaliter sensu apprehendimus, quam in his quae supernaturaliter fide suscipimus. Videmus enim quod suscipit aliquo modo mensuram et modum a materia, omne receptae, ut dicitur in libro de causis...."

15 Ibid., f.17rb: "Numquam ergo quod est secundum rem substantia erit accidens secundum rem, nec econverso, et quod secundum rem quid, numquam erit secundum rem quale vel quantum. Sed sicut quod est secundum rem quale vel

ents) can be quantified *secundum modum* only through the inherence of, and qualities through inherence in, quantity (so that the division of substance or qualities into parts and their extension is posterior in the order of explanation to their conjunction with indeterminate and dimensive quantities, respectively), Giles insisted that the parts of substance/quality are distinct from those of quantity.[16] Thus, even if the former could not exist apart from real conjunction with quantity, the intellect can distinguish them and signify the former apart from the latter, so that 'quantified substance,' 'quantified matter,' 'extended whiteness' signify no essence other than substance/matter/whiteness, respectively.[17] Yet even if mode adds no new thing (*res*) to what it

---

quantum potest habere quendam modum relativum, sic quod secundum rem est quid, potest habere quendam modum qualem vel quendam modum quantum, et quod secundum rem est substantia, potest habere quendam modum accidentalem, et econverso."

16 Ibid., *Propositio* XXVIII, f.17va: "Notandum ergo, quod licet extensio per se et primo competat quantitati, et nihil extendatur nisi mediante quantitate, tamen aliae sunt partes quantitatis a partibus eorum, quae per quantitatem extenduntur. Videmus nam albedinem extendi per superficiem, secundum quam extensionem, quanta est superficies, tanta est albedo. Ideo dicitur in *Praedicamentis* quod dicimus albedinem multam eo quod superficies multa sit; si tamen superficies ab albo divideretur, partes albedinis essent aliae a partibus superficiei. Et quia ad alietatem partium sequitur alietas extensionis, dicere possumus quod extensio secundum partes albedinis est alia ab extensione secundum partes superficiei.... Nam licet sint partes in albedine solum propter partes superficiei, tamen quia vere ipsa albedo extenditur extensione superficiei, ex quo albedo differt realiter a superficie, et alia est essentia albedinis ab essentia superficiei, partes albedinis oportet essentialiter differre a partibus superficiei. Cum ergo ipsa materia extendatur extensione quantitatis, et cum dividitur materia quanta simul cum quantitate dividitur materia, sicut cum dividebatur superficies alba, simul cum superficie dividebatur albedo, oportet partes materiae esse alias a partibus quantitatis, sicut partes albedinis erant aliae a partibus superficiei. Licet ergo materia non habeat partes nisi per quantitatem, aliae tamen sunt partes materiae aliae quantitatis."

17 Ibid., *Propositio* XXIX, f.18ra: "Quicquid enim est extensum, vel est quantitas, vel hoc habet ex quantitate, ut induit quendam quantitativum modum, sed huiusmodi modus nullam essentiam addit supra naturam rei nec trahit rem extra

modifies, it makes a real difference whether the thing is thus modified or not.[18]

According to Giles's account of conversion (in section III.1 above), only the substance of Christ's Body is present by the power of the sacrament; His quantity and other accidents, only by natural concomitance (Ibid., *Propositiones* III & VI, f. 2va & 4rb). It is thus not circumscriptively in place, because it is not related to place by its own quantity, in such a way as to be whole in the whole place and parts in the parts.[19] Nor is it definitively in place, because it is not located in such a way that

---

> praedicamentum.... Non ergo huiusmodi extensio addit aliquam naturam supra essentiam albedinis.... Rursum talis extensio quia non addit aliquam essentiam supra naturam albedinis, nec diversificat essentiam eius, non trahit albedinem in aliud praedicamentum...."

18 Ibid., f. 18rb: "Non ergo diversificat praedicamentum modus superadditus naturae rei. Non tamen debemus concedere quod nullam differentiam realem faciat talis modus. Si enim albedo posset habere esse praeter quantitatem et habere esse non extensum, realiter differret a se ipsa, ut haberet esse extensum, et ut fundaretur in quanto. Dicere ergo possemus quod extensio accidit albedini, quia albedo per se non est quid extensum, sed accidit ei extensio: est enim extensa per quantitatem. Rursum ipsa extensio est aliquid receptum in albedine, quia modus rei est aliquid receptum in natura rei ... huiusmodi extensio facit realem differentiam in albedine, nec tamen dicit aliam essentiam ab essentia albedinis ... si albedo haberet esse secundum modum non extensum (ut dicebatur) realiter differret a seipsa ut ei extensio competeret ... sic quia partes materiae sunt aliae a partibus quantitatis, extensio competens materiae consideratae secundum suas partes, non dicit aliquam essentiam superadditam materiae: sed solum nominat quendam modum, quem acquirit materia, eo quod est quantitatis subiectum...."

19 Ibid., *Propositio* IV, f. 2vb: "Nam quod aliquid alicubi circumscriptive existat, hoc est quia quantitas locati sive illud, quod per locatum in loco existit, univoce comparatur ad quantitatem loci et ad locatum ipsum, et ideo corpora existentia in loco per quantitatem propriam circumscriptive in loco existunt, eo quod ratio quanti univoce dicitur de corpore locati et locantis ... circumscriberetur ibidem, ita quod pars esset in parte et totus in toto." Cf. *Propositio* V, f. 3va: "loco circumscribi dicitur, cum per quantitatem propriam comparatur ad locum, et ratio quanti univoce reperitur in quantitate locantis et locati...."

Marilyn McCord Adams

it could not be elsewhere simultaneously.[20] Rather it is determined to place through the quantity of the species.[21] And it is whole under the whole species, and whole under each part. Refining Aquinas, Giles differentiated essential totality (the whole expressed by the definition) and quantitative totality (all of the parts produced by the thing's indeterminate dimensions), and insisted that the Body of Christ is not only whole in the whole and whole in each part the first way (just as the substance of bread was before conversion) but also the second way (Ibid., *Propositio* IX, ff. 5va-6ra). Nevertheless, the Body of Christ is not thereby present to infinitely many parts, not for Aquinas's reason (that the continuum is infinitely divisible only in potentiality, and not in act), but because the Body of Christ is present only where the species of bread are present, and bodies of a given kind have 'least' and so finitely many parts (i.e., parts such that were they to be divided the remaining parts would not be bodies of that species) (Ibid., *Propositio* X, f. 6rb-6vb; cf. *Propositio* XI, f. 7ra-b). Again, distinguishing position (*situs*) which is a distinct category involving the relation of the parts of a thing to the parts of place, from position that is a differentia of quantity involving the order of the parts of a thing to its whole, Giles concluded that the Body of Christ in the Eucharist has the latter but not the former.[22]

---

20 Ibid., *Propositio* V, f. 3va: "diffiniti in loco" = "loco diffinitur cum habet finitam magnitudinem, et per eam comparatur ad locum."

21 Ibid.: "determinari ad locum" = "res determinatur ad locum, cum magnitudo illa, per quam in loco esse ponitur, est finita, et non est sua substantia."

22 Ibid., *Propositio* VI, f. 4ra: "... Cum ergo habitum sit quantitatem Corporis Christi non esse in sacramento ex vi sacramenti, cum nihil convertatur in ipsam, sed solum ex naturali concomitantia, quia Corpus Christi sine quantitate propria esse non posset ex quo substantia panis est conversa in substantiam corporis, et ponitur substantia corporis in altari per huiusmodi conversionem existere, oportet quantitatem propriam, quae suum subiectum non deserit, ibi esse.... Cum ergo sumatur positio quae est differentia quantitatis, prout corpus habet esse quantum et partes ordinantur ad totum, positio vero quae est praedicamentum sumatur, prout aliquid est alicubi quantitative, et partes eius comparantur ad locum, manifestum est quod declarare volebamus videlicet, Corpus Christi,

3. The Term of Conversion

Aquinas identified the term of conversion as the Body of Christ; his warrant, none other than the dominical utterance, '*Hoc est corpus meum*.' Nevertheless, given his unitarian convictions about substantial form, it is difficult to render this claim consistent with his contention that the soul is present under the species only by natural concomitance. Giles confronted this problem squarely. Mustering the courage of his unitarian convictions, he explicitly drew and endorsed their philosophical consequences. If neither the soul of Christ nor His accidents are present in the Eucharist by the power of the sacrament, the only thing left to be thus present is that with which the soul unites to make something one per se: viz., organized matter. Organized matter is neither prime matter, nor the aggregate of quantity and matter, but matter in its quantitative mode.[23] Sometimes it looks as if he had only indeterminate quantity in mind (and hence matter, insofar as it is divided into parts, but not insofar as it is extended). Other times, since organized matter is the complement of intellectual soul, it seems that he thought of matter, modified by both indeterminate and dimensive quantity.[24] Giles

---

ut est sub hostia habere positionem, quae est differentia quantitatis, cum quantitas sua det ei esse quantum, cum non seserat ordinem quem habet ad subiectum, non tamen habere positionem, quae est praedicamentum, cum dictum corpus non existat sub hostia quantitative, eo quod sua quantitas deserit ordinem, quem habet ad exteriora, cum substantia non sit ibi mediante quantitate, sed quantitas mediante substantia."

23 Ibid., *Propositio* XXVIII, f. 17vb: "... Si igitur in materia quanta est dare partes alias a partibus quantitatis, oportet partes illas alias ex quo non significant essentiam quantitatis importare solam essentiam materiae ... materia sic accepta a talibus partibus dicit materiam organizatam, quia materia organizata potest dici corpus...."

24 Ibid., *Propositio* XXVIII, f.17va: "Notandum ergo, quod licet extensio per se et primo competat quantitati, et nihil extendatur nisi mediante quantitate, tamen aliae sunt partes quantitatis a partibus eorum, quae per quantitatem extenduntur. Videmus nam albedinem extendi per superficiem, secundum quam extensionem, quanta est superficies, tanta est albedo. Ideo dicitur in *Praedicamentis*

deployed his notion that the parts of matter and their extension are distinct from those of the quantities that divide and extend them, to uphold the theological consensus that the quantity of the Body of Christ is not sacramentally present. To the obvious remaining question, of whether organized matter can be called 'body,' Giles replied in the affirmative that the term 'body' can be taken three ways: (i) for three (as opposed to one or two) dimensions, and so for something properly in the category of quantity;[25] (ii) for the composite of matter and the form of corporeity, which is a genus in the category of substance;[26] and (iii) for organized matter,

---

quod dicimus albedinem multam eo quod superficies multa sit; si tamen superficies ab albo divideretur, partes albedinis essent aliae a partibus superficiei. Et quia ad alietatem partium sequitur alietas extensionis, dicere possumus quod extensio secundum partes albedinis est alia ab extensione secundum partes superficiei.... Nam licet sint partes in albedine solum propter partes superficiei, tamen quia vere ipsa albedo extenditur extensione superficiei, ex quo albedo differt realiter a superficie, et alia est essentia albedinis ab essentia superficiei, partes albedinis oportet essentialiter differre a partibus superficiei. Cum ergo ipsa materia extendatur extensione quantitatis, et cum dividitur materia quanta simul cum quantitate dividitur materia, sicut cum dividebatur superficies alba, simul cum superficie dividebatur albedo, oportet partes materiae esse alias a partibus quantitatis, sicut partes albedinis erant aliae a partibus superficiei. Licet ergo materia non habeat partes nisi per quantitatem, aliae tamen sunt partes materiae aliae quantitatis." Cf. *Propositio XXX*, f. 19ra: "Cum igitur materia ut existit in Christo, sit aliquid extensum et organizatum, et habeat quendam modum quantitativum, et competat ei habere partes, quae partes non dicunt aliam essentiam ab essentia materiae, cum quaelibet pars materiae sit materia, constat materiam existentem in Christo esse quid realiter compositum, cum realiter habeat partes."

25 Ibid., *Propositio XXVI*: "Uno modo, corpus est ipsae tres dimensiones; sicut enim magnitudo habens unam dimensionem est linea, et habens duas est superficies, sic magnitudo habens tres dimensiones est corpus; propter quod corpus sic acceptum nihil aliud est quam trina dimensio" (f.16rb). "Corpus primo modo sumptum est quantitas, est nam in genere quantitatis secundum rectam lineam" and not by reduction (f.16rb).

26 Ibid., *Propositio XXVI*, f. 16rb: "Secundo, corpus nominat compositum ex materia et forma corporeitatis, et sic corpus est genus ad quodlibet animal.... Corpus vero

which is under the substantial form of animal and informed by the soul and thus in the category of substance by reduction.[27] Giles observed that *'corpus'* in *'Hoc est corpus meum'* refers to an essential part of a whole animal, and so understood is not truly predicable of Christ. Since 'body' taken the first two ways is thus predicable, the third must be the intended sense (Ibid., f. 16ra-b).

Does not this interpretation jeopardize the characterization of sacramental conversion as transubstantiation, in which one whole substance is converted into another whole substance, form to form, and matter to matter? Giles scrambled ingeniously to interpret this formulation. First, since forms are educed from the potency of matter, there is some sense in which they may be said to exist in the matter even when they do not actually inhere in it. What created agents can educe from the potency of matter, God can reduce to the potency of matter, and such reduction is no more to be equated with annihilation than natural eduction is with creation. God could then convert the matter into the Body of Christ in the way described above (in section III.1). Since — according to Giles — Divine power can act on matter considered in itself and prior to its individuation, it can make the soul of Christ to inhere in and thereby individuate the matter, with the result that indeterminate and/or dimensive quantity divide it into parts and/or distribute them. But — Giles claimed — those parts of matter (though naturally posterior both to the soul of Christ that individuates them and the quantity that divides them) are as distinct from the substantial form of Christ's human nature as they are from the parts of quantity. Moreover, if God could do this successively, He could also do it instantaneously.[28]

---

sumptum secundo modo, prout dicit materiam cum forma corporeitatis est in genere substantiae secundum rectam lineam."

27 Ibid.: "Tertio modo, corpus dicit ipsam materiam" (f.16rb). "... [C]orpus sumi potest tertio modo, secundum quod nominat ipsam materiam organizatam, quae est sub forma animalis, et informatur ab anima, et sic acceptum corpus est in genere substantiae non directe ... sed per reductionem..." (f.16va).

28 Ibid., *Propositio* XXXIII, f. 22ra: "Sic ergo poterit Deus totam substantiam panis

Remarkable as it is, this account still seems to renege on the notion that transubstantiation involves the conversion of substantial form into substantial form. For on the unitarian view, the only substantial form in Christ is His intellectual soul, which is denied by all to be a (partial) term of the conversion. Giles admitted that his story is odd, but identified his only alternative as pluralism about substantial forms — a theory which he found downright unintelligible.[29]

Interestingly enough, this explanatory venture brought Giles to the edge of yet another metaphysical brink. For since "God can do more than our intellect can understand," "perhaps someone might say that God could conserve the parts of matter in existence without those

in solam materiam convertere, quia poterit formam panis in potentiam materiae reducere, et facere quod illa materia informetur illa eadem forma, quae est existens in Christo, et tunc materia illa conversa erit in materiam, quae est in Christo. Et quia forma reducta in potentiam materiae non dicitur annihilata, si deus converteret materiam illam, in quam reducta est forma panis, in materiam existentem in Christo, quodammodo totam substantiam panis in solam materiam convertisset. Cum ergo effective loquendo, deus possit immediate facere quod mediate facit, si potest totam substantiam panis convertere in solam materiam, reducendo formam panis in potentiam materiae, poterit absque tali reductione talem conversionem facere; immo quia secundum converti et passive (ut in praecedenti propositione dicebatur) non plus est forma et materia panis quam materia solum; si potest deus convertere materiam panis in materiam Corporis Christi, poterit immediate totam substantiam panis convertere in solam materiam existentem in Christo, absque eo quod prius secundum intellectum inducatur forma panis in potentiam materiae...."

29 Ibid., *Propositio* XXXIV, f. 23ra-b: "Nam ponere multas formas in composito habet multas difficultates secundum se, quas solvere nescio.... Rursum multa inconvenientia mihi insolubilia hanc positionem sequuntur.... Istam ergo positionem de multitudine formarum non intelligo, nec tamen in his, quae sunt fidei minus assentio, cum ad talia requiratur captivitas intellectus. Quid ergo dicamus? Scio quod panis substantia convertitur in verum Corpus Christi, et in illud idem numero quod in caelum ascendit, et verum Corpus Christi sumimus in altari. Hoc Christus tradidit, hoc etiam ecclesia tenet, si aliis hoc non sufficit, mihi sufficit. Cui ergo non sufficit, salvus fundamentis fidei, cum reverentia et timore investiget, quale sit illud corpus; ego autem malo in mea simplicitate persistere, quam de arduis temere iudicare."

parts of quantity."[30] Then again, "perhaps this is impossible," so that God cannot do it.[31] The doubt raised, Giles quickly backed off, pleading the irrelevance of the issue to his subject.

4. *The Possibility of Separate Accidents*

So far as separate accidents are concerned, Giles adopted the limited goal of showing the Faith not to be unreasonable.[32] Generally speaking, he observed,

> The whole reason why we say that an accident cannot exist per se, is that it depends on its subject. Therefore, in proportion as accidents depend more and less on their subjects, so it is more and less difficult to maintain that the accidents exist per se....[33]

Adopting the strategy of 'divide and conquer,' he first distinguished successive accidents (such as motion) whose *esse* is *fieri*, from permanent accidents (such as quantity and quality) all of whose parts can exist at once.[34] So far as the former are concerned, Giles found it

---

30 Ibid., *Propositio* XXXIII, f. 21vb: "...Deus tamen plus potest facere, quam intellectus noster intelligere, quia potest facere accidens esse sine subiecto, licet hoc non possimus intelligere. Sic forte diceret aliquis quod deus posset convervare in esse partes materiae absque partibus quantitatis; licet forte non possimus intelligere partes materiae, non intellectis partibus quantitatis...."

31 Ibid., f. 21vb: "...Sed si hoc ... non potest deus, quia forte non habet rationem possibilis, quod actu existant partes materiae absque partibus quantitatis, non tamen propter hoc tollitur veritas quaesita...."

32 Ibid., *Propositio* XXXIX, f. 26va: "positio fidei de existentia accidentis absque subiecto non irrationabilis si diligenter videatur modus ponendi...."

33 Ibid., *Propositio* XXXVI, f. 24ra: "tota causa, quare dicimus accidens non posse per se esse, est quia a subiecto dependet. Ideo secundum quod magis et minus dependeat accidentia a suis subiectis, sic est magis et minus difficile sustinere, quod possint accidentia per se esse, loquendo de accidentibus permanentibus, quia de successivis nulla est quaestio; planum nam est successiva sine subiecto esse non posse."

34 Ibid., *Propositio* XXXV, f. 23rb: "Accidentia successiva, quorum esse est in fieri,

obvious that they cannot exist without a subject — motion without anything mobile, the Eucharistic fraction without anything being broken — either naturally or miraculously. Later he explained that successives have their essential unity from their subject and are individuated through it.[35] Among permanent accidents, he reckoned with Aquinas that all but quantity depend on their subjects for individuation.[36] Here Giles hesitated a bit: as to permanent accidents that are not individuated per se but through their subjects, "it is either impossible that they exist per se without it, which implies a contradiction, or it is at least difficult to hold that they do."[37]

Assuming the defensive posture of rebutting arguments against the possibility of separate accidents, Giles reasoned that if the permanent accident of quantity is individuated of itself, and the other accidents are individuated through inhering (directly or indirectly)

---

adeo a substantia dependent, quod nec naturaliter nec miraculo fieri potest, quod habeant per se esse. Si ergo frangatur hostia consecrata oportet fractionem illam fundari in aliquo susceptivo." Cf. f.23va: "Totalitas nam permanentium consistit in simultate partium ... totalitas successivorum non est in simultate partium, sed in ordine partium.... Et iste ordo de necessitate requirit mobile et successivum, numquam enim esset prius et posterius in motu, nisi aliquid variaretur secundum prius et posterius ... quia totalitas successivorum est in ordine partium, fieri non potest quod sit aliquod successivum et non sit talis ordo...."

35 Ibid., *Propositio* XXXVIII, f.26ra: "accidentia ... successiva conservantur in esse per subiectum et quasi formaliter habent essentialem unitatem per subiectum, et individuantur per ipsum...."

36 Ibid., *Propositio* XXXVI, f. 24ra: "Cetera accidentia per sua subiecta individuationem suscipiunt, sola quantitas dimensiva seipsa est haec, quae ut individuetur, subiecto non indiget; ex parte ergo individuationis impugnari non poterit, cum in hoc sacramento possit quantitas per se esse."

37 Cf. Ibid., f. 24ra: "Cetera vero accidentia permanentia potissime difficultatem habent, quod non possint per se esse, quia per subiecta individuantur...Omnia ergo illa accidentia quae per sua subiecta individuantur, vel est impossibile quod per se existant absque eo quod contradictionem implicent, vel est valde difficile sustinere...."

in it, then the objection from individuation will fail.[38] Nor does the fact that accidents are naturally conserved in existence by their subjects, automatically mean that they could not exist per se by Divine power.[39] It all depends on the nature of their subject's causal contribution. For Divine omnipotence entails that whatever God can do by means of a created efficient or final cause, God can do all by Himself without it.[40] Likewise, God is the non-inherent formal exemplar cause of all creatures.[41] Nevertheless, God cannot Himself be the material or the inherent formal cause of any creature.[42] Thus, God can replace the subject in its efficient causal role of preserving the accidents in existence. Giles's provisional conclusion was that if the subject's efficient causality of the accident is the only obstacle, God can conserve the accident in existence without its subject.[43] Replying to the general argument, that *inesse* is definitive of the essence of accidents,

---

38 Ibid., *Propositio XXXVI*, f. 24ra: "... si possumus ostendere quod non omnia accidentia individuantur per sua subiecta, et quod quantitas individuetur per se, ex parte individuationis non poterit veritas huius sacramenti impugnari, ex hoc quod quantitas per se existat...."

39 Ibid., *Propositio XXXVII*, f. 24va: "Omnia accidentia per sua susceptibilia conservantur propter quod nullum accidens potest naturaliter per se esse. Sed per hoc non habetur quod virtute divina in hoc sacramento non possit accidens per se subsistere, si nihil aliud obviaret."

40 Ibid., f. 24va: "...secundum genus causae efficientis, quicquid potest deus mediante creatura, potest non mediante illa...." Cf. f. 24vb: "et quod dictum est de causa efficiente veritatem habet de causa finali...."

41 Ibid., f.24vb: "Sic etiam in causa formali dicere possumus, prout deus est causa formalis rerum. Est autem deus forma exemplaris rerum et non inhaerens...."

42 Ibid., f.24vb: "...Est enim una creatura respectu alterius in duplici genere causae secundum quod genus causae deus nullius est causa, videlicet in genere causae materialis et formalis inhaerentis; sive loquamur de materia ex qua sive in qua deus nullius est materia...."

43 Ibid., f.25ra: "...si nihil aliud obviat quod accidens non posset esse sine subiecto, nisi quia subiectum est causa efficiens accidentis, inquantum accidens oritur ex principiis subiecti et per subiectum reservatur in esse ... si potest Deus mediante subiecto, conservare accidens in esse, poterit ipsum sine subiecto conservare ...

Giles followed Aquinas's approach but used his own terminology. He claimed that *inesse* is a mode of being that naturally pertains to accidents; but — barring further objections — some accidents (viz., quantity) can by Divine power have the mode of being that pertains to substance.[44] Rather what pertains to accidents, as opposed to substance, by their very nature is the aptitude for inhering. If God miraculously conserves it in existence without a subject, so that it does not actually inhere, the aptitude for inherence nevertheless remains.[45]

---

sic naturaliter accidens conservatur in esse a deo mediante subiecto, cum quicquid effectivitatis est in subiecto, totum reservetur in deo. Si ergo nihil aliud obviat, quare accidens sine subiecto esse non possit, nisi quia per subiectum conservatur, poterit deus miraculo, sua virtute conservare accidens in esse sine subiecto, quod naturaliter per subiectum in esse conservat ... virtute divina potest accidens per se subsistere." Cf. *Propositio* XXXVIII, f. 26rb: "Totus ergo difficultas quare quantitas non videtur posse esse sine subiecto sumitur, quia per subiectum conservatur in esse. Si ergo nihil aliud obviat, ut ostensum est, poterit virtute divina, in sacramento altaris quantitas per se esse — quod declarare volebamus...."

44 Ibid., *Propositio* XXXIX, f. 26rb: "contradictionem non implicat accidens sine subiecto esse, ex eo quod subiectum facit ad productionem eius ... nec contra-dictionem implicat, si ponimus accidens absque subiecto esse, ex eo quod subiectum facit ad modum essendi accidentis, ut quia competit accidenti inesse, quia est in subiecto, cum res unius praedicamenti modum alterius possit habere...."

45 Ibid., *Propositio* XLI, f. 28va: "Sciendum ergo quod causa quare accidens absque subiecto non potest intelligi, non proprie sumitur propter ipsum inesse actuali-ter, sed propter ipsam aptitudinem, quam habet accidens, ut subiecto insit...vir-tute divina ablata sit ab eo actualis inhaerentia; tamen quia aptitudo inhaerendi inseparabiliter concomitatur naturam accidentis, cum illud accidens maneat accidens, et non sit amota ab eo natura propria, non est amota ab eo aptitudo inhaerendi...." Cf. f. 28vb: "non competit illi accidenti per naturam suam quod non insit, sed per miraculum quantum est de natura sua semper est aptum natum inesse...." "Cum ergo accidens non possit intelligi sine subiecto propter aptitudinem, quam habet, ut insit.... Aliud enim est cognoscere de re quid est; aliud est cognoscere ipsam esse, de substantiis enim separatis scimus, quia sunt; quid autem sunt, scire non possumus...." & "Cum ergo natura et quiditas sint obiectum intellectus, intelligere accidens est intelligere naturam et quiditatem accidentis; si aptitudo inhaerendi concomitatur ipsam naturam et quiditatem et

5. Eucharistic Species and Their Causal Interactions

Turning to the physical cum metaphysical problems in accounting for the changes observed in the consecrated host, Giles appealed to his layer-like analysis of the structure of bodies. Given that the qualities inhere immediately in quantity, quantity functions as the matter and quality the form in alteration.[46] Similarly, his distinction between indeterminate and dimensive quantities allowed him to locate the former as the subject of changes of the latter in condensation and rarefaction.[47] Likewise for diminution, which occurs when the host is divided into parts that do not have the same determinate dimensions as the whole had (Ibid., f. 31va-32rb). Because the theological tag that the Body of Christ remains so long as the species remain was construed by Giles to mean "as long as the indeterminate quantity remains," he could easily explain how real presence persists through alteration and changes of dimensive quantity. As for generation and corruption, Giles tried to make Aquinas's claim — that they occur naturally without further miracle, because quantity receives the power of the substance

---

sublata actuali inhaerentia ab accidente, non tollatur aptitudo inhaerendi, non poterit intelligi quiditas accidentis, et per consequens non poterit intelligi ipsum accidens sine aptitudine inhaerendi, data quod actualiter non insit...."

46 Ibid., *Propositio* XLIII, f. 30rb: "Notandum ergo quod tota causa quare unum accidens non potest esse subiectum alterius accidentis, nisi hoc habeat virtute materia, quae ponitur esse primum subiectum, et etiam tota causa, quare omnis transmutatio praesupponit materiam, sumitur ex eo quod accidentia absque materia in esse conservari non possunt.... Poterit ergo quantitas, si potest habere per se esse, sine materia ab una qualitate in aliam transmutari et esse subiectum diversarum qualitatum sine materia...." Cf. f. 30vb: "...materia dicit quid in potentia et habet rationem subiicibilis, forma vero dicit quid in actu et habet rationem activi ... sed quantitas quae habet rationem subiecti magis se tenet ex parte materiae; qualitas vero, quae habet rationem activi, magis se tenet ex parte formae...."

47 Ibid., *Propositio* XLIV, f. 30vb: "Non augmentata Corporis Christi substantia, circa sacramentum altaris per rarefactionem et condensationem contingere poterit motus augmenti, quia dimensiones indeterminatae determinatis dimensionibus sunt subiectae."

Marilyn McCord Adams

along with its mode of existence — plausible by producing an analogy with the generation of animals. In particular, Giles contended that a thing can act by the power of the substance apart from real conjunction with it. For just as the semen of the lion acts by the power of the substance to produce the embryo lion even though the substantial form of lion does not inhere in it; so the accidents of the bread act by the power of the substance even though they do not inhere in it (Ibid., *Propositiones* XLV, f. 33rb-34rb, & XLVIII, f. 36vb-37ra).

IV John Duns Scotus: New Philosophical Perspectives

For Scotus, too, the theology of the Euchrarist involved a complex interaction among doctrine, empirical evidence, and philosophical (both metaphysical and physical) theory. A faithful son of the Church, Scotus felt bound to the truth of explicit statements in Scripture and Church pronouncements, and to their evident entailments. But he also agreed that "miracles should not be multiplied beyond necessity." One should not opt for intellectually problematic construals where straightforward interpretations of doctrinal tenets are available, because this creates obstacles to Faith for philosophers as for all those committed to a life of reason.[48] Not surprising, then, if Scotus's alternative philosophical convictions should have issued in fresh theological assessments.

1. Becoming Present

Reasserting theological consensus that the real presence of the Body and Blood of Christ on the altar under forms of bread and wine is the doctrinal tenet fundamentally at stake (Ibid., d.10, q.1, nn.3-4; Wadding 8, 488). Scotus agreed that transubstantiation — the change of one whole substance (which is one per se) into another (which is one per se), without any persistent common metaphysical constituent (Ibid.,

---

48 John Duns Scotus [1], *Op.Ox.* IV, d.11, q.3, n.5; Wadding 8, 606; cf. nn.14-15; Wadding 8, 618.

d.11, q.1, n.2; Wadding 8, 586) — is metaphysically possible. For substance can be annihilated and so cease to be without remainder, and substance can be created with all of its parts new (Ibid., d.11, q.1, n.4; Wadding 8, 587). Likewise, Scotus concurred, transubstantiation is not an Aristotelian change (Ibid., d.11, q.1, n.10; Wadding 8, 590), but one possible only by Divine power, which alone can bring a whole from non-being into being, and vice versa (Ibid., d.11, q.1, n.4; Wadding 8, 587). It follows that only those things whose being and non-being are totally subordinate to Divine power, can be the terms of such conversion, and hence that any creature can be thus converted into any other (Ibid., d.11, q.2, n.3; Wadding 8, 597), but Divinity neither converted nor converted into (Ibid., d.11, q.2, n.3; Wadding 8, 597).

Nevertheless, Scotus rejected Aquinas's contention that transubstantiation is the only philosophically viable theory that can explain eucharistic real presence. (i) First and decisively, transubstantiation as Aquinas understands it is not sufficient to account for real presence. (a) For, according to him, the term of sacramental conversion is the substance of the Body of Christ, not its presence on the altar. Since the substance is naturally prior to its presence, to explain the former is not thereby to account for the latter (Ibid., d.10, q.1, n.6; Wadding 8, 498). (b) Even if one did allow that conversion of substance could spill over to account for accidents in the term of change, Scotus found Aquinas's application of this idea far-fetched. If A is converted into B, wouldn't it be more natural to suppose that the condition of A was converted into the condition of B as well, rather than that A is converted to B in such a way that the conditions of A pertain to B (Ibid., d.10, q.1, n.8; Wadding 8, 499)? (c) Again, if the quantity of the bread were converted into the quantity of the Body of Christ, the Body of Christ would not thereby have the location that the bread had circumscriptively (so that the whole was present to the whole place and the parts to the parts of place). Therefore, why would the Body of Christ thereby be present where bread was present definitively (Ibid.)?

(ii) Moreover, contrary to Aquinas, it is not necessary to 'flee' to transubstantiation to explain real presence either (Ibid., d.10, q.1, n.9; Wadding 8, 501). Scotus agreed that 'The Body of Christ is here' and 'The Body of Christ is not here' could not be true successively apart from any real change (Ibid.). Distinguishing between acquiring and losing a place, he envisioned three scenarios: (a) when a moving body expels another, there are four changes (each loses a place and each acquires a new place); (b) when a moving body does not expel another (as in the case of Christ's glorified body which walks through doors, etc.), there are two changes (the Body of Christ loses a place and acquires a new place, but the doors stay put); (c) when a body acquires a new place without either expelling another body or losing its old place, there is one change (Ibid.). But how, apart from Aquinas's sacramental conversion, could any real change be involved in this last case?

Scotus's answer explicitly appealed to his theory of relations. Drawing on his distinction between intrinsic and extrinsic relations (where the existence of the relata is sufficient for the former, but not the latter), he maintained that being present is just being the foundation/term of extrinsic relations of presence; being newly present, being newly the foundation/term thereof apart from any other change. Consequently, God can make the Body of Christ to be newly present on the altar(s) by bringing about a new relation of presence, quite apart from any conversion of one substance into another (Ibid., d.10, q.1, n.8; Wadding 8, 499). Theologically, Scotus seems to have operated within the ground-rule that the glorified Body of Christ is impassible and so undergoes no change at all in sacramental conversion. In one passage, Scotus hesitated to say that the real presence involves a '*novus respectus*' in the Body of Christ.[49] On balance, he seems to have decided in favor of recognizing a new relation both in the species to the Body of Christ and in the Body of Christ to the

---

49 Ibid., d.10, q.1 n.2; Wadding 8, 502: "Necesse est ponere saltem aliquam respectum extrinsecum advenientem, qui scilicet non necessario sequatur fundamentum et terminum posita in actu quia omnis respectus, sic consequens necessario est intrinsecus adveniens...ergo respectus potest advenire extrinsecus de novo, sine alio quocunque novo, vel in fundamento vel in termino. Sic ergo non est inconveniens Corpus Christi esse de novo praesens alicui non habenti novam formam absolutam, nec novum respectum respectu eius, vel si habet huiusmodi novum respectum, pari ratione, et Corpus Christi habebit novum respectum eius...."

species. Should there be philosophical scruples about calling a mere change in relatives (*respectus*) a *mutatio*, Scotus refused the linguistic quibble, but insisted that the new extrinsic relations are sufficient ground in reality to allow "The Body of Christ is not here" to be first true and then false (Ibid., d.10, q.1, n.17; Wadding 8, 506).

2. The Manner of Presence

Turning to analyze real eucharistic presence in more detail, Scotus took over Giles's distinction between position which is a differentia of quantity (the order of parts to one another and to their whole) and categorial position (the order of the parts of a body to the parts of place, which accounts for a body's containment in place). To convince us of their logical independence, Scotus invites us to agree that God could make a quantified body (whose parts were ordered to one another and to their whole) outside the universe and hence not contained in any Aristotelian place (Ibid., d.10, q.1, n.14; Wadding 8, 505). Again, Scotus maintained, if a nature is contingently related to the forms of a genus taken one by one, it is contingently related to the whole genus. But the fact of locomotion shows that bodies are contingently related to each categorial position. Concluding that they are contingently related to categorial position, he found it perfectly intelligible that the whole should bear an external relation of coexistence with the whole of a place, without its parts bearing such external relations to the parts of the place (but not without any of the intrinsic relations between the parts of the body and the parts of the place) (Ibid., d.10, q.1, n.16; Wadding 8, 506). Thus, the parts of the Body of Christ are not present on the altar, each by their own extrinsic relation of presence, but rather they are present by a single relation of presence that is founded on their whole.[50]

---

50 Ibid., d.10, q.1, n.17; Wadding 8, 506: "totum quantum habens eodem modo suas partes extra se invicem in toto, potest habere unicam praesentiam sui et omnium

Marilyn McCord Adams

Aquinas and Giles of Rome had combined the doctrine of real presence with the metaphysical axiom that a single body cannot have categorial position in two places at once, to conclude that the Body of Christ must be present on the altar(s) in some special way. Scotus inverted the thought process: the doctrine of real presence provokes reflection on the nature of body that issues in his rejection of the bi-location 'axiom.'[51] Given the premiss of Divine omnipotence (Ibid., d.10, q.2, n.5; Wadding 8, 511), Scotus mounted two 'a fortiori' arguments. (a) First, he insisted, there is no less difficulty involved in two bodies existing in one place simultaneously than one in two. In either case, the obstacle would seem to be the notion that a body occupies place through a mutual commensuration of their parts, so that the capacity of body to be present to place, and of the place to body are both exhausted. But, Scotus observes, doctrine requires us to affirm the former (in the cases of the virgin birth and the risen Christ's walking through doors). So the latter must be possible by Divine power as well. (b) Again, wherever God can make a natural substance exist under a mode opposed to its natural mode, God can make it under its natural mode (because the former is miraculous and the latter is not). But God makes the Body of Christ to be present on many altars simultaneously under a mode opposed to its natural mode. Therefore, God can make the Body of Christ (and hence any body) to be present and extended in many places (Ibid., d.10, q.2, n.9; Wadding 8, 512).

(c) Rejecting as childish the objection that bi-location is unimaginable (Ibid., d.10, q.2; Wadding 8, 513), Scotus turned to consider the

---

partium ad aliquod unum extra indivisibile, vel quantumcumque modi cum divisibile, ita quod ibi non est alia praesentia alii parti et alia alii...."

51 Note Scotus's own comment at Ibid., d.10, q.3, n.4; Wadding 8, 528-9: "forte ille qui negant Deum posse facere corpus suum in pluribus locis, aliter quam per conversionem sub sacramento, negarent etiam hoc, nisi quia fides dicit hoc. De modo autem isto essendi, scilicet non quantitative vel non dimensive, vel localiter, non video, si potest fieri idem in pluribus locis non sub modo naturali, quin etiam possit fieri modo naturali, cum in primo sint duo miracula, in secundo tantum unum...."

issue from a metaphysical point of view. Once again, he pointed out that presence to a place is a matter of extrinsic relations. (i) It might be thought that a single thing cannot be the foundation of more than one relation of a given species simultaneously. But nature offers many counter-examples to this where intrinsic relations are concerned: e.g., Socrates's whiteness is simultaneously the foundation of his similarity to Plato and Aristotle and difference from Brownie the donkey and Blackie the dog. Likewise, the same part of a body is simultaneously below, above, behind, and in front of many others. A fortiori, this thesis has no presumptive force where extrinsic relations are concerned (Ibid., d.10, q.2, n.25; Wadding 8, 525-6). (ii) Likewise, the naturally prior is not numerically multiplied because of the multiplication of the naturally posterior. But a body and its dimensions are naturally prior to their accidental and contingent extrinsic relation to place (Ibid., d.10, q.2, n.11; Wadding 8, 513; cf. n.12; Wadding 8, 514). Thus, Scotus saw no positive metaphysical reason why we should suppose that the capacity for extrinsic relations of presence, whether of a body (the body's parts) or a place (the parts of place), should be exhausted by mutual relations to a single body (Ibid., d.10, q.2, n.12; Wadding 8, 514).

Scotus filled out his conclusion — that it is "absolutely possible for God to make the same body located in different places simultaneously," inasmuch as such location involves only "a certain extrinsic relation founded on one quantified thing in relation to another quantified thing circumscribing it" (Ibid., d.10, q.2, n.11; Wadding 8, 513) — with several corollaries. First, Scotus insisted, whatever is essentially prior to location in place, exists in the body uniformly and not varied in different places (Ibid., d.10, q.2, n.13; Wadding 8, 518). Likewise, its active and passive causal powers remain the same. Thus, a patient existing in two places and relevantly close to one active cause in each will be affected the same way as if it existed in a single place and were relevantly close to both active causes there. For example, if water existed simultaneously in London and Rome and were close to a cooling agent in London and a heating agent in Rome, its resultant temperature would be the same as if both cooling and heating agents were relevantly close to it in London. Likewise, an agent existing in two places and relevantly close to an appropriate patient in each, will produce the same effects as if it were located in a single place and both patients were present there (Ibid., d.10, q.2, n.13; Wadding 8, 518). Scotus used the latter against a series of bogus counter-examples, intended to show that bi-location would produce insuperable problems for physics (Ibid., d.10, q.2, n.16-17; Wadding 8, 519-20; cf. n.22; Wadding 8, 524). He also conceded the un-Aristotelian sounding conclusion that God could make the Body of Christ to be present everywhere simultaneously, once again, through extrinsic relations of presence (Ibid., d.10, q.2, n.14; Wadding 8, 519).

Aquinas had explained that only the Body of Christ is present "by the power of the sacrament," whereas the quantity, soul, and Divinity of Christ are there by natural concomitance, on the ground that only the substance of the Body of Christ is the term of the conversion. Scotus recognized the distinction: "something pertains to Christ insofar as it is here, which would pertain to it even if it were nowhere other than here," while "something pertains to it here concomitantly, that pertains to it primarily insofar as it is elsewhere and pertains to it as here only because of the identity of subject and form."[52] But he denied that the mere fact that quantity is not the primary term of the change would be enough to sort it among the merely concomitant features and so to keep it (from Aquinas's point of view) out of metaphysical harm's way. For, according to Aquinas, quantity is one of those accidents necessarily consequent upon corporeal nature, and so will accompany a body wherever it goes. Aquinas should have used Giles's distinction between two sorts of position to explain how the quantity can be really present without being extended on the altar(s).

For his own part, Scotus maintained that of itself the Body of Christ is really indifferent as between the sacramental and natural modes of existence, i.e., as to whether it has or lacks categorial position in the

---

52 Ibid., d.10, q.5; Wadding 8, 547: "Respondeo primo, dicitur aliquid inesse Christo, ut hic, quod sibi inesset, si nusquam alibi esset nisi hic, concomitanter autem dicitur aliquid sibi inesse hic, quod primo inest sibi, ut alibi, et ex hoc sibi inest, ut hic propter identitatem subiecti et formae."

place to which it is present. For God can cause it to exist without anything that does not pertain to it essentially, and categorial position pertains to body accidentally and contingently (Ibid., d.10, q.4, n.4; Wadding 8, 533). Thus, it is logically possible that Christ's Body be sacramentally present somewhere and yet naturally present nowhere (e.g., before the Incarnation, or if He had ceased to exist in the natural way after the Incarnation) (Ibid., d.10, q.4, n.5; Wadding 8, 533). Again, God could make the Body of Christ to be sacramentally present, without any of the absolute forms to which it is conjoined (e.g., intellectual soul, body, quantity) being thus present (Ibid., d.10, q.4, n.14; Wadding 8, 542). For this would merely be a question of these absolute forms not being included in the whole related by an extrinsic relation of presence to the relevant place.

3. The Fact of Transubstantiation?

Granted that the theory of transubstantiation is aetiologically irrelevant to eucharistic real presence, does authority nevertheless require that it be held as a fact? Scotus denies any cogency to Aquinas's arguments (see section II above) for the affirmative. Dismissing the grammatical argument from Scripture — that the truth of '*Hoc est corpus meum*' requires the absence of bread for pronoun agreement and demonstrative clarity — as a red herring, Scotus notes that grammatically '*hoc*' could refer to *hoc accidens* as much as to *hoc corpus*; yet everyone agrees that the accidents remain (Ibid., d.11, q.3, n.10; Wadding 8, 609). Besides, other Scriptural passages favor the presence of the bread: e.g., "*Ego sum panis vivus*" (John 6:35) and "*Panis, quem frangimus, nonne communicatio corporis Christi est?*" (I Cor 10:16). As to the putative incongruities, he observes that if the remaining accidents do not turn eucharistic adoration into idolatry, the presence of the bread wouldn't either (Ibid., d.11, q.3, n.9; Wadding 8, 608). Again, the real tension with fasting regulations arises from experience: everyone knows that people are nourished by consecrated hosts, whatever the correct theory of real presence may be (Ibid., d.11, q.3, nn.9-10; Wadding 8, 608).

Nevertheless, Scotus did let authority decide the issue in favor of transubstantiation. Not the authority of Scripture, but of a conciliar

Marilyn McCord Adams

document — Innocent III's pronouncement in the Fourth Lateran Council — which none of Scotus's eminent predecessors had taken as decisive.[53] His methodological comment reflects a high doctrine of ecclesiastical authority, and belies cynicism about medieval hermeneutics and the malleability of authority's wax nose:

> Suppose you ask why the Church wished to choose such a difficult interpretation of this article [of Faith], when the words of Scripture can be preserved by an interpretation of this article that is easier to understand and that has a greater appearance of truth.
> I reply that the Scriptures are expounded by the Spirit by which they were created. Thus, we must suppose that the Church catholic expounded them by the very spirit by which the Faith was handed down to us — viz., the Spirit of Truth — and thus led chose this interpretation, because it is true. For it was not within the power of the Church to make this true or not true, but within the power of God who instituted [the sacrament]. Rather, as we believe, led by the Spirit of Truth, the Church made explicit the interpretation handed down to it by God.[54]

4. The 'How' of Transubstantiation

According to Scotus, Giles's detailed accounts of how transubstantiation occurs, fail the test of philosophical coherence by jumbling the explanatory priorities and posteriorities. The issue becomes clearer if we borrow Scotus's apparatus of instants of nature. Matter consid-

---

53 Ibid., d.11,q.3, n.15; Wadding 8, 618-19: "dicendum quod Ecclesia declaravit istum intellectum esse de veritate fidei in illo Symbolo edito sub Innocent III in Concilio Lateranensi. Firmiter credimus etc. sicut allegatum est superius; ubi explicite ponitur veritas aliquorum credendorum, magis explicite quam habebatur in Symbolo Apostolorum, vel Athanasii, vel Niceni. Et breviter, quidquid ibi dicitur esse credendum, tenendum est esse de substantia fidei, et hoc post istam declarationem solemnem factam ab Ecclesia." Cf. James H. McCue, 'The Doctrine of Transubstantiation from Berengar through Trent: The Point at Issue,' *Harvard Theological Review* 61 (1968) 385-430. Curiously, in treating the doctrine of the Trinity, Scotus once again over-interprets Lateran IV, as requiring the tenet 'tres res sunt una res,' when the document speaks of 'alia et alia persona,' not 'alia et alia res.'

54 John Duns Scotus [1], Op.Ox. IV, d.11,q.3, n.15; Wadding 8, 619

ered in itself and prior to the inherence of nature would be dated at n1; matter considered insofar as indeterminate quantity inheres in it at n2; insofar as determinate quantity inheres in indeterminate quantity and extends it, at n3; etc. Giles's mistake was to attribute to matter at n1 features it acquires only at later instants of nature. (a) Thus, when Giles said that God converts the matter of the bread into the matter of the Body of Christ, by acting on the matter considered as it is prior to individuation, he located the action at n1. When — in the interests of giving substance to the *'ex pane'* — Giles described the action as converting this matter (i.e., that of the bread) to that (viz., that of the Body of Christ), he re-located the conversion at n2. Scotus mounted reductios to the effect that Giles can't have it both ways (Ibid., d.11, q.3, n.17; Wadding 8, 620; cf. n.20; Wadding 8, 620). (b) Again, Giles's unitarian attempt to identify the term of conversion with organized matter assigned matter 'organized' features that it has only at n2 and possibly n3, while considering matter apart from the forms which inhere in it to produce these features, i.e., as it is at n1.[55] Scotus reckoned unitarian inability to identify an adequate term of transubstantiation, among the arguments in favor of pluralism regarding substantial forms (Ibid., d.11, q.3, nn.31-2; Wadding 8, 632).

Beyond these concerns, Scotus thought the strength of Giles's strategy — of connecting the bread and Christ's Body via the matter — was its weakness. On the one hand, it makes transubstantiation seem too much like generation (Ibid., d.11, q.3, n.20; Wadding 8, 621). Again, Giles's explanation — that the bread is not annihilated, because its form remains in the potency of the matter — would imply the impossibility of God's annihilating any corruptible substance, without annihilating every other corruptible substance; for the matter of any corruptible substance is in potency with respect to any sub-

---

55 Ibid., d.11, q.3, n.29; Wadding 8, 631. Indeed, given Aquinas's and Giles's views about individuation, this is not the only priority paradox generated by unitarianism: for substantial form inheres in individuated matter, and individuation depends on the inherence of indeterminate quantity; so the inherence of substantial form must be both posterior to that of quantity, and prior to it, inasmuch as accidents are naturally posterior to substance.

Marilyn McCord Adams

stantial form it could naturally acquire (Ibid., d.11, q.4, n.5; Wadding 8, 659).

For Scotus, Divine action is what links the two terms. The bread ceases to exist altogether, yet is not annihilated but converted into the Body of Christ, which acquires no new substantial *esse* but only *esse hic* (in the manner described in sections IV.1 and IV.2 above) (Ibid., d.11, q.4, n.8; Wadding 8, 661-2).

5. The Ontological Status of Accidents

Scotus's novel response to general arguments that *inesse* is essential to accidents, was that such a conclusion would destroy the Philosopher's own distinction between absolute and relative accidents (i.e., quantity and quality, as opposed to all the others) (Ibid., d.12, q.1, n.10; Wadding 8, 717-18). *Inesse* is not a proper *passio* of accident (Ibid., d.12, q.1, n.21; Wadding 8, 723). Following Giles, Scotus distinguished between aptitudinal and actual inherence, and identified the former as the essential feature (Ibid., d.12, q.1, n.7; Wadding 8, 711). Eschewing worries about material causality, Scotus insisted that in the natural order of things accidents depend on their subjects only as external, efficient causes of their continued existence (Ibid., d.12, q.1, n.9; Wadding 8, 717). Aristotle's comments about necessary dependence reflected his belief (not shared by Christians) that the natural order of causes is necessary (Ibid., d.12, q.1; Wadding 8, 717-18; cf. n.15; Wadding 8, 720). In fact, however, God can supply the efficient causal power of the subject and conserve the accidents in existence all by Himself (Ibid., d.12, q.1; Wadding 8, 717-18; n.15; Wadding 8, 720).

Scotus's own view that individuation is not through quantity but a non-categorial positive entity ('*haecceitas*') freed him to reconsider the metaphysical possibilities for independence among accidents of different kinds. Acknowledging the common layer-like view of bodies, Scotus distinguished the proximate from the ultimate subject of inherence, where the latter role is restricted to substance but the former taken by one accident in relation to another (Ibid., d.12, q.2, n.15; Wadding 8, 733). Once again, the division between absolute and relative accidents is key. Any accident can exist without its ultimate subject by Divine power, but no relative can exist without inhering in its proximate subject (because relatives by definition must have terms) (Ibid., d.12, q.2, n.14; Wadding 8, 713). As for absolute accidents, Scotus argued that existence without inherence is as possible for quality as for quantity. (a) In a series, dependence on the first is more essential than dependence on what is posterior. But according to Aquinas and Giles, quantity depends on substance, the first subject, whereas quality depends on quantity. Therefore, dependence on a subject seems more essential to quantity than to quality (Ibid., d.12, q.2, n.9; Wadding 8, 731). (b) Again, Scotus correlated the capacity for actual non-inherence with ontological perfection. But quantity seems not to enjoy a general ontological superiority over accidents. For instance, spiritual qualities can belong to nobler substances than quantity can belong to (Ibid., d.12, q.2, nn.9-11; Wadding 8, 731). Nor is quantity more like substance than quality. Rather substance has two aspects — the subject role, and the agent role; quantity (as inactive) is more like substance the first way, whereas qualities resemble it more the second way (Ibid., d.12, q. 2, n.12; Wadding 8, 732).

Venturesome in mapping the metaphysical possibilities, Scotus was indecisive about what happens in fact. On the one hand, he cited the common opinion — exemplified by Aquinas and Giles — according to which "quantity is an absolute essence distinct from the essence of corporeal substance and quality" and quantity exists in the Eucharist without any proximate subject, while qualities exist in quantity as a proximate subject (Ibid., d.12, q.2, n.15; Wadding 8, 733). On the other hand, he noted the unusual view (perhaps held by Godfrey of Fontaines among his predecessors and championed among his successors by William Ockham) that "the quantity of corporeal substance is nothing other than the essence of that substance, and the quantity of color is nothing other than the color, etc." According to it, "quality here [i.e., in the Eucharist] is not in quantity, but rather is quantity," i.e., "the quantity of the quality" (Ibid., d.12, q.2, n.15; Wadding 8, 734).

6. The Accidents of the Bread and their Causal Interactions

Scotus joined the consensus that the accidents of the bread have all the active causal powers they had before, but rejected Aquinas's interpretation of it — that the accidents remain the instrumental causes of substance because God transfers to the species the *virtus* by which the substance acted — as multiply confused. (a) First, Scotus pressed the metaphysics of this *virtus*-transfer: Is the *virtus* something absolute, or relative? No substantial absolute, because the substance of bread exists no longer. No accident, because one accident could not confer on others the causal power they lacked by virtue of being accidents (Ibid., d.12, q.3, n.5; Wadding 8, 741). Were Aquinas to reply that the *virtus* of the substance is to be identified with its *esse*, and that very *esse* in which the species shared prior to consecration is the one preserved in them after consecration, Scotus would have responded with his battery of arguments against Aquinas's real distinction between *esse* and *essence*. For Scotus, the *esse* of the accidents is really identical with them, before, during, and after the consecration; it is metaphysically impossible for them to share in the esse of substance in the required way. Nor will Giles's analogy with animal reproduction — that we say the semen acts by the power of the substance, even though there is no metaphysical conjunction involved — suffice. For either 'by the power of the substance' requires to be parsed in one of the excluded ways, or it is merely an improper way of speaking. (b) Again, how could the eucharistic species continue to be instrumental causes of substance, when the substance no longer exists (Ibid., d.12, q.3, n.6; Wadding 8, 741-2)?

Scotus's own opinion was that the accidents never were instrumental causes, but always had active causal powers of their own. Distinguishing three categories of action — (i) the generation of substances, (ii) the production of accidents in intentional *esse* in sensation, and (iii) the production of accidents in real existence in a patient that has contrary accidents — Scotus insisted that their powers in categories (ii) and (iii) are unaffected by the absence of the bread. As for (i), on the other hand, Scotus insisted, the accidents never had sufficient causal power to generate substance. The reason is that that amount of causal power is criterial for ontological perfection,[56] and accidents

---

56 Ibid., d.12, q.3, n. 16; Wadding 8, 745: "nescirem probare aliquem ordinem entium, imo nec quod primum ens esset perfectissimum."

are ontologically inferior to substance. Accidents do alter substances to prepare the way for substantial change. But the power of substantial form to resist corruption is greater than that of any accident to produce a (higher degree of) a contrary quality, so that there is no degree of alteration at which the corruption of the substantial form of the altered object necessarily follows (Ibid., d.12, q.3, nn.23-5; Wadding 8, 751).

Experience shows that the consecrated host not only acts, but is acted upon. Here Scotus adhered to the fundamental principle of Aristotelian physics, that natural change requires a patient to be acted upon and to persist through the change, for the underlying reason that natural efficient causes require the concurrence of the passive power of the matter to receive forms (Ibid., d.12, q.4, n.23; Wadding 8, 768). The theoretical options, therefore, are to identify subjects for the observed changes, or to declare them miraculous. The latter will have to be embraced, for qualitative changes if qualities do not inhere in quantity, and for condensation and rarefaction if this involves the production of new quantities (Ibid., d.12, a.4, nn.19-20; Wadding 8, 766). Likewise, miraculous is the presence of substance (e.g., of worms or ashes) when the species cease to exist (Ibid., d.12, q.6, n.14-15; Wadding 8, 782-3). Scotus met theological scruples against multiplying miracles in the Eucharist beyond those signified in the formula of consecration itself, with the suggestion that all such supernatural changes are covered by the original Divine decree according to which (i) the substance of the bread ceases to exist, but (ii) the accidents change in ways phenomenologically indistinguishable from those that would have occurred had the substance of the bread remained, and (iii) the Body of Christ comes to be and remains present under the original accidents but also any replacements associated with such changes (Ibid., d.12, q.4, n.21; Wadding 8, 767).

V William of Ockham on the Sacrament of the Altar:
Further Philosophical Surprises

Ockham, too, recognized that although the doctrine of real presence and its approved interpretation in terms of transubstantiation cannot be established by natural reason;[57] nevertheless, the articulation of these claims pertains as much to philosophy as to theology, requires an understanding of Aristotle as much as of Scripture, the Fathers, and the determinations of the Church.[58]

1. The Placement Problem Revisited

Ockham was perhaps most critical of his predecessor's accounts of the relation of the Body of Christ, really present in the Eucharist, to place.

a. Critique of Aquinas. Following Scotus, Ockham rejects Aquinas's conclusion that sacramental conversion is the only possible explanation of the presence of the Body of Christ on the altar. (i) Mounting a new argument that it is not necessary, Ockham reasoned that what God can conserve, bracketing anything else, He can also produce without anything else. But God can conserve the Body of Christ under the species without the substance of the bread. Therefore, He could make the Body of Christ to be there even if the substance of the bread had never been there and so had never been converted.[59] (ii) Nor would such sacramental conversion be sufficient apart from any other change in the Body of Christ. For a body cannot be in a new place where it didn't exist before without changing place. Likewise, relations are distinct if their foundations and/or terms are distinct. Thus, the Body of Christ will be the foundation of a presence-relation distinct from that founded on the bread (Ibid.; OTh VII, 63-4). (iii)

---

57 William Ockham [5], *Tractatus de Corpore Christi*, c.3; OTh X, 93

58 William Ockham [6], *Tractatus de Quantitate*, Prologus; OTh X,4.

59 William Ockham [3], *Quaest. in IV Sent.* q.6; OTh VII, 63

Further, Ockham questioned how it is supposed to be that sacramental conversion makes Christ's Body present to place only mediately, by means of the species of the bread. For generally, if F pertains to x primarily, and pertains to y by means of x, this is because of some sort of union between x and y. For example, fire is said to heat, because the quality heat, to which heating activity properly pertains, inheres in fire; and God the Son is said to suffer because of His hypostatic union with Christ's human nature, which suffers properly speaking. But Aquinas upheld the theological consensus which denies any union between the Body of Christ and the accidents of the bread (Ibid.; OTh VII, 64).

b. Quantitative vs. Categorial Position? Equally incomprehensible from Ockham's point of view was the distinction, sponsored by Giles and Scotus, between quantitative and categorial position. Ontologically, they seem to have assumed that place is a container really distinct from a body and its parts, and that relations of order and presence are likewise really distinct relations. Thus, if God made the body without any place-containers (say if it were the only body in creation), it would exist without any relations of presence to really distinct containers, and yet its parts would still bear relations of internal ordering to one another. Analogously, in the world as it is, the whole body could bear a relation of presence to the containing place, without each of the parts having their own individual relations to parts of the container.

Ockham admitted that if places and presence-relations were such *parvae respectus*, God could create, in the world as it is, a body whose parts were internally ordered and yet did not bear any relation to place.[60] But he finds this conclusion absurd, a veritable reductio of such ontological commitments, pitting against it as he does his fundamental intuition that distance between parts necessarily implies location in place. (i) Thus, he admitted, Giles and Scotus are right to remember that Aristotle divides the category of quantity between

---

60   William Ockham [4], *Quodlibeta* IV, q.18; OTh IX, 392-5

those that have and those that lack position. But his paradigms of the former were lines, surfaces, and bodies, all of which have parts at a distance from one another, and have "position somewhere (*situm ... alicubi*)" according to the Philosopher's own words.[61] (ii) Again, what sort of internal order could the parts of body have to one another? Ockham could think of five: (a) situation (above, behind, etc.); (b) perfection; (c) part/whole (e.g., the eye is part of the head); (d) causal (one the cause of another); (e) natural priority or posteriority. The last four sorts are not differentia of the genus of quantity, but the first implies location.[62] (iii) Again, Scotus himself admitted that "this order of parts in the whole cannot exist without the distance of one part from another";[63] likewise, for him, it involves the parts being shaped into organs, so that the Body of Christ remains organic even under the sacrament. But neither of these can be had without relation to place (Ibid.; OTh VII, 68, 70). (iv) Again, where there is order among distant parts, there can be locomotion — which is impossible without relation to place (Ibid.; OTh VII, 69). Zeroing in with a masterful ad hominem, (v) Ockham diagnosed Scotus's positive argument as invalid. For if it follows from the contingency of a body's relation to each position in place, that it is contingently related to categorial position in general, it equally follows from the contingent relation of body to each order of parts to the whole, that body is contingently related to the category of quantity (Ibid.; *OTh* VII, 69-70; *Quodlibeta* IV, q.18; *OTh* IX, 392-3).

c. Ockham on Quantity and Placement. Ockham's own intuitions about sacramental presence were shaped as much by an allegedly Aristotelian view of the ontological status of quantity, as by various Biblical miracles. Working from the 'more reasonable' position that quantity is nothing really distinct from substance and quality — a view which he

---

61 *Quaest. in IV Sent.* q.6; *OTh* VII, 67-8; cf. *Quodlibeta* IV, q.18; *OTh* IX, 392

62 *Quaest. in IV Sent.* q.6; *OTh* VII, 67; *Quodlibeta* IV, q.18; *OTh* IX, 389-90

63 *Quaest. in IV Sent.* q.6; *OTh* VII, 68

recited, attributed to Aristotle, endorsed and then conditionally endorsed, assuming it is not contrary to Ecclesiastical pronouncements — Ockham streamlined the distinction between circumscriptive (being whole in the whole place and part in the parts) and definitive location in place (being whole in the whole place and whole in each part),[64] and claimed that the Body of Christ exists immediately (Ibid.; *OTh* VII, 97) and definitively in the places where the consecrated hosts are.[65] Twin puzzles require clarification here: (i) how can numerically the same body exist as a whole in many places at once? and (ii) how can numerically distinct bodies (parts) exist in the same place simultaneously?[66] He met the first (i) with an argument from analogy. Consensus, both philosophical and theological, admitted that the intellectual soul can be whole in the whole of a place and whole in each of its parts; likewise, that an angel exists definitively in place. Ockham saw no more difficulty in a body's existing whole in the whole place and whole in each of many parts, and hence no greater problem in a single body's existing definitively in many (discontinuous) places at once.[67] Biblical miracles — the virgin birth, the Risen Christ walking through doors and ascending through the unriven heavens[68] — notify us of the possibility of the second (ii). Ockham's understanding of Aristotleian physics — according to which condensation involves existence in the same place of parts of body which were in different places earlier—provided reason to think so. Imitating Aristotle's own inference, Ockham argued that if two parts can exist in the place simultaneously, then any number can; and if that is so of parts, why not also of distinct bodies (Ibid.; *OTh* IX, 452)? Continuing these speculations on the metaphysics of body, Ockham concurred with Scotus that if numerically the same body can

---

64 *Quaest. in IV Sent.*, q.6; *OTh* VII, 65. Cf. Giles's tri-partite distinction in section III.2 above.

65 *Quodlibeta* IV, q.31; *OTh* IX, 451

66 *Quaest. in IV Sent.* q.6; *OTh* VII, 79; cf. *Quodlibeta* IV, q.31; OTh IX, 452

67 *Quaest. in IV Sent.* q.6; *OTh* VII, 79

68 *Quodlibeta* IV, q.31; *OTh* IX 453

exist in many places at once definitively, it is even easier for it to be in multiple locations circumscriptively.[69] As for the paradoxes in physics (e.g., numerically the same water relevantly proximate to a heating agent in Rome but not in London) raised against this inference, Ockham cross-referenced Scotus's reply (see section IV.2 above), but then argued by analogy for a remarkable alternative solution: why should there be any more difficulty in a substance existing in a place where its really inherent accident does not exist, than in the Divine Word's existing in many places (due to Divine omnipresence) where His assumed nature does not? Indeed, "just as the Divine Word is said to be unlimited with respect to place, because the Divine essence is everywhere in itself, by its own power; so corporeal substance is unlimited, because it can exist in many places at once, even everywhere, by the power of God and not by its own power."[70]

Returning to the Body of Christ in the Eucharist, Ockham claimed his theory of 'definitive placement' saves the theologians' tag, that it is not quantified there; a body is quantified on Ockham's theory, when it is circumscriptively in place (Ibid.; *OTh* VII, 80-1; *Quodlibeta* IV, q.31; *OTh* IX, 454. Cf. *Tractatus de Quantitate*, q.iii; *OTh* X, 78-9). Likewise, Ockham thought, his estimates of the possibilities of bi-location easily handle the traditional claim that the Body of Christ exists extended (circumscriptively) in heaven, and (definitively) on many altars simultaneously.[71] But how can his theory allow the Body of Christ to remain differentiated and organic on the altar, if figure requires distance and distance implies extension in place? Ockham bit the bullet, admitting that neither the Body of Christ nor its parts have any shape on the altar. All the same, they retain their differentiation as to material dispositions (accidents and powers still inhere in one part as opposed to another) and so do their causal powers, even

---

69 *Quaest. in IV Sent.*, q.6; *OTh* VII, 97. Cf. *Tractatus de Corpore Christi*, c.7; *OTh* X, 103-5

70 *Quaest. in IV Sent.* q.6; *OTh* VII, 99

71 *Quaest. in IV Sent.* q.6; *OTh* VII, 88; cf. q.8; OTh VII, 147

when they are all located in the same place. For Ockham, the latter is enough to warrant the label 'organic' (Ibid., q.6; *OTh* VII, 89; *Quodlibeta* IV, q.31; *OTh* IX, 453-4). The thrust of his thought experiments should have led him to admit that God could make a corporeal nature exist somewhere definitively without its simultaneously existing anywhere circumscriptively. Conceding this for living bodies would reverse Aristotle's sense of the natural priorities: viz., that the shape and relevant disposition of bodies is naturally prior to the inherence of souls and their consequent powers.

Surprisingly, Ockham's alternative metaphysics of quantity with his consequent denial that the remaining bread qualities inhere in really distinct quantity, were opposed as doctrinally out of bounds — a fact that prompted Ockham's (surely correct) protest that neither the Bible, nor the Fathers, nor any Ecclesiastical document had made the more common philosophy of body religiously obligatory.[72]

2. Present by Transubstantiation?

Focusing on the sacrament of the altar, Ockham defined transubstantiation as the change in which one substance, *a*, succeeds another substance, *b*, where *b* ceases to exist simpliciter and *a* comes to exist under the accidents that belonged to *b*.[73] Like Scotus, he commented on its obvious metaphysical possibility: "for it is not incompatible with Divine power to destroy a substance in itself and to conserve its accidents, and [to bring it about] that [another] substance immediately coexist with those accidents without their informing it."[74] As to

---

72 William Ockham [6], *Tractatus de Quantitate*, q.iii; *OTh* X, 65, 70-71; and William Ockham [5], *Tractatus de Corpore Christi*, cc. 1-2; *OTh* X, 89-92.

73 William Ockham [3], *Quaest. in IV Sent.* q.8; *OTh* VII, 136: "successio substantiae ad substantiam desinentem esse simpliciter in se, sub aliquibus accidentibus propriis substantiae praecedenti...."

74 Ibid.; *OTh* VII, 136-37: "Possibilitas istius apparet, quia non repugnat potentiae divinae destruere substantiam in se et conservare accidentia et quod substantia eisdem accidentibus non eam informantibus immediate coexistat."

what in fact happens in the Eucharist, Ockham agreed with Scotus that the theory of transubstantiation has one serious competitor: viz., consubstantiation, according to which the substance of the bread remains. Not bothering to cite arguments pro and contra, Ockham simply declares that consubstantiation is not contrary to the Bible.[75] Moreover, he insisted, it is more reasonable from a philosophical point of view. For "of all the difficulties that are supposed to follow from this sacrament, the greatest is that an accident exist without its subject";[76] whereas consubstantiation "saves and avoids" all such difficulties.[77] Nevertheless, Ockham recognized unanimity of theological opinion against it, and joined Scotus in reading Lateran IV as determining in favor of transubstantiation,[78] obviously sympathetic to the premiss of the objector who writes:

> A plurality of miracles should not be posited without necessity.
> But there is no necessity for positing that the substance does not remain, since the Body of Christ can be present there sacramentally just as well whether the substance of the bread remains or not.
> Therefore, etc.[79]

Ockham replied, in effect, that it does not always please God to follow 'Ockham's Razor.' Apparently, it was revealed to the Church that the

---

75 Ibid.; *OTh* VII, 139; cf. William Ockham [4], *Quodlibeta* IV, q.30; *OTh* IX, 450. Cf. *Tractatus de Corpore Christi*, c.6; *OTh* X, 99-101.

76 *Quaest. in IV Sent.* q.8; *OTh* VII, 139: "est rationabilior et facilior ad tenendum inter omnes modos, quia pauciora inconvenientia sequuntur ex eo quam ex aliquo alio modo. Quod patet, quia inter omnia inconvenientia quae ponuntur sequi ex isto sacramento, maius est quod accidens sit sine subiecto...."

77 *Quodlibeta* IV, q.30; *OTh* IX, 450

78 *Quaest. in IV Sent.*, q.8; *OTh* VII, 139; cf. *Quodlibeta* IV, q.30; *OTh* IX, 450.

79 *Quodlibeta* IV, q.30; *OTh* VIII, 448-9: "pluralitas miraculorum non est ponenda sine necessitate, sed non est necessitas ponere illam substantiam non manere, cum aequaliter potest corpus Christi ibi esse praesens sacramentaliter, manente substantia panis sicut ipsa non manente; igitur etc."

Eucharist is another case where God chooses to do with more what could be done with fewer.[80]

If transubstantiation is God's method, what are the terms of this change? Aquinas had claimed they were the substance of the bread and the Body of Christ, and insisted that the latter undergoes no change in the conversion, but only the former. Ockham rejected both suggestions. First, the primary terms of any change must be incompossible, whereas the substances are not. Rather, so far as the bread is concerned, the terms are *esse* and *non esse*; for Christ's Body, *non esse hic* and *esse hic*. Thus (as noted in section V.1 above) the Body of Christ changes place, not by losing any but by acquiring a new one.[81] For Ockham, it was a merely verbal issue, whether one says that the bread is annihilated because reduced to *purum nihil*, or not annihilated because its ceasing happens in a context that otherwise conforms to the definition of 'transubstantiation' (Ibid.; *OTh* VII, 148).

Aquinas had maintained that only the first and proper term of transubstantiation was present "by the power of the sacrament," whereas what is really united with that first term is present "by natural concomitance" only. Ockham responded that this distinction can be rendered well or badly. Badly, on analogy with that between the house which is the formal term of building and its whiteness which is a term per accidens. On the contrary, Ockham thought, there is a numerically distinct transubstantiation for every really distinct thing which is united in Christ to make something one per se. Consequently, before the death and after the resurrection of Christ, the soul is the per se term of its own transubstantiation. But during the triduum, when the soul of Christ was separated from His Body, it would not have been present on the altar at all (Ibid.; *OTh* VII, 140-1). Rather, the first term of transubstantiation is the one primarily intended by the agent of transubstantiation, the one such that if it were

---

80 Ibid.; *OTh* IX, 450: "aliquando ponenda sunt plura miracula circa aliquid ubi posset fieri per pauciora, et hoc placet Deo. Et hoc constat Ecclesiae per aliquam revelationem, ut suppono; ideo sic determinavit."

81 *Quaest. in IV Sent.* q.8; *OTh* VII, 141-2, 145

present and separated from everything else, transubstantiation would still occur. Thus, the Body of Christ is the first term of transubstantiation, because God intends to convert the substance of the bread into the Body of Christ, and transubstantiation would occur even if the Body were present and the soul was not, but not vice versa.[82]

3. Separate Accidents

After identifying separate accidents as the biggest philosophical disadvantage of transubstantiation, Ockham gave the topic short shrift. He did not bother to rehearse, much less to reply to the now-familiar arguments that *inesse* is essential to accidents generally. Although he doubtless presupposes it, I have found no explicit mention of the distinction between aptitudinal and actual inherence. Ignoring worries about material causality, he adopted without fanfare the solution that the subject is only a secondary efficient cause of the conservation of its accidents, and what God does with it, He can do without it, all by Himself.[83]

Ockham's interest perks up when it comes to putative differences in accidents so far as the metaphysical possibility of 'separate' existence is concerned. Following Scotus, Ockham recognizes no difference between quality and quantity on this score. For quantity is not really distinct from substance and quality. Thus, the quantity that is really the same as a quality can exist without a subject if and only if the quality whose quantity it is can (Ibid.; *OTh* VII, 153). For those who insist that quantity is a thing really distinct from substance and quality, Scotus's arguments (in section IV.5 above) should convince. Rejecting putative counter-examples to these general conclusions, Ockham found no impossibility in God's making acts of understanding and willing apart from any subject (Ibid.; *OTh* VII, 155).

Likewise, if metaphysics teaches that some accidents "determine themselves to their subjects," this means that they cannot exist in

---

82 Ibid.; *OTh* VII, 142; cf. *Quodlibeta* IV, q.29; *OTh* IX, 447, for a similar distinction.

83 *Quaest. in IV Sent.* q.8; *OTh* VII,154-5, 59

subjects of other species, not that they cannot exist without any subject at all (Ibid.; *OTh* VII, 157-8). Thus, Ockham concluded, if quantity is nothing really distinct from substance and quality, God can make quality without substance and extend its parts in place. If quantity is taken to be a distinct kind of thing, then God can make quality without quantity and quantity without substance (Ibid.; *OTh* VII, 154).

What about relative accidents (*respectus*)? One objector worried that Ockham's arguments will apply to them as much as to absolute accidents (Ibid.; *OTh* VII, 155) — contrary to what Giles and Scotus had maintained. Ockham agreed both with his predecessors that relatives necessarily include a reference to their terms, and with the objector that his arguments would apply as much to relatives as to absolutes.[84] Did Ockham intend this throw-away remark as a quiet reductio of the notion that relative accidents are *parvae res*?

4. Causal Interactions

Ockham thought the interesting question, so far as the active causal powers of the accidents are concerned, was whether the separate accidents can function as agents in the generation and corruption of substances, the way they did before the consecration. Once again, philosophical disagreements about relations among co-acting causes come into play. Where Aquinas had styled accidents as instruments of substance in generation and corruption, a role they supposedly retain via the miraculous *virtus*-transfer; Scotus had awarded them the role of preparatory causes, while denying — on grounds of ontological hierarchy among others — that they ever had the power to generate or corrupt substance. By contrast, Ockham insisted that accidents can be immediate partial causes of generating and corrupt-

---

84 Ibid.; *OTh* VII, 155-6: "Ad secundum potest dici quod non est simile, quia respectus necessario dicit habitudinem et ordinem ad subiectum suum, ideo non potest poni sine subiecto, sicut potest accidens absolutum. Tamen rationes adductae aequaliter probant de respectu sicut de accidente absoluto, quod non sic dicit ordinem ad subiectum suum."

ing substances. No matter whether they are separate or conjoined to subjects, they cannot be the total causes for the general metaphysical reason that God is an immediate efficient partial cause of every created effect, and God alone has power to be the total cause of any effect.[85] To be sure, Ockham conceded, this causal role for accidents cannot be demonstrated. But observed correlations, make it reasonable to assign accidents the role of efficient partial causes: for when the accidents are present, many things are produced and many corrupted which would not be produced or corrupted in their absence.

> And it seems that this could not be unless the accidents had some activity for producing those effects or corrupting [those things]. Otherwise every way of proving one thing to be the cause of another would perish....[86]

The argument from experience would be even better if we could observe cases where substances are present without their accidents; but such are neither naturally nor supernaturally available to us (Ibid.; *OTh* VII, 169-70).

So far as undergoing change is concerned, all agreed that the species remain susceptible of locomotion. Problems arise about quantitative and qualitative change, and about the possibility of generating a new substance from them. (i) Looking first at the condensation and rarefaction of the accidents, Ockham argued that if quantity is nothing really distinct from substance and quality, these changes merely involved locomotion of the parts to be closer to (even in the same place as) or more distant from one another (Ibid.; *OTh* VII, 174-5). If quantity were a thing really distinct from substance and quality, Ockham contended, condensation and rarefaction would involve the production of a totally new quantity — which would be miraculous, for the familiar Aristotelian reason that every created agent requires a patient on which to act (Ibid.; *OTh* VII, 177).

---

85 Ibid., q.9; *OTh* VII, 169, 170-72; cf. William Ockham [2], *Quaest. in II Sent.* q.6; *OTh* V, 89-92.

86 *Quaest. in IV Sent.* q.9; *OTh* VII, 169

(ii) Turning next to corruption, Ockham departed from the common opinion — that natural agents cannot corrupt separate accidents, because the latter can only be annihilated — to mount a clever argument that natural agents can annihilate but not create. Natural agents cannot create, he suggested, because they are indifferently related to indefinitely many effects of a given kind, and they always act to the limit of their powers when the situation is appropriate. What keeps them from actually producing indefinitely many effects is that they aren't appropriately related to indefinitely many patients. But all non-existent creatables as *purum nihil* are on a par, so that if they could create any of them, nothing in the situation would prevent them from creating all of them. Things susceptible of annihilation are not uniformly related to natural agents, however. Thus, assigning them the power to annihilate things of a certain sort would not automatically result in their all being actually annihilated (Ibid.; *OTh* VII, 178-9). More intuitively, why should destructive power have to rely on the concurrence of a material cause, just because generative power does (Ibid.; *OTh* VII, 179)? Thus, when the host turns color, the created cause destroys the old color, but God acts as total immediate cause to create the new one (Ibid.).

Properly speaking, nothing can be generated from the accidents by either God or creatures, because there is no matter to persist through the change (Ibid.; *OTh* VII, 179-80). Nevertheless,

> With respect to His absolute power, God can make matter to exist there without form, and form without matter, and the whole composite; and [He can bring it about] that the accidents inform that composite or matter, just as it pleases Him. (Ibid.; *OTh* VII, 180)

Thus, when the host "turns to" worms, "God creates the matter there from which the form of worm is educed."[87]

(iii) Qualitative change involves a variation on the same themes. If quantity is nothing really distinct from substance and quality, then no created agent can intensify an existing or create a new quality, but

---

87 *Quaest. in II Sent.* q.6; *OTh* V, 97.

Marilyn McCord Adams

a created agent can reduce or corrupt a quality existing there.[88] If quantity were a really distinct thing, then both intensification and reduction, generation and corruption could occur naturally, because — according to the common opinion — quantity would serve as a subject to persist through the change (Ibid.; *OTh* VII, 180).

Ockham agreed with Scotus that:

> God has instituted that the Body of Christ will remain under the accidents, so long as there remain either the same accidents as were in the consecrated host at first, or others that could naturally perfect that same substance of bread if it had remained there.... (Ibid.; *OTh* VII, 190)

Ockham mocked worries about the above changes involving too many new miracles, by asking what 'new' and 'old' mean in this context. For God wills whatever He wills by a single immutable, eternal (and hence 'old') act. On the other hand, some of its objects are new every morning (Ibid.; *OTh* VII, 191).

VI Conclusion

My beginning is my ending: relations between the doctrine of transubstantiation and later medieval Aristotelian philosophy are complex. Even this all too partial survey, of four philosophers and four problem areas, resists ready generalizations. All four thinkers took transubstantiation, separate accidents, and sensory phenomena as givens demanding to be somehow integrated with the tenets of Aristotelian metaphysics and physics. Their struggles with these difficulties sparked imaginative developments of hylomorphism: from the Aegidian/Scotistic distinction between two kinds of position, to Giles's flirtation with the idea that God could preserve matter divided and extended without really inherent quantity, from Scotus's arguments for the ontological parity between quantity and quality to Ockham's willingness to work with substance and quality alone.

---

88 *Quaest. in IV Sent.* q.9; *OTh* VII, 181

Likewise, wrestling with the placement problem eventually broke the hold of dogmas against multiple location (of many bodies in one place, or one in many places).

The problems in physics proved less tractable, and their attempts to solve them apparently less fruitful. The effort (sponsored by Aquinas and Giles) to take transubstantiation seriously as a distinct species of change was abandoned by the Franciscans, who in effect dissolved it into the conjunction of several other kinds of change. Attempts by Aquinas and Giles to explain some causal interactions in terms of a *donum superadditum* for the separate accidents, gave way in Scotus and Ockham to the frank admission of miracles, all subsumed under a general Divine eucharistic policy.

By far the biggest factor in their doctrinal disagreements remains their strikingly divergent philosophical intuitions. And so this essay adds evidence for what may no longer need proving: that thirteenth- and fourteenth-century Aristotelian philosophy was far from univocal.

Bibliography of Primary Sources Referred To

Albertus Magnus

[1] *Opera Omnia*. A. Borgnet, ed. Paris: Vives 1890.

Algazali

[1] *Logica et Philosophia*. Venice: 1506; facsimile ed. Frankfurt: Minerva G.M.B.H. 1969.

Ammonius

[1] *In Aristotelis Categorias Commentarius*. A. Busse, ed. *Commentaria in Aristotelem Graeca*, vol. 4, pt. 5. Berlin: Reimer 1895.

[2] *In Aristotelis De Interpretatione Commentarius*. A. Busse, ed. *Commentaria in Aristotelem Graeca*, vol. 4, pt. 5. Berlin: Reimer 1897.

[3] *Commentaire sur le 'Peri hermenias' d'Aristote: Traduction de Guillaume de Moerbeke*. G. Verbeke, ed. *Corpus Latinum Commentariorum in Aristotelem Graecorum*, vol. 2. Paris: Beatrice-Nauwelaerts; Louvain: Publications Universitaires de Louvain 1961.

Anonymous

[1] Incerti Auctores, *Quaestiones super Sophisticos Elenchos*. S. Ebbesen, ed. *Corpus Philosophorum Danicorum Medii Aevi* VII. Copenhagen: Gad 1977.

Aristotle

[1] *Categoriae et Liber de Interpretatione*. L. Minio-Paluello. Oxford: Clarendon 1966.

[2] *Aristotelis Latinus I 1-5. Categoriae vel Praedicamenta*. L. Minio-Paluello. Leiden: E.J. Brill 1961.

[3] *De Anima*. W.D. Ross, ed. Oxford: Clarendon 1956.

[4] *Metaphysics*. W.D. Ross, ed. Oxford: Clarendon 1953.

Bibliography

[5] *Aristoteles Latinus XXV 2. Metaphysica Lib.I-X, XII-XIV. Translatio Anonyma sive 'Media.'* G. Vuillemin-Diem, ed. Leiden: E.J. Brill 1976.

[6] *Nicomachean Ethics*, in *The Ethics of Aristotle*. John Burnet, ed. London: Methuen 1900.

[7] *Aristotelis Latinus XXVI 1-3. Fasciculus Quartus. Ethica Nicomachea Translatio Roberti Grosseteste Lincolniensis sive 'Liber Ethicorum.'* B. Recensio Recognita. R.A. Gauthier, ed. Brussels; Leiden: E.J. Brill 1973.

[8] *Physica*. W.D. Ross, ed. Oxford: Clarendon 1950.

[9] *Aristotelis Topica et Sophistica Elenchi*. W.D. Ross, ed. Oxford: Clarendon 1958.

[10] *Aristoteles Latinus VI 1-3. De Sophisticis Elenchis*. B.G. Dod, ed. Leiden: E.J. Brill; Brussels: Desclee de Brouwer 1975.

[11] *Analytica priora et posteriora*. W.D. Ross, ed. Oxford: Clarendon 1964.

Augustine

[1] *De Libero Arbitrio*, in *Aurelii Augustini Opera* II, 2 (*Corpus Christianorum, Series Latina* XXIX). W.M. Green, ed. Turnholt: Brepols 1970.

[2] *De Magistro*, in *Corpus Scriptorum Ecclesiasticorum Latinorum*, vol. 77.

Averroes

[1] *Epitome in Librum Metaphysicae Aristotelis* in *Aristotelis Opera cum Averrois Commentariis*. Venice: 1562-74; reprint Frankfurt: Minerva 1962.

Avicenna

[1] *Avicenna Latinus: Liber de Anima, seu sextus de naturalibus*, 2 vols. S. Van Riet, ed. Louvain: Peeters; Leiden: E.J. Brill 1968-72.

[2] *Metaphysica* in *Avicenne perhypatetici philosophi ac medicorum facile primi opera*. Venice: 1508; reprint Frankfurt: Minerva 1961.

Boethius

[1] *Commentarii in librum Aristotelis Peri hermenias*, 2 vols. Karl Meiser, ed. Leipzig: 1877; reprint New York and London: Garland 1987.

[2] *In Categorias Aristotelis libri quatuor*, in *patrologiae Cursus Completus. Series Latina*, vol. 64. J.-P. Migne, ed. Paris: 1891.

Boethius of Dacia

[1] *Modi significandi sive Quaestiones super Priscianum maiorem*, vol. 1 of *Boetii Daci Opera. Corpus Philosophorum Danicorum Medii Aevi*, vol. 4. J. Pinborg, H. Roos, and S.S. Jensen, eds. Copenhagen: Gad 1969.

Descartes

[1] *The Philosophical Writings of Descartes*, 2 vols. John Cottingham, Robert Stoothoff, and Dugald Murdoch, trans. Cambridge: Cambridge University Press 1984.

Dexippus

[1] *In Aristotelis Categorias Commentarium*, in *Commentaria in Aristotelem Graeca*, vol. 4, pt. 2. A. Busse, ed. Berlin: Reimer 1888.

Elias

[1] *In Aristotelis Categorias Commentarium*, in *Commentaria in Aristotelem Graeca*, vol. 18, pt. 1. A. Busse, ed. Berlin: Reimer 1900.

Giles of Rome

[1] *Theoremata de Corpore Christi*. Rome: 1554.

John Duns Scotus

[1] *Opus Oxoniense*, in *Opera Omnia*, vols. 5-18. L. Wadding, ed. Lyons: 1639; reprint Hildesheim: George Olms 1968.

[2] *In libros Elenchorum Quaestiones*, in *Opera Omnia II*. Paris: Vives 1891.

[3] *In librum Praedicamentorum Quaestiones*, in *Opera Omnia I*. Paris: Vives 1891.

John Locke

[1] *An Essay Concerning Human Understanding*. Peter H. Nidditch, ed. Oxford: Clarendon Press 1975.

Lambert of Auxerre

[1] *Logica (Summa Lamberti)*. F. Alessio, ed. Florence: La Nuova Italia Editrice 1971.

Bibliography

Martin of Dacia

[1] *Martinus de Dacia Quaestiones super librum Perihermenias*, in *Martini de Dacia Opera, Corpus Philosophorum Danicorum Medii Aevi*, vol. 2. H. Roos, ed. Copenhagen: Gad 1961.

Peter of Spain

[1] *Tractatus called afterwards Summule Logicales*. L.M. de Rijk, ed. Assen: Van Gorcum 1972.

Philoponus

[1] *In Aristotelis Categorias Commentarium*, in *Commentaria in Aristotelem Graeca*, vol. 13, pt. 1. A. Busse, ed. Berlin: Reimer 1898.

Priscian

[1] *Prisciani Institutionum grammaticarum libri XVIII*, in *Grammatici Latini*, vols. 2-3. Martin Hertz, ed. Leipzig: 1855; reprint Hildesheim: Olms 1961.

Robert Kilwardby

[1] *Notule super Periermenias Aristotelis*, in 'Robert Kilwardby's Writings on the *Logica Vetus* Studied with Regard to Their Teaching and Method.' P. Osmund Lewry, ed. PhD diss. Oxford: 1978.

[2] *De ortu scientiarum*. A.G. Judy, ed. Oxford: The British Academy; Toronto: Pontifical Institute of Medieval Studies 1976.

Simon of Faversham

[1] *Quaestiones super libro Elenchorum*. S. Ebbesen, T. Izbicke, J. Longeway, F. del Punta, E. Serene and E. Stump, eds. Toronto: Pontifical Institute of Medieval Studies 1984.

[2] *Quaestiones super libro Perihermenias*, in *Magistri Simonis Anglici sive de Faverisham Opera omnia, Opera logica*, vol. 1. Pasquale Mazzarella, ed. Padua: C.E.D.A.M. 1957.

Simplicius

[1] *In Aristotelis Categorias Commentarium*, in *Commentaria in Aristotelem Graeca*, vol. 8. C. Kalbfleisch, ed. Berlin: Reimer 1907.

[2] *Commentaire sur les Categories d'Aristote. Traduction de Guillaume de Moerbeke.* A. Pattin, ed. Louvain: Publications Universitaires de Louvain; Paris: Beatrice-Nauwelaerts 1971.

Thomas Aquinas

[1] *Opera Omnia.* Rome: Commissio Leonina; Paris: Vrin 1989.

[2] *Scriptum super Sententiis.* P. Mandonnet, ed. Paris: Lethielleux 1929.

[3] *Summa Theologica.* P. Caramello, ed. Torino: Marietti 1952-56.

[4] *Summa contra gentiles.* P. Marc, C. Pera, and P. Caramello, eds. Torino: Marietti 1961.

[5] *Quaestiones disputatae de anima.* P.P.M. Calcaterra and T.S. Centi, eds. Torino: Marietti 1949.

[6] *Quaestiones disputatae de malo.* P. Bazzi and P.M. Pession, eds. Torino: Marietti 1949.

[7] *Quaestiones disputatae de spiritualibus creaturis,* in *Tractatus de spiritualibus creaturis.* Text et docum. L. Keeler, ed. Rome: Series philos. 1946.

[8] *Quaestiones disputatae de veritate.* R. Spiazzi, ed. Torino: Marietti 1949.

[9] *Quaestiones disputatae de virtutibus in communi,* vol. II. P. Bazzi, M. Calcaterra, T.S. Centi, E. Odetto, and P.M. Pession, eds. Torino: Marietti 1965.

[10] *Quaestiones Quodlibetales.* R. Spiazzi, ed. Torino: Marietti 1956.

[11] *In Aristotelis librum De anima commentarium.* A.M. Pirotta, ed. Torino: Marietti 1959.

[12] *Expositio super librum Boetii De Trinitate.* B. Decker, ed. Leiden: E.J. Brill 1955.

[13] *In librum beati Dionysii De divinis nominibus expositio.* C. Pera, P. Caramello, and C. Mazzantini, eds. Torino: Marietti 1950.

[14] *In decem libros Ethicorum Aristotelis ad Nicomachum expositio.* R.M. Spiazzi, ed. Torino: Marietti 1949.

[15] *In duodecim libros Metaphysicorum Aristotelis expositio.* M.-R. Cathala and R.M. Spiazzi, eds. Torino: Marietti 1950.

[16] *In libros Peri Hermenias.* R.M. Spiazzi, ed. Torino: Marietti 1955.

[17] *In Aristotelis libros Peri hermenias et Posteriorum analyticorum expositio cum textu et recensione leonina,* 2nd ed. R.M. Spiazzi, ed. Torino: Marietti 1964.

[18] *Expositio in evangelium Joannis.* Torino: Marietti 1952.

Bibliography

William Ockham

[1] *Opera Philosophica et Theologica ad fidem codicum manuscriptorum edita.* St. Bonaventure, NY: Franciscan Institute, St. Bonaventure University 1967-86.

[2] *Quaestiones in librum secundum Sententiarum (Reportatio)*, in [1] vol. V. G. Gal and R. Wood, eds. St. Bonaventure, NY: St. Bonaventure University 1981.

[3] *Quaestiones in librum quartum Sententiarum (Reportatio)*, in [1] vol. VII. R. Wood, G. Gal, and R. Green, eds. St. Bonaventure, NY: St. Bonaventure University 1984.

[4] *Quodlibeta Septem*, in [1] vol IX. J.C. Wey, ed. St. Bonaventure, NY: St. Bonaventure University 1980.

[5] *Tractatus de Corpore Christi*, in [1] vol. X. C.A. Grassi, ed. St. Bonaventure, NY: St. Bonaventure University 1986.

[6] *Tractatus de Quantitate*, in [1], vol. X. C.A. Grassi, ed. St. Bonaventure, NY: St. Bonaventure University 1986

Index